Paul D. Fotegno

REVOLUTIONARY FEMINISM

D0814738

Also by Gary Kelly

THE ENGLISH JACOBIN NOVEL, 1780–1805
ENGLISH FICTION OF THE ROMANTIC PERIOD, 1789–1830
WOMEN, WRITING, AND REVOLUTION, 1790–1827

Revolutionary Feminism

The Mind and Career of Mary Wollstonecraft

GARY KELLY
Professor of English
University of Keele

St. Martin's Press
New York

REVOLUTIONARY FEMINISM: The Mind and Career of Mary Wollstonecraft
Copyright © 1996 by Kelly, Gary
All rights reserved. No part of this book may be used or reproduced
in any manner whatsoever without written permission except in the
case of brief quotations embodied in critical articles or reviews.
For information, address:

St. Martin's Press, Scholarly and Reference Division,
175 Fifth Avenue, New York, N.Y. 10010

First published in the United States of America in 1992
Reprinted with minor alterations 1996

Printed in Great Britain

ISBN 0–312–12904–1

Library of Congress Cataloging-in-Publication Data applied for

Contents

Preface

In her life and writing Mary Wollstonecraft addressed the problematic relation of subjectivity and society, 'mind' and the state, ideology and culture, especially for women. In order to cope with this problem in her own life, as the internalization of class and gender difference, Wollstonecraft developed a feminism for her age. Modern feminisms continue to be preoccupied with this problem and ways to resolve it; indeed, as Cora Kaplan points out, modern feminism's interest 'in the psychic life of women as a crucial element in their subordination and liberation' begins with Wollstonecraft.

This book is a reading of Mary Wollstonecraft's 'mind' and career in relation to the cultural revolution that founded the modern state in late eighteenth-century Britain. That revolution was led by the professional bourgeoisie and created new kinds and orientations of class, gender and culture, especially during the Revolutionary decade of the 1790s. Inspired by the Revolutionary crisis, Wollstonecraft aimed to re-revolutionize the cultural revolution and its construction of 'woman' as a cultural figure and as a prescription for women. In order to do so she focused on central issues of the cultural revolution – the 'mind' of women, their careers in society and the relation of both to the state – and she offered her own 'mind' and career as exemplary, in and through her writing. Because it was through writing in particular, the instrument of the bourgeois cultural revolution, that women internalized their own subjection, it was through writing that Wollstonecraft had to challenge the social and cultural order oppressing women.

As a Revolutionary feminist writer Wollstonecraft had to write in ways that would disrupt the gendered hierarchy in writing – including style, genre and discourse – that reproduced women's oppression. Yet she had to write in ways that would reach the widest possible readership if she were to revolutionize the 'reading public', and especially women. The result was that her writing has often been seen as incompetent and inartistic rather than experimental and revolutionary; I try to point out the ways Wollstonecraft challenged the gendered order of writing, including standards of 'competence' and 'artistry', as an essential task of her Revolutionary feminism.

Research for this book began many years ago, assisted by a fellowship from the Killam Foundation of the Canada Council. Since then my research has been supported by grants from the Social Sciences and Humanities Research Council and a McCalla research professorship from the University of Alberta. I could not have done the research without help from staff at the Bodleian Library, the British Library, the Pforzheimer Library at the New York Public Library, and Bruce Peel Special Collections at the University of Alberta. I also wish to thank Lord Abinger for permission to use the manuscripts now deposited in the Bodleian Library. This book would not have been possible without the many before me who have written on Wollstonecraft and her times; my debt to these predecessors is only partially indicated in the notes. Friends and family have also done much to make the book possible, particularly Audrey and Peter Ryan, Vera and Albert Levine and my wife. I dedicate this book to my daughters, Alice and Christabel.

Keele

1
Gender, Class and Cultural Revolution

Mary Wollstonecraft was a Revolutionary feminist – an advocate of the rights or claims of women in a specific revolutionary situation. There were two related aspects of that situation: the French Revolution and the cultural revolution that founded the modern state in Britain.[1] Many cultural revolutionaries in Britain saw the Revolution in France, at least in its early stages, as an example of what they themselves could achieve. But the British cultural revolution was itself a field of struggle in which the fortunes of various contestants, including Revolutionary feminism, were influenced by the changing course of the French Revolution. Paradoxically, the Revolution soon turned against feminists in France, yet it was also used as a reason to reject feminism, along with other forms of 'innovation' or 'French principles', in Britain.

The British debate on the French Revolution was part of the struggle for power within the British cultural revolution and it was conducted through writing, one of the cultural revolution's main instruments. Thus it was necessarily through writing, or print, that Wollstonecraft aimed to intervene in both the French Revolution debate and the cultural revolution in her own country, to turn them in the direction of a feminism for the Revolutionary decade. She did so not only by advancing feminist arguments in writing, but by challenging the entire male-dominated institution of writing in her time. She used the available resources of style, genre and discourse to show that the limited education, experience and professional opportunities assigned to women in both the pre-Revolutionary order and the British cultural revolution could lead not to subordination but to feminist consciousness, and the emancipation of women. Wollstonecraft's Revolutionary feminism was a writing revolution, exemplified and conducted in writing.

'Feminism' and 'revolution' are of course problematic terms. As Philippa Levine points out, 'The definition of feminism in the historical context is . . . fraught with difficulties.'[2] 'Feminism' in

1

the usual modern sense – advocacy of the rights or claims of women – did not come into the English language until the campaign for women's electoral rights in the 1890s, but it can be argued that there were feminisms in Britain before then, such as Renaissance feminism, seventeenth-century court and anti-court feminism, mid-eighteenth century Bluestocking feminism, and feminisms within cultural movements such as Sensibility and Evangelicalism.[3] After 1800 there was a Romantic nationalist feminism and, later still, socialist feminism, mid-nineteenth century movements for women's legal and educational rights and the later campaign for women's suffrage, giving rise to the modern use of the word 'feminism'. Each of these feminisms was conditioned by different social and historical circumstances, different horizons of possibility.

'Revolution' usually means a sudden or violent transformation in the established order and Wollstonecraft lived in an age of such revolutions, but some revolutions are less sudden. The Revolutionary feminists of the 1790s advocated the rights and claims of women within an intense debate over a sudden and violent revolution, and within the longer revolution that founded the modern state in Britain. This cultural revolution was not sudden or massively violent, but it transformed the culture, society and political structure of Britain, and naturalized this order for individuals in daily life and experience. Within this cultural revolution gender difference was a major issue, deeply implicated in other major revolutionary issues and in the struggle to define and lead the classes by and for whom the cultural revolution was being carried out.[4]

Social class may be taken as a particular historical phenomenon rather than a transhistorical social reality, a manifestation of social conflict rather than the cause of it, as different social groups come to see themselves having common interests, identity and opponents.[5] The cultural revolution of the late eighteenth century was carried out by and for the bourgeoisie or middle classes – the 'middle ranks' or 'middling sort', as they were then called – led by the professional class. Their revolution aimed to remake society in their own image and interests by imposing their culture, or forms of it, on other classes. But their cultural revolution was conditioned by their own changing experience of social conflict and the politics of culture. In the middle decades of the eighteenth century, bourgeois social critics, along with others, attacked court government and culture as well as emulation of court culture by the gentry and middle classes. Toward the end of the century, and especially in the 1790s, they also attacked the lower classes, both urban and rural, whom they saw as either subordinated to court culture or challenging for political power, if not for social and cultural domination in their own right. Yet the professional cultural revolution owed much to these different class rivals.

The professional bourgeoisie were especially marked by relations with their 'betters' – the landed classes. Historically, the professionals had been closely associated with these classes and dependent on them.[6] The aristocracy and gentry placed second and third sons in the professions – careers often controlled by the landed classes through patronage. But the professions also offered upward social mobility to the commercial and mercantile middle classes. The gentry married first daughters off within their own class to secure family alliances and thus build a broader base of power through patronage; second and third daughters could be married off to useful and promising professional men or sons of well-to-do commercial or manufacturing families. Heiresses of the commercial and manufacturing classes raised their families' status by marrying into the gentry and brought new money for agrarian capitalism and the conspicuous consumption that affirmed the gentry's power and prestige.

The professional bourgeoisie were an increasingly distinct group within the middle classes from the seventeenth century on, but their increasing power and prestige in the eighteenth century were due to the pre-eminence of the landed classes. The latter had established their power with the Glorious Revolution of 1688 and used it to enhance their prosperity through capitalist land management, improved production and technological advance. Some of the new prosperity went into the traditional gentry culture of conspicuous consumption, which in turn increased the numbers, wealth and status of the professionals who provided administrative, cultural and personal services.[7] Economic expansion also led to the growth of towns, where most professionals lived and which they came to dominate; in fact, they were often called 'the town gentry'.[8] These developments enabled professional people to develop distinctive identity, interests, culture and values. Increasing distinctness accompanied increasing sense of distinction, or social importance and dignity. Other differences reinforced these distinctions, as with the religious Dissenters who had been legally and socially excluded from most patronage and power since the seventeenth century.[9]

Yet in the last three decades of the century there was an increasing sense of class conflict. Increased social distinction and economic opportunities led to increased social frustration for those professional people not in élite professions or well-connected to the gentry-dominated system of patronage that still controlled economy and state.[10] Because of this domination, membership in the gentry continued to be the aim of socially ambitious individuals and groups, and those who could not quite make it into the gentry emulated them socially and culturally or challenged their domination. While social and cultural changes were enhancing the status and power of the professional class, they also increased distinctions within the middle classes. Middle-class emulation of their 'betters' and desire for upward social mobility led to increasing disdain for the 'lower orders' and sharper distinctions between the professions, the commercial and manufacturing bourgeoisie and mere 'tradespeople'. The increasing numbers and wealth of the professionals also widened gaps between 'learned' professions such as law and the clergy, 'gentlemanly' professions such as the military, and professions still associated with crafts or trades. Even in the law there was a strong distinction between the élite barristers and the mere attorneys.

There was increased hostility between the lower classes and the others, arising from the shift to a wage economy, accelerated enclosure of common lands, abandonment of customary doles, suppression of popular sports, pastimes and festivals, exclusion of the 'vulgar' from public spaces in towns, and the development of 'standard' forms of language and culture from which the lower classes were excluded.[11] Furthermore, economic development and improved communication between the regions of Britain made their social, historical, cultural and religious differences more noticeable. The growing towns were very different from one another. People of all classes retained strong local loyalty and regional identity, which could cut across an emergent sense of national solidarity and common interest within a particular social class. Many events gave prominence to these social divisions, including the Jacobite rebellions, unrest in Ireland, antiquarian and folklore movements, the rise of local presses, the rise of the 'reading public', the feminization of literature and culture, the Gordon Riots and other disturbances.

Then events of the 1790s, such as the debate on the French Revolution, political unrest in Scotland and open rebellion in Ireland, formation of organized lower-class opposition to government, the association of religious Dissent with sympathy for the Revolution, and the debate on women's rights, revealed dangerous regional and social divisions in Britain and within the professional and middle classes.[12] Meanwhile, events in France showed how a professional middle-class revolution could go wrong. Nevertheless, in the 1780s and 1790s some middle-class and professional people were ready to form a coalition with the literate, politicized artisan classes in order to carry out a middle-class revolution: overthrow of the court system, the patronage system and the hegemony of the upper classes. Such circumstances sharpened both the struggle for leadership within the professional and middle classes and these classes' competition with other classes.

In this conflict of loyalties, identities and distinctions, gender difference was increasingly important and complex.[13] The extent to which women identified with or distinguished themselves from the men of 'their' class or social group was and is a difficult question. R. S. Neale argues that 'while men might have the illusion of freedom, women never could', for 'all family relationships, marriage, love and morality were determined by, and the servants of, property; they were facets of total alienation'. Thus 'the value stance expected of women may be encapsulated in the word propriety – one might say that among the landed classes propriety was to women as property was to men'.[14] This may have been even more the case for women of the professional class, whose capital and property were, in the first instance, intellectual and moral – of the the 'mind' – the basis of 'propriety' as conduct.

Within the professional middle class gender differences also parallelled and reinforced class differences. Wives of merchants and tradesmen could participate in their husbands' businesses but wives of professional men could not.[15] The leisured and cultivated 'lady' of the landed classes was distinguished from the mere 'woman' because she possessed a class-based culture that exhibited the status and wealth of the men and families of her class. Therefore she was emulated by middle-class women, and many socially ambitious middle-class men wished their women to become 'ladies'. Yet the sacrifice of women to mere family interest and ambition – that is, the interest and ambition of men – was widely deplored in all classes. The courtly lady who used or was used in sexual intrigue for political ends – the so-called 'mistress system' of court politics and patronage – was widely condemned, and the upper-class or would-be upper-class coquette symbolized the decadence and injustice of the court system.

It is true that women subordinated within the upper classes could seem parallel to a bourgeoisie that felt itself subordinated by the upper classes. On the other hand, since women were subordinated in all classes they would seem to have good reason to betray family or class in order to marry up the social scale or to be seduced by a more powerful and (therefore) attractive social superior. Both quasi-feminist sympathy for women and anti-feminist resentments and fears are represented in plays, novels, newspaper scandals and trials for adultery and 'crim. con.' during the century. 'Woman' could either symbolize a class's own sense of its weakness or embody its ideal image of itself. The ideal was developed as 'domestic woman', representing the values and practices of the professional middle class in particular, as distinct from what was seen as the merely public and social sphere dominated by the upper classes.[16] 'Domestic woman' was a figure embodying social and cultural values, but it affected women because of their role in everyday domestic life, social customs and relations, habits and patterns of consumption, and the class-based exercise of choices and distinctions.

In living out such distinctions cultural consumption was increasingly important, for economic and technological change were creating another revolution: the commercialization of culture which made possible or necessary a greater range of consumer goods and services, a larger field for exercise of the social distinctions and conflicts just described.[17] New modes of manufacture and marketing were intertwined even before the Industrial Revolution, and were dependent on social emulation, the fashion system, a culture of novelty and patterns of consumption stemming from the dominant landed gentry, aristocracy and court class. A wide range of products and services, including professional ones, flourished on historic patterns of emulation, but the commercialization of culture made cultural revolution more obvious, more comprehensive and more powerful.

Like the cultural revolution, the consumer revolution was a field of struggle. The landed class's culture of conspicuous consumption was related to court culture of display and magnificence. Bourgeois social critics saw such display as an instrument of power, dazzling the common people and blinding them to the corruption and decadence of court government. Display was also politically dangerous for the gentry and middle classes because it conflicted with rational use of capital and forced its victims into the court patronage system, to recoup over-expenditure on display or 'luxury' by means of sinecures, 'places', offices of state, monopolies and commercial privileges. Together, 'luxury' and the patronage system were thought to undermine both the merit system and the market system, be it a market in goods, services or talent. The 'men of merit', that is, the professional men, dependent on intellectual capital, had the greatest stake in the critique of display, 'luxury' and 'fashion', but upper-class losers in the patronage system also joined this critique in a temporary coalition with bourgeois cultural revolutionaries.

Members of the middle classes who succumbed to 'luxury' or 'fashion' were in double jeopardy. They lacked the public credit and base of family financial support available to members of the landed classes, and had to manage their capital carefully or risk falling into the ungenteel lower middle classes or even lower. Moreover, commercialized consumption reproduced and disseminated upper-class culture by providing consumers in other classes with cheaper versions of the novelties being consumed by their 'betters'. These novelties covered a great range of material culture and 'manners', including clothing, dinnerware, health products and services, arts and architecture, travel, 'correct' pronunciation, education, courtship practices and so on. Thus criticism of fashion, luxury and display addressed both upper-class culture and emulation of that culture by the middle classes and, later, the lower classes. Women were thought to play an important role in fashion, luxury and display, partly because of their role in court culture. Numerous eighteenth-century satires depict a woman ruining her husband or family through extravagant emulation of her 'betters'. The fashionable woman symbolized the middle classes' emulation of their 'betters' through cultural consumption; but she also represented the consumer revolution's commodification of women, making them into objects as well as agents of conspicuous consumption for competing men and social classes.

A major form of cultural consumption was print. Yet print culture was historically associated with the professional middle class and in the eighteenth century became a major way of disseminating their cultural revolution. The 'rise of the reading public', much commented on at the time, was facilitated by increasing numbers of circulating libraries, publishers and booksellers, newspapers and magazines.[18] Well-appointed circulating libraries, exclusive book clubs and stylish but inexpensive reprints also enabled middle-class people to participate in book culture as a genteel avocation.[19] Literary culture, as distinct from merely professional writing, was both an aspect of the consumer revolution and a way of disseminating it, for miscellany magazines and 'books of the day' – especially novels – purveyed information on manners, fashion, high society, public issues, the arts, 'proper' language and so on to readers who would otherwise find it unobtainable. Even when this fashion system was being condemned in some magazine or novel, readers were learning how the system worked, and bourgeois social critics often saw 'books of the day' as disseminators of ideology and culture hostile to their own interests. Print could be seen to both foster and disable the sense of common interest and nation-wide identity among the 'reading public' – the professional and other middle classes.

Since Renaissance Humanism at least, these classes had participated with the upper classes in literature as a broad, classically based culture.[20] But in the eighteenth century literary culture moved from domination by aristocratic coteries and patronage to domination by the market-place and the 'reading public'. 'Literature' ceased to mean predominantly 'the extant writing on a particular subject' and came to have its modern sense of 'written verbal art'. Yet 'literature' was increasingly commercialized, specialized and professionalized, while maintaining a façade of genteel belletrism. The professional class had a vested interest in literature in both main senses. Many professionals specialized in the interpretation and production of literature in the older sense, from Holy Scripture to official documents, contracts, legislation, technology, plans and projects, and scholarly or scientific research of various kinds. But many professionals needed literature in the new sense for the social aspects of their work, associating with cultivated patrons, employers and colleagues through a broad, shared literary culture. More importantly, literature in both senses made up a discursive order that enabled the professional bourgeoisie, who were widely scattered through Britain, to communicate among themselves according to a shared set of assumptions and conventions, thereby reproducing themselves daily, in the act of reading, as members of a national class.

A sense of common identity, transcending local ties and limits, could readily be conveyed through print. Ephemeral periodicals such as newspapers and magazines repeatedly made a common culture available – daily, weekly or monthly – to widely scattered professional and middle-class readers, through their nature as much as through their contents. Print culture seemed superior to both the oral, communal culture of the lower classes and the social culture of the landed classes. Lower-class culture had to be reinforced by frequent contact in everyday life; upper-class culture depended on social contacts in country and town houses, and at seasonal social, political, judicial and administrative gatherings. The rise of what Benedict Anderson calls 'print capitalism' gave the professionals and their followers greater potential to become a national class than their social rivals – unless those rivals also participated in the new print culture.[21] But if they did so, it would be on the terms of the professional people who increasingly commanded print culture as the 'reading public'.

Literature in the new sense addressed a wider readship than narrowly professional writing. Writing as verbal art supplemented and validated writing on a particular, usually professional subject, ennobling it by association. Yet 'written verbal art' was also in some ways writing as an end in itself, distinct from and transcending mere professional writing. Literature as *belles-lettres*, a genteel avocation, especially in the older, aristocratic literary culture, seemed to relegate professional writing to a merely utilitarian, vulgarly middle-class sphere. But in the latter half of the eighteenth century literature as verbal art was becoming professionalized, while remaining distinct from other professional writing, and validating the entire domain of writing as professional craft and art.[22]

In Mary Wollstonecraft's lifetime both print culture and literature became the class property of the professional bourgeoisie, used as instruments in a class-based cultural revolution. But print culture and literature were also divided by gender distinctions. The learned discourses and noble genres were conventionally reserved for men, both as practitioners and readers, and included theoretical and abstract writing such as philosophy, science, political economy, aesthetics and rhetoric; scholarly writing such as

natural science, technology, topography, encyclopaedias, historiography, classical studies, biblical studies, textual criticism and
editing, and literary and other criticism in the arts; controversial
writing such as political polemics or theological disputations; and
the noble or sublime genres such as tragedy and epic. By contrast,
most women writers kept to kinds of writing that could be seen as
extensions of women's domestic range of education and experience: useful and practical subjects, and lighter, entertaining, desultory, occasional and personal forms of *belles-lettres*. These included
educational writing and books for children; conduct books for girls
and young women; devotional verse and prose; comedy; verse
narrative; poems of domestic or quotidian life and subjective experience; and of course prose fiction, seen in the later eighteenth
century as *the* women's genre. The gendering of writing reinforced
and was reinforced by the domestication of women of the middle
and upper classes. 'Books of the day' or ephemeral, entertaining,
'polite' kinds of literature were especially associated with women,
strengthening the association of women with the fashion system.
The gendering of writing left women in a paradoxical relationship
to it – at once merely domestic and merely 'fashionable'.

Though print and literary culture were class property, divided
by gender, highly commercialized and implicated in social emulation, they were also major disseminators of the professional
middle-class cultural revolution. In this cultural work women
writers played an important if undervalued role, partly because the
genres left to women popularized the professional cultural revolution and made it available to a wide range of 'the reading public'.
Writing was also highly suited for representing central themes and
practices of the cultural revolution, particularly the subjective self,
the 'domestic affections' and domesticity and the 'national' community. These themes were appropriated from other social classes
but made to embody the values, self-image and interests of the
professional middle classes and their followers. These themes
were subjects of controversy and conflict in the cultural revolution,
but before 1800, at least, they were often expressed through a
particular construction of the figure 'woman', in which women
writers could reasonably claim interest and expertise.

Practices of subjectivity, or what Michel Foucault calls 'technologies of the self', can be found even in early historic cultures,
and such practices may in fact have been made possible by
writing.[23] But in the middle third of the eighteenth century there

was rapid development of subjectivity as complex, autonomous, authentic and pre-social or extra-social.[24] This idea of the self was appropriated from late Renaissance and seventeenth-century court culture, or rather from oppositional and marginal culture within court society.[25] By the early eighteenth century much courtly literature depicted subjectivity as true personal merit in the face of the merely public, social, political rank of court personages, a refuge from and a critique of mere courtliness. Significantly, court literature often embodied this subjectivity in a heroine. For a woman could represent anyone, man or woman, subject to domination, courtship or seduction by another – usually more powerful and male. Such a model of subjectivity could also appeal to the non-courtly classes, whether gentry or bourgeoisie, lower down the chain of court patronage or frustrated in attempts to infiltrate other patronage systems.

Subjectivity was a social practice paradoxically pretending to be extra-social; but writing seemed to solve the paradox. Writing and reading are solitary practices but they are also cultural and social practices available to anyone who is literate. The 'rise of the reading public' coincided with a rapid and diverse development in the writing of subjectivity, from Lockean 'mental philosophy' to religious devotional literature, from personal lyric poetry to Rousseauist autobiography, from Sentimental novels to political theories of the 'rights of man' based on the 'natural' inviolability of the personal self. As appropriated by the professional class, subjectivity was equated with the kind of moral discipline and intellectual training necessary to professional men who had to make their way in a hostile, competitive, seductive and uncongenial social world. This moral and intellectual discipline was represented as 'virtue' and 'reason' – words that recur often in eighteenth-century philosophy and social criticism, including the writings of Mary Wollstonecraft.

This culture of subjectivity realized through writing distinguished and defended the middle-class individual from both upper and lower classes. The 'lower orders' were depicted as lacking in developed, complex subjectivity; their 'merely' social and communal culture was seen as parallel to the 'merely' social, courtly, fashionable society of the upper classes. Thus subjectivity was used by the bourgeois cultural revolution to counter a social, public and political domain thought to be occupied by the dominant but 'merely' social courtly upper classes on one hand and by the unindividualized, communal and subordinated lower classes on the other.

The bourgeois cultural revolution used the 'domestic affections' and domesticity in a related way, to provide authentic social relations for the subjective self, in contrast to what were seen as the vitiated, self-interested, exploitative social relations of a courtly society. The domestic affections subsumed friendship as well as family relations, for ideas of 'family' and 'friend' were themselves altered by the cultural revolution.[26] The upper-class family was seen as an unofficial joint stock company based on the landed estate, the lower-class family as a collective and communal production unit. The cultural revolution refashioned both as the family based on conjugal, parental and filial relations, excluding servants and more distant relations and excluding obvious economic production from the home. This kind of family was based on neither landed property nor communal production, but was to 'produce' – or reproduce – the moral and intellectual individual suited for middle-class and especially professional life.[27] Nevertheless, this reproduction was to be different for males and females: the former were to be trained for professional and public life while the latter were to be trained as companions for such men and as sustainers of the authentic domestic realm. 'Friend' ceased to mean someone sharing or assisting in a material, social or political interest, and came to mean someone with mutual moral, intellectual and emotional interests. In these new senses family and friends were appropriated from upper-class and lower-class culture by being domesticated and feminized.

Domesticity was the daily culture of family and friends in the new sense. It included the idea of home as a refuge from a hostile and competitive social world. It included the constitution of the quotidian, local and particular as 'real' life in contrast to the courtly and cosmopolitan, which were represented as artificial, fantastic and a mystification of 'reality'. It included 'domestic education', or the development of the moral and intellectual self necessary to master a competitive, seductive social world. Domesticity included the cult of the cottage or bourgeois pastoral, the separation of home from place of work, and the rise of the suburb. It led to domestication of the arts – parlour music rather than concert or ceremonial music; drawing and watercolour rather than formal painting; genre painting rather than history painting; engravings rather than paintings; private theatricals and closet drama rather than the public theatres; privatization of formerly public spaces; gardening that could be carried out by the individual without large income and gardening staff; family reading; needlework; and a host of other activities.[28] This domesticity may have originated in various aristocratic and bourgeois practices, but it contrasted with courtly social relations – the mistress system, 'gallantry', libertinism, mingled sexual and political intrigue and notorious intrafamily rivalries, such as the hostility between George III and his son the Prince of Wales. The literature of domesticity developed with the rise of the professionals in the 1730s and 1740s and became a flood in the second half of the century, from the novels of Samuel Richardson through Rousseau's *La nouvelle Héloïse* to the 'conversation poems' of Coleridge.

Subjectivity, the domestic affections and domesticity together formed the basis for new ideas of national identity, community and culture.[29] Older forms of national identity, as loyalty to a ruling dynasty, had given way in Britain to national identity as a complex of social, economic, political and regional 'interests'. These 'interests' were dominated by the ruling class as a network of interrelated families based on large landed estates. 'Patriotism' in the eighteenth century often meant opposition of the landed interest to a court faction supposedly leading king and country to domestic ruin and to defeat by external enemies, trading competitors and imperial rivals. In the latter part of the century, however, national identity and culture were represented as residing in 'the people' and rooted in domestic affections and social sympathies of particular kinds.

Great Britain was a complex state whose disparate regional cultures seemed to find expression in antiquarianism, local natural history, 'popular antiquities' or folklore, literary 'fakelore' or forgeries such as Macpherson's 'Ossian' and Chatterton's poems, and collecting and imitating popular ballads. In fact, these activities assimilated the local and regional to a national culture of writing commanded by the professional bourgeoisie. Writing transformed local and regional class cultures into apparently classless ones by transposing them from speech communities to the national community of print. Transcribing the oral culture of the common people transformed it into a culture subject to the interests and expertise of the professional middle class.[30] The 'imagined community' of the nation that could only be experienced in print was an alternative to the 'political nation' of large landed families who controlled national politics and local administration. It was also an alternative to the 'nation' as the common people, especially during the Revolutionary decade of the 1790s.

Women, or rather 'woman', had a central place in these major themes of the professional middle-class cultural revolution. 'Woman' was a figure or persuasive device in the rhetoric of cultural transformation rather than the actual women of any class or all classes.[31] 'Woman' linked the major themes of the bourgeois cultural revolution and was therefore central to the rhetoric of revolution. Some women, especially in the professional and other middle classes, saw themselves in this figure of 'woman', participated in it or helped construct it in writing. Other women, including Mary Wollstonecraft, argued that 'woman' oppressed women and betrayed the middle-class cultural revolution. 'Woman', like other themes and figures, was both an instrument of the cultural revolution and a field of struggle within it.

For one thing, 'woman' was a major figure for the new subjectivity. In courtly literature woman is often represented as a vessel of feeling. Excluded from the public, political and martial spheres and subordinate in the ceremonial of court life (except by dynastic accident), women were associated with the private, personal, aesthetic and amorous domains. Because love was seen as a personal and aesthetic experience, not a public or political one, courtly amorous culture was often depicted as presided over by women. Professional middle-class culture of the eighteenth century appropriated woman in this role, but dropped the associations with sexual-political intrigue and modified courtly love to romantic love as a personal, subjective absolute.[32] Yet elements of courtly 'gallantry' remained, and it was these that Revolutionary feminism attacked.

Woman as emblem for both romantic and courtly love was an ambiguous figure – both subject and object in an upper middle-class culture that was ambivalent about the courtly culture it was appropriating and refashioning. In professional culture, and increasingly in the culture of the commercial and manufacturing bourgeoisie and the master artisans, women were excluded from the public domain and restricted to the domestic sphere. Yet this restriction was thought to exaggerate their emotional, affective, subjective development. The ambiguous character of woman as emblem of subjectivity and romantic love also shows that woman represents more than femaleness or femininity. Woman was sub-

ject *par excellence*, to be courted yet denied independence, equality
and power, and thus could stand for the bourgeois subject regardless of sex and for the bourgeoisie in general, especially if subjectivity were equated with desiring inwardness in any individual or
the social class as a whole.

Such desiring inwardness is the seducible element, open to
ideological penetration and subjection by the social other. In professional middle-class culture woman as subject was a counter to
the public, social, political domains seen to be dominated by the
social other. But woman was also a figure for class anxiety and
uncertainty, cast as erotic desires and relations, amorous seductions and betrayals. For this reason 'woman' became a central
topic of concern in the various Enlightenments – movements of
social and cultural criticism emphasizing 'reason' as an objective
and transcendent criterion against 'unenlightened' culture of both
court and common people. In the Enlightenments' gendering of
intellectual and cultural values, woman as desiring subject often
represented 'unreason'.[33]

For this reason woman was redefined as domestic in order to
appropriate the positive values she represented for the Enlightenments as social critiques of the Old Regime.[34] The culture of
Sensibility, or Sentimentalism, which was based on Enlightenment
rationalism and materialism, developed the two themes of subjectivity and domesticity in a wide-ranging feminization of culture in
the 1770s and 1780s, to some extent in opposition to the mascu-
linist values of the Enlightenments.[35] Woman is defined as domestic in order to confine her there, in contrast to negative figures of
femininity: the too public, too political, independently desiring
woman of the courtly upper classes; the too social, 'managing'
woman of the commercial and trading bourgeoisie; and the
labouring, sexually available woman of the servant and other
lower classes.[36]

'Woman' constructed for a particular class interest and culture
was then made to stand for women of all classes. Nature as biology
was invoked, not for the first or last time, to extend woman's
physical roles as mother and wife to the moral and social domain of
the domestic affections. As friendship came to be seen as less a
business or social relationship and more a personal, affective one,
woman was made responsible for the home as a place fostering the
extra-domestic friendships of husband and other family members.
Yet female friendships outside the family caused anxiety to many

social critics. Domestic woman became a female version of the professional man, distinguished from woman as partner in a family-owned business and woman as ornament in courtly upper-class life. She was to be a non-labouring worker, overseeing the household, the management and early education of children, and encouraging various class-based cultural values and practices. Woman of the professional bourgeoisie was to provide a moral-intellectual service, ostensibly without remuneration. In this too she was a female version of the male professional, requiring the same kind of self-discipline and method ('virtue' and 'reason'), but not the same intellectual training, and working in a distinct, parallel sphere.

To fulfil this role, however, domestic woman required a proper education. A decorative and aesthetic role was retained for her in emulation of upper-class woman. Education in the decorative and entertaining arts, or 'accomplishments', was to make domestic woman a proper companion for the professional man after the rigours of his professional work and after his trying experiences in a hostile and competitive public social world. This function was parallel to that of woman in court culture, but domestic woman was also to have a form of the moral and intellectual training required by professional men. This would guard her from excessive courtliness, from questioning her lot, from temptation to a more glamorous social life and from personal or domestic extravagance damaging to the family interest. The exact nature of domestic woman's training was debated, but its general aim was to distinguish her from both courtly upper-class woman and vulgarly middle-class or lower-class woman, yet to exclude her from the public sphere and assign her a subaltern role in the professional middle-class family. She was assigned a diminutive or domestic version of the intellectual and artistic culture of men. Because of her restricted sphere of experience and observation, domestic woman was supposed to be a specialist in 'real life', local observation, the detail of quotidian life, domestic heroism and the 'trivial sublime', or intimations of grandeur and transcendence in common life. In short, domestic woman was a figure for distinguishing traits of professional middle-class culture; but by being domestic she was also distinguished and firmly subordinated within that culture.

This domestication of culture and social relations was important for the reconstruction of the national identity, culture and destiny in the interests of the professional bourgeoisie. The site of the essential, authentic national identity was shifted from the public and political sphere to the domestic and personal, in order to wrest the power to define the national interest from the courtly and landed classes. This process was important for the cultural revolution's ability to respond to events outside Britain, especially the French Revolution. Even before the 1790s woman's role in the 'national' culture was seen as an extension of her central role in domesticity, and Britain's vicissitudes abroad were represented by their effects on domestic relations and affections, and on woman as wife, mother, sister and daughter. During the 1790s and the Revolutionary aftermath of Romantic nationalism woman was also made the repository of national 'folk' culture, as the essence and unifying element in a society that Revolutionary threat, domestic political upheaval, feminist protest, regional revolt and international crisis revealed to be dangerously divided by class, region and gender.

Prescriptions for the construction of domestic woman can be found everywhere in writing of the period. Yet the plentifulness of such prescriptions suggests that woman was also emblem of the professional middle class's ideological, social and cultural vulnerability and sense of powerlessness, and therefore that women were seen as a problem in those classes. These prescriptions took the form of conduct books – instructions for the construction of woman for the bourgeois cultural revolution. The conduct books in turn merely gave systematic statement to themes widely diffused in literature of all kinds, including philosophy, history, essays, plays and especially novels.[37]

One of the most reprinted conduct books was *The Lady's New Year's Gift; or, Advice to a Daughter* by George Savile, Marquis of Halifax, first published in 1688, the year of the Glorious Revolution. Just over a century later, in another revolutionary year, Wollstonecraft published an extract from it in her anthology *The Female Reader*. Halifax, like most conduct-book writers, recommends religion to allay the dangerous passions, personal and social, to which women were supposed to be subject. Passion is what rebels against difference as oppression and desires the social other through a mingled erotic and social drive. As Halifax puts it, 'A devout mind hath the privilege of being free from passions, as some climates are free from all venomous kinds of creatures.' Poison or venom was a common figure for the silent, invisible, perverting or fatal operation of alien ideology. Behind Halifax's platitude is a sophisticated understanding of the social and personal function of religion for the subjugated and divided, be they a class, a race or a sex.[38] Halifax then prescribes a domestic role for women, rooted in nature and divine will, and advises against excessive socializing, gaudy dress and self-display – attributes of courtly society. In order to fulfil their domestic role, women are told to 'get understanding, and practise virtue', but Halifax is less specific on how this should be done than later conduct writers would be. 'Reason' and 'virtue' commonly represent the intellectual and moral training used to subject women within professional middle-class culture and to secure them against seduction from above or contamination from below.

Halifax's views continued to appeal to the professional middle classes, but they were modified and even challenged. In 1696 Mary Astell, in *An Essay in Defence of the Female Sex*, declared that 'souls are equal'. Mind should therefore be developed in women as well as men if women were to gain salvation and also play their role in emergent professional middle-class culture. Similar views were widely disseminated in the early eighteenth century through such advocates of fusing genteel and professional cultures as *The Spectator*. In 1739 'Sophia, a Person of Quality' argued in *Woman Not Inferior to Man* that the difference between the sexes was due to education, custom and circumstances. Relying on a Lockean materialist epistemology, she (if she was a she) argues that women have more delicate senses than men and, since all knowledge is acquired through the senses, women should 'at least keep pace' with men in learning and should be debarred from no profession, including the military. Like the Revolutionary feminists half a century later, she condemns the appropriation of courtly subjection of women by the professional middle class.

By mid-century 'domestic woman' had been constructed for the professional middle-class revolution, not only in Britain but also in France and elsewhere on the Continent.[39] This movement coincided with the emergence of the professional middle class as a major social and cultural force, but the ambivalence in middle-class patriarchy between courtly woman and domestic woman remained.[40] For example, the Scottish Enlightenment philosopher David Hume asserted the importance of women to national culture, but did so by appropriating aspects of courtly woman and courtly gallantry. In his essay 'Of the Rise and Progress of the Arts and Sciences' (1742) he argues that the modern age had superior 'politeness', or intellectual culture, because 'modern notions of *gallantry*, the natural produce of courts and monarchies', enabled 'the company of virtuous women' to modify the natural harshness of the male character. Hume opposes confining women to the domestic sphere because their polishing influence on men would be lost. This Enlightenment sociology of 'progress' in 'the arts and sciences' is an *embourgeoisement* of court culture, fusing courtly and bourgeois values and practices in a feminization of culture.

The most influential appropriation of courtly woman for the bourgeois cultural revolution, even in Britain, was that of Jean-Jacques Rousseau. He was the leading writer of the intellectual and cultural movement known as Sensibility, related to and overlapping the Enlightenment.[41] In his novel *La nouvelle Héloïse* (1761) and his educational quasi-novel *Émile* (1762) Rousseau idealizes domestic woman and the domestic affections and contrasts them with the corrupt courtly mistress system and gender relations based on coquetry and gallantry which filtered down through the rest of society by the process of social emulation. In his influential essay on political theory, *Du contrat social* (1762), he takes the family based on domestic affections as the model for the state. Rousseau follows the Enlightenment and Protestant Nonconformist view of woman as an equal soul and mind with man; but he also asserts that woman has a different moral and intellectual character. Whereas man thinks, reasons and abstracts, woman feels, sympathizes and puts into practice. Therefore woman should obey man; but lest man become a tyrant, woman may use coquetry to achieve a balance of power. Within the family and state man should have ultimate authority, modified by woman's kind of knowledge, not through reasoning, for that is man's domain, but by woman controlling her erotic desire in order to govern man's and thereby influence his judgement. In this way Rousseau appropriates the courtly mistress system of political and amorous intrigue to bourgeois domesticity.

Rousseau's influence on the construction of domestic woman in Britain was reinforced by Dr James Fordyce's *Sermons to Young Women* (1766). Fordyce was a man of the Scottish Enlightenment and a popular preacher, and his combination of familiar conduct-book precepts with Rousseau's domestication of courtly woman took *Sermons* through at least twenty editions by 1800. Following Hume, he envisages woman gentrifying man through a bourgeois

form of courtly love called 'honourable love': 'that great preserv-
ative of purity, that powerful softener of the fiercest spirit, that
mighty improver of the rudest carriage, that all-subduing, yet all
exalting principle of the human breast, which humbles the proud,
and bends the stubborn, yet fills with lofty conceptions, and
animates with a fortitude that nothing can conquer'. Such love is
contrasted to 'that false and vicious gallantry which gains ground
amongst us every day' and which is 'effeminate' rather than
feminized. Fordyce goes on to link the influence of woman
through 'honourable love' to the national destiny, particularly in
the face of the historic enemy, France, which Britons equated with
court government and court culture.[42] The themes, arguments and
even the words and rhythms of Fordyce's 'honourable love' passage would be echoed in Edmund Burke's paean to 'antient chivalry' in *Reflections on the Revolution in France*, thereby making this
appropriation of courtly woman central to the counter-Revolution.
Not surprisingly, Rousseau, Fordyce and Burke were all objects of
Mary Wollstonecraft's feminist polemic in the 1790s.

Thus 'woman' was a central figure in the rhetoric of the cultural
revolution – so important that the cultural revolution could be seen
as a feminization of culture, advancing the claims and position of
women, permitting women to participate in the cultural revolution, and even taking the form of feminist movements such as
Bluestocking feminism, Enlightenment feminism, Sentimental
feminism, Evangelical feminism and Revolutionary feminism, each
of which proposed a somewhat different figure of 'woman' and her
attendant 'rights' as part of the bourgeois cultural revolution. But
men of the revolutionary classes could also see themselves in these
figures. 'Woman' could signify differently to men and women in
the cultural revolution, yet both could read themselves in that
figure, and in this way were brought together in the revolution. In
fact the cultural revolution was not only class-based but gender-
biased. 'Woman' of the cultural revolution oppressed middle-class
women in ways not found in the classes which the revolution
attacked, and as Margaret Walters writes, 'during the eighteenth
century, when some women were beginning to articulate their
rights, the distinction between the sexes was in fact becoming
harder and sharper', and middle-class women 'more firmly excluded from public affairs and the world of work'.[43] For this reason
'woman' was not only a powerful figure in the rhetoric of cultural

revolution but a field of struggle, fought over by factions contending for leadership and definition of that revolution.

Mary Wollstonecraft attempted the most thorough feminist transformation of the cultural revolution in her time, though her career and her feminism were made possible by that revolution. She was constructed as a self-divided being by the interlocked class and gender distinctions of her society, but this very division enabled her to recognize that culture, language, discourse and identity were not free spaces for the natural play of individuality but structured by power relations of several kinds in order to shape personal and social identity in the interests of dominant social groups, be these groups defined by class or gender, or both.[44] Accordingly, she constructed an identity and career as social critic in order to cope with her self-division and attack the social and cultural causes of it. Inevitably, this identity was paradoxical in terms of her culture – a woman of 'mind', 'a woman who has thinking powers', a 'female philosopher'.

The cultural revolution made possible Wollstonecraft's identity as social critic, as a woman of 'mind'; she then turned her 'mind' to one of the few professional careers available to women – that of professional writer. The French Revolution then provided the occasion for turning her 'mind' and career to Revolutionary feminism. As Virginia Woolf puts it,

> The Revolution . . . was not merely an event that had happened outside her; it was an active agent in her own blood. She had been in revolt all her life – against tyranny, against law, against convention. . . . The outbreak of the Revolution in France expressed some of her deepest theories and convictions.

Or as Toril Moi puts it, Wollstonecraft's 'essay on the rights of woman was made possible by the emancipatory if bourgeois-patriarchal ideas of *liberté, égalité* and *fraternité*'.[45]

'Mind' is a key word in Wollstonecraft's life and writings, and by it she meant the moral-intellectual being required by professional men. As she defined it, 'mind' included reason and imagination, feeling and critical thought, according to the full definition in Johnson's *Dictionary*. She accepted that most women's careers would be domestic – nurturing professional culture, reproducing it in the next generation and disseminating a diminutive version of it to the lower ranks who came within women's domestic sphere. But she argued that women needed 'mind' themselves if they were to fulfil the career prescribed by the cultural revolution's ideal of 'woman'. Wollstonecraft also argued that some women should be allowed to enter professions outside the home, and she even suggested that, to further their civism and patriotism, women should have electoral rights. But the central argument of her Revolutionary feminism was the need for distinct but parallel careers of 'mind' for (middle-class) men and women, if the professional middle class were to revolutionize society in their own image and interests, especially in a time of Revolutionary crisis.

Ultimately, Revolutionary feminism became a casualty of that crisis. It exposed contradictions in the cultural revolution in Britain, as far as women were concerned and involved. But at a time of sharply increased competition within the cultural revolution for leadership and power, such exposing of contradictions could seem dangerous to the revolution itself. The 1790s saw increased resistance not only to feminism but to the feminization of culture within the British cultural revolution, just as the French Revolution of 1793 to 1795 aimed to reverse the supposed feminization of culture and politics in the Revolution of 1789 to 1792. The failure of the first phase of the French Revolution, which corresponded to the character and aims of the bourgeois cultural revolution in Britain, led to a withdrawal from Revolutionary feminism in Britain along with withdrawal from coalition with 'progressive' elements of the upper and lower classes. In the 1790s most British cultural revolutionaries turned to 'femininism' or even anti-feminism; Revolutionary feminism and its immediate heirs were marginalized, suppressed or adopted by rival revolutionary programmes.

2

Self, Social Conflict and Writing

Mary Wollstonecraft's family background and upbringing gave her sharp experience of the regional, class, gender, and cultural divisions of late eighteenth-century Britain. She was born in 1759, the second of seven children, into a middle-class urban family that had been rising for several generations.[1] The Wollstonecrafts were in the London silk manufacture but by mid-century moved up from trade to become rentiers; her mother's family were mercantile middle-class Irish Protestants. Her father decided to move the family further up socially by becoming a gentleman-farmer just outside London. But like so many other chasers after gentility, he soon succumbed to the proverbial evils of social emulation: bad management, personal excesses and eventually social downfall. The family kept moving from one place to another in search of financial stability and social advancement, and by 1768 they were at Beverley in Yorkshire.

Here Mary Wollstonecraft received some formal education, and letters of this period show her to be socially and culturally ambitious. She is concerned about her own social status, and professes 'true' friendship against that 'according to the opinion of the world'.[2] She even repeats the conduct-book commonplace that the highest form of friendship is conjugal. She expresses self-criticism and self-doubts that would become aggravated and at times paralysing in later life. She adopts Sentimental poses to bolster her sense of herself – a trait she later turns into a rhetorical ploy in her books.[3] Similarly, she claims to write in a true expressive manner – 'what I have written flows spontaneously from my pen' (p. 61). She is interested in current practices of courtship, coquetry, gallantry and marriage, though she disdains both courtly amorousness and bourgeois 'prudery' – later to be major themes of her feminism. In these early letters she also shows an interest in writing itself and experiments with epistolary form, a variety of expressive and rhetorical devices and writing's potential for constructing an identity transcending mere social relativities.

But her father's financial and emotional 'extravagance' (as she later called it) accelerated the family's social and domestic decline. In order to economize he moved to Laugharne in Wales and then to Walworth near London. The stress of social failure led him to abuse his own family, though his 'passions' were seldom directed against Wollstonecraft herself; but she felt acutely both the humiliation of the family's slide down the social scale and the agony of the family's internal disintegration.[4] Though strong-willed, she suffered neurasthenic attacks during these years and at many times of crisis thereafter – a common resort, socially and philosophically sanctioned at the time.[5]

One recourse continued to be intellectual improvement. Such self-improvement led to relations of 'domestic affection' outside her own family, often with mentor figures, both male and female. At Hoxton, north of London, she was befriended by a clergyman named Clare and his wife who helped her to augment her limited formal education and thereby to face the grim reality that women of her class had few careers outside marriage. Her family's resources went to preparing her older brother Edward for the law, and Wollstonecraft resented this bourgeois version of primogeniture. Her brother was also concerned about respectability and this alienated her from middle-class social values and practices.

Her other recourse continued to be friendship. In the mid-1770s Wollstonecraft became friends with Frances Blood (always known as Fanny), like her, the daughter of a family ruined by a father's extravagance. In 1779 Wollstonecraft described her as one 'whom I love better than all the world beside. . . . She has a masculine understanding, and sound judgment, yet she has every feminine virtue' (*Letters*, p. 67). Meanwhile Wollstonecraft's father's affairs 'were so embarrassed by his misconduct that he was obliged to take the fortune that was settled on' his children (*Letters*, p. 66). Her older brother set up as an attorney in the City and married, but was reluctant to help his brothers and sisters. Wollstonecraft's two sisters Elizabeth (called Eliza or Bess) and Everina went to a boarding-school. Wollstonecraft planned to live with Fanny Blood, who was a competent artist, and perhaps open a school.

In 1778 she took one of the few jobs open to her, as lady's companion to a well-to-do merchant's wife living at Windsor and Bath. She was treated well but felt the social ambiguity of her position, somewhere between true companion and upper servant. At Bath and Windsor she also had ample opportunity to observe social emulation and distinctions of class and gender. Bath was England's leading fashionable resort and Wollstonecraft looked down on its fashionable social life, preferring intimate friendship and the domestic affections. She wrote from Windsor in 1780:

> I am very indifferent to the opinion of the world in general; – I wish to retire as much from it as possible – I am particularly sick of genteel life, as it is called; – the unmeaning civilities that I see every day practiced don't agree with my temper; – I long for a little sincerity, and look forward with pleasure to the time when I shall lay aside all restraint. (*Letters*, pp. 71–2)

Like many other middle-class people, she made a virtue of necessity and sought an alternative to a social world in which she had no status and could not compete.

Her sense of social isolation, alienation and lost social status later enabled her to develop the 'detached' or 'objective' stance necessary to the social critic, the Enlightenment demystifier of the hegemonic, the taken-for-granted, naturalized and legitimized as the established order. For the time being, like many others, she compensated for her situation with friendship, family duty, books, self-reflection and a broad humanitarianism. She took increasing responsibility for the education, employment and careers of her sisters, her brothers and even friends such as Fanny Blood's brother George. Intellectual self-improvement increased her prospects of employment but also enabled her to theorize her own character and social situation, legitimizing alienation as 'philosophical', or the result of a superior, critical consciousness.

She saw herself as a divided personality, internalizing the social ambivalence of her own social class toward their social superiors and explaining it in terms of the moral-intellectual commonplaces of later eighteenth-century middle-class culture. She also fluctuated between self-blame and intense if unfocused aspiration, between haughtiness – leading George Blood to nickname her 'the Princess' – and self-abasement. Not surprisingly, she often suffered from mental and emotional exhaustion and apathy – social frustration taking the form of physical complaints, often regarded as 'female ailments', permitted to the oppressed by the social culture of her day. Hence she sought self-affirmation and legitimization through 'philanthropy' – a prominent theme in liberal branches of Sensibility. She saw general love of mankind (as well as animals) as an extension of the domestic affections: 'I would wish to cherish a universal love to all mankind, but the principal part of my heart must be occupied by those who have for years had a place there' (*Letters*, p. 70).

Philanthropy was related to her other compensation, devotional religion. Like many socially marginalized people, she sought to suppress social anger with stoical, providential faith and to transfer social ambition and personal desire on to the transcendental plane of divine approval and life after death. She was more than nominally a member of the Church of England and took seriously the Church's doctrine that both true faith and good works are necessary to obtain salvation. In the 1780s she became closely associated with intellectual and political leaders of the liberal wing of English Dissent, but the moral and ethical culture of Anglicanism continued to be important in her intellectual development and her work and made her resist the agnosticism, radical theorizing and philosophical materialism of many cultural revolutionaries she came to know in later years.

In the early 1780s she had further experience of gender difference. In 1780 she left her job as lady's companion to nurse her mother through her last illness. This traditional female responsibility was especially onerous because she had tried to break her dependence on identity through the family; her mother was also a difficult patient. After her death Wollstonecraft moved to Walham Green to be with Fanny Blood, but then went to help the older of her two sisters, Elizabeth, through the last stages of her pregnancy. In October 1782 Eliza had married Meredith Bishop, son of a well-to-do family of shipwrights and himself engaged in overseas trade. After bearing her daughter she developed post-partum depression and aversion to her husband. Wollstonecraft could not mediate between the uncomprehending husband and the distraught wife and mother. She decided to help her sister flee, and early in 1784 the two ran away to lodgings elsewhere in London.

She knew that a husband had complete legal rights over his wife and children and that according to conduct books and social convention a wife was supposed to bear with a husband, however bad. She herself claimed to 'hold the marriage vow sacred'; she also knew she would be condemned as 'the *shameful incendiary* in this shocking affair of a woman's leaving her bed-fellow . . . In short 'tis contrary to all the rules of conduct that are published for the benefit of new married Ladies' (*Letters*, p. 86). 'Incendiary' means an agitator, particularly 'one who stirs up civil strife'. The sarcastic reference to conduct books shows awareness of the gap between women's actual domestic lives and such books' prescriptions for domestic woman.

The injustice of conjugal sexual and emotional relations in her own class was soon reinforced for her. After she extricated Eliza from her marriage she set up a school north of London to ensure independence for herself, her sisters and Fanny Blood. The school was combined with a boarding-house for women and their children, and required attention to business, a reputation for 'respectability' and a subservience to clients that Wollstonecraft found irksome. The responsibility fell mostly on her shoulders, causing her further anxiety. Fanny Blood had an 'understanding' with Hugh Skeys, but he feared his family would disapprove of marriage to an impecunious young woman of ungenteel family connections. Wollstonecraft saw Skeys as excessively 'prudent' in his narrowly bourgeois concern for money and respectability at the expense of love. Skeys and Blood finally married in February 1785 and left for Lisbon; Fanny became pregnant, though she was in poor health. Wollstonecraft must have felt that Skeys's expecting his wife to bear him a child as soon as possible was inconsiderate and dangerous. Wollstonecraft went to Portugal in the autumn of 1785 to be with her friend during childbirth, but Fanny and her infant died in late November and Wollstonecraft returned to England a month later. She knew that her absence from the school might hasten its failure, as turned out to be the case. Fanny's fate dramatized again the injustice, inequality and physical vulnerability that was the lot of women in marriage, and pointed up again the limitations of petty bourgeois propriety and 'prudence'. Through these vicissitudes Wollstonecraft was taking up a social and cultural position distant at once from the fashionable, courtly upper class and from what she saw as the petty, self-interested, vulgar, mercantile middle classes.

This self-construction as a social critic was reinforced at Newington Green in the mid-1780s by her widening social sphere and intellectual contacts, such as the Reverend Richard Price, a leader of the English Nonconformist Enlightenment and spokesman for various causes of political and social reform.[6] Price's moral, social and political philosophy, systematized in his *Review of the Principal*

Questions in Morals (1758, revised 1769 and 1787) and popularized in a number of sermons and political tracts, became the basis of Wollstonecraft's own philosophy, leading to her Revolutionary feminism of the 1790s.[7] Summarizing the tradition of liberal Dissent, Price argues that spiritually all humans are equal, and that mortal life is a probationary state in which moral character and ethical conduct determine one's fate in eternity. To act according to God's will one must be able to exercise moral judgement, and this requires moral and intellectual education and personal liberty. Price carried this philosophy into many domains of human and social life, and applied it in several philanthropic, liberal, reformist causes, including the independence of the American colonies and relief of Dissenters from the civil disabilities imposed on them in the seventeenth century.

An important woman-friend at this time was associated with the same tradition of thought. Sarah Burgh was the widow of Dr James Burgh, Dissenting Academy lecturer and moral and educational writer, whose works may also have been studied by Wollstonecraft. Mrs Burgh acted as a patron, loaning Wollstonecraft money for her projects of independence and opening further contacts with English Dissent and its progressive, reformist Enlightenment. Another valuable friend was the Reverend John Hewlett, an intellectual Anglican clergyman. He tried to help her career in 1783 by introducing her to Samuel Johnson, long known as patron and mentor of women writers and intellectuals. Through this widening circle of professional middle-class friends, Wollstonecraft accelerated her own intellectual development and improved her professional prospects.

She herself acted as a patron when she could, trying to find 'places' for her friends and relations, and exhorting them to 'improvement' so that they could take advantage of opportunities she turned up. On her return from Portugal and the collapse of the school her own women-friends tried to find her a job, and she was hired as governess to the daughters of Lord and Lady Kingsborough of Mitchelstown in county Cork, Ireland. But before she went to Ireland in the autumn of 1786 she finished a conduct book for girls and then through Hewlett met Joseph Johnson, the leading publisher of the Nonconformist Enlightenment, who published the book and played a major role in the rest of her career.

Thoughts on the Education of Daughters: With Reflections on Female Conduct, in the More Important Duties of Life was published early in 1787 and belongs to a long tradition of conduct books for women. Women writers in this tradition follow the same principles and topics set forth in books by men, such as Halifax's *Advice to a Daughter* (1688) and Fénelon's *Traité de l'éducation des filles* (1687; English translation, 1707). But there are differences. Whereas the men admonish and exhort, books such as Lady Sarah Pennington's *An Unfortunate Mother's Advice to Her Absent Daughters* (1761) and Hester Chapone's *Letters on the Improvement of the Mind, Addressed to a Young Lady* (1773) also sympathize and console, view women's lot gloomily, recommend intellectual and moral development as defence against the inevitable disappointments of a woman's life, criticize women contaminated by vulgarity or corrupted by courtliness, and often use imperative verbs and words such as 'must' and 'only'.

Wollstonecraft knew Pennington's and Chapone's books and printed several passages from Chapone in her *Female Reader* (1789), such as : 'The principal virtues or vices of a woman must be of a private and domestic kind. – Within the circle of her own family and dependants lies her sphere of action.'[8] Yet Chapone, like Wollstonecraft, insists that women are not naturally inferior to men (quoted in *The Female Reader*). Not surprisingly, Wollstonecraft echoes Chapone in her private letters of the 1780s and even in *A Vindication of the Rights of Woman*. Conduct books sometimes projected women's role beyond domesticity, as in Sarah Trimmer's *The Œconomy of Charity* (1787), ostensibly a proposal for women of the upper and middle classes to extend their domestic and educational role from the home to society at large, by setting up a network of institutes for education and employment of otherwise 'idle' lower-class men and women. In fact conduct literature is the context for Revolutionary feminism, defining woman as domestic yet insisting on her human dignity and her importance to both private life and the fate of the nation

Like its predecessors, *Thoughts* is more ambitious than it looks, popularizing current philosophical, theological and cultural issues in a comprehensive critique of class and gender relations. For example, like other educational writers Wollstonecraft warns against moral and cultural contamination by the lower classes, especially servants, who are often left to supervise middle-class children.[9] She views the lower classes themselves as child-like and recommends they be treated as children.[10] On this point class and gender distinctions overlap: women who lack moral and intellectual training resemble the lower orders in being 'superstitious', improvident, opportunistic, impulsive, merely social and gullible. By contrast, the properly educated woman is rational, provident, realistic, self-disciplined, self-conscious and critical, resembling the professional man who is the unstated social and cultural norm.

Therefore Wollstonecraft's prescription for the construction of woman is patterned on education for males, especially those who must accumulate moral and intellectual capital for professional life. Accordingly, she prescribes 'exercise' of mind and body. Physical exercise is recommended as the foundation of mental exercise and vigour, according to contemporary materialist philosophy of the physical, sensory basis of moral and intellectual being. Through physical exercise women will avoid the sickly delicacy of courtly women; by implication, men will also find it more difficult to treat women as they are in court society. Wollstonecraft's insistence on vigorous exercise for females goes beyond most conduct books and participates in the *embourgeoisement* of the female body – the appropriation or construction of the female body for middle-class culture. She is also more insistent than her predecessors that women acquire critical thought similar to that required by professional men (p. 22). Women should learn to reflect on their own experience to build an independent self (p. 111). 'Taste' and the arts should be acquired as forms of critical thought rather than genteel ornaments. This includes writing, critical thought applied through language: 'Writing well is of great consequence in life as to our temporal interest, and of still more to the mind; as it teaches a person to arrange their thoughts, and digest them' (p. 46).

Writing and reading thus make the 'mind' independent of the 'senses' and those 'passions' that open the self to court culture and social emulation. But novels cause 'affectation', or emulative conduct; encourage 'sensibility', or a pretended nobility of soul; produce 'a false taste' that makes solid reading seem 'dull and insipid'; unfit 'the mind' for domestic life and duties; and teach courtly love which makes women 'insignificant' or mere sexual prey, enslaving them subjectively. Because men hold all social, legal and political power, courtly love gives women the illusion and sometimes the reality of power. Nevertheless, love can be resisted (p. 84); indeed, as a physical passion it has no place in a good marriage (pp. 97–8), for it merely re-sites the 'mistress system' in the home. Wollstonecraft even argues that marriage in itself harms women because, paradoxically, it deprives them of struggle with the wider social world, a struggle that men must engage in daily (p. 100).

She argues that women, like professional men, must develop moral-intellectual being as critical consciousness, even though, like other conduct writers, she envisages women's 'profession' as companionate and egalitarian marriage, the basis for reproducing gentrified professional middle-class culture, and thus the basis of the state. But in contrast to men conduct writers she leaves this topic to consider ways women can compensate for inevitable disappointment in life. These include two attributes necessary for successful professional life – intellectual cultivation and moral discipline – as well as religion, which is neither a flight to the transcendental nor an alternative to social rebellion, but a way to heroize women's impossible social position. These compensations constitute the only power available to women and other socially oppressed groups: power over one's self, legitimated divinely, transcendentally and non-socially.

Wollstonecraft closes her book on this note, rejecting both the 'fine Lady' of court culture and the fallen woman who is the 'fine Lady's' failed emulator, rejecting both upper-class 'vice' and lower-class 'folly' for the paradisal culture of the revolutionary middle classes, which is not yet of this world:

> Our pursuits and pleasures should . . . prepare us for a state of purity and happiness. There vice and folly will not poison our pleasures; our faculties will expand, and not mistake their objects; and we shall no longer 'see as through a glass darkly, but know, even as we are known'. (p. 160)

Appropriately, she ends by quoting the biblical conduct writer, St Paul. Nevertheless, *Thoughts* points toward Wollstonecraft's Revolutionary feminism of the 1790s. It is a thorough application of the women's conduct-book tradition, with its pessimism about the earthly prospects for women of the middle class – the class of most women conduct writers. It also recommends a version of professional men's culture for women but envisages no real social role for such women. Like the other conduct books, *Thoughts* leaves women in an impasse; but it was a short step to resolving that impasse with something like Revolutionary feminism.

Stylistically Wollstonecraft also anticipates her polemical

writings of the Revolutionary decade through a gender-based decorum of style and composition that exemplifies her argument on the intellectual and moral condition of women. Her preface declares that her style will validate her social critique:

> I am afraid, indeed, the reflections will, by some, be thought too grave; but I could not make them less so without writing affectedly; yet, though they may be insipid to the gay, others may not think them so; and if they should prove useful to one fellow-creature, and beguile any hours, which sorrow has made heavy, I shall think I have not been employed in vain.

'Reflections' are instances of critical thought; 'writing affectedly' and 'the gay' are instances of the courtly; and being 'useful' and 'not employed in vain' are instances of the professional. The wish to 'beguile any hours, which sorrow has made heavy' is not a pious, sentimental hope but an intention to speak from one sorrow (the author's) to another (the reader's) – both sorrows implicitly arising from the condition of women. Thus the preface sets a course for useful social criticism in an answerable style.

The main text is composed in a loose, desultory form, as indicated by the title – 'Thoughts . . . With Reflections'. But the sections of the book have a rational pattern, the growth and education of a woman in relation to the vicissitudes of her life, from education in 'The Nursery' (the first section) to entry into social life in 'Public Places' (the last section). In between, the book prescribes construction of the moral, intellectual and social self in 'Moral Discipline', 'Exterior Accomplishments', 'Artificial Manners', 'Dress', 'The Fine Arts', 'Reading', 'Boarding Schools' and 'The Temper'. The section 'Unfortunate Situation of Females, fashionably educated, and left without a Fortune' notes that for most women 'settling' in life means marriage, for there are few professions open to them. 'Love' and 'Matrimony' are described gloomily, leading to 'Desultory Thoughts' on the value of religion, and 'The Benefits which Arise from Disappointments'. The last seven sections consider woman's domestic, moral, ethical and social life after marriage, including 'On the Treatment of Servants', 'The Observance of Sunday', 'On the Misfortune of Fluctuating Principles', 'Benevolence', 'Card-Playing', 'The Theatre' and finally 'Public Places'.

But *Thoughts* avoids resembling a treatise or philosophical inquiry and purports to be desultory, occasional and *ad hoc* because it purports to speak to the practical, daily, continuing reality of its female readers, who are in any case conventionally excluded from philosophical, abstract enquiry and argument. For this reason *Thoughts* is also intermittently autobiographical, sustaining the authority of a woman writing on women, even where the author has no direct experience, such as of motherhood and breast-feeding. Suckling one's own infants stimulates maternal feeling, she declares: 'I have even felt it, when I have seen a mother perform that office; and am of opinion, that maternal tenderness arises quite as much from habit as instinct' (p. 4). The movement of thought here is characteristic – from a reported experience to a general principle or 'opinion'. But the passage also exemplifies her simple programme for the self-education of women – reflection on one's personal everyday life. Similarly, she repeatedly validates a generalization by a personal reference, beginning 'I have seen . . .'.

This kind of validation is also seen in passages of lyrical ex-pressivity, as when the writer describes the loneliness of the educated and cultivated woman forced into a degrading profession such as governess (pp. 74–5). These passages aim not only to avoid 'affectation' but to display the plenitude of self that is the goal of her educational system, a plenitude that may be produced from the impasse of women's condition. Such passages often move toward or away from generalizations of experience in the form of the maxim rather than the syllogistic argument. Young women were advised to read collections of maxims because they were thought to need guiding principles but could not themselves reason out such principles. Wollstonecraft uses maxims in *Thoughts* and elsewhere as an emblem of women's intellectual culture, as the appropriate form for women's 'reflections' on their daily and domestic experience.

Other rhetorical devices observe the same decorum. She uses examples from common life, often with a biblical echo, rather than learned or philosophical ones, as when she writes that the mind 'will not lie fallow; promiscuous seeds will be sown by accident, and they will shoot up with the wheat, and perhaps never be eradicated' (pp. 17–18). She is fond of analogies to natural pro-cesses, as when she writes: 'Intellectual improvements, like the growth and formation of the body, must be gradual' (p. 17). She uses recurrent images, such as veils and dress to suggest the way the self conceals or reveals itself through culture and custom, for good or ill. Such images aim to persuade through repetition rather than argument. Quotations, references and allusions are few, and come from well known works such as Locke on education, the writings of A. L. Barbauld and Sarah Trimmer, the epistles of St Paul, Nicholas Rowe's popular 'she-tragedy' *The Fair Penitent* and Shakespeare's *King Lear*, heroic drama and 'classic' English poets such as Thomson and Pope. She is sparing of rhetorical flourishes, in keeping with the avoidance of 'affectation'. She uses alliteration to fashion a resounding phrase, writing that 'many women always retain the pretty prattle of the nursery, and do not forget to lisp, when they have learnt to languish' (p. 8). Here alliteration achieves sarcastic edge with 'pretty prattle' while suggesting that the effeminization and courtization of women link the infantilism of lisping to the coquetry of languishing.

The language, style and form of *Thoughts* aim to show the kind of 'mind' that it calls for women to acquire; the implication of this discursive move is that the way out of the impasse of women's condition is to become like the author of *Thoughts*, whom the reader might suppose to be, by virtue of her very authorship, that rare being: a woman professional, independent of domesticity. This probability implicitly challenges the apparently conventional prescription for domestic woman that the book sets forth. Such a challenge would not be made explicit, however, until the 1790s. Although *Thoughts* is not a major book it takes up the conduct-book tradition and orients it toward Revolutionary feminism. It impressed Joseph Johnson, who already had writers such as A. L. Barbauld and Sarah Trimmer in his list, and the fact that it was soon to be published may have obtained for Wollstonecraft an important advance in her career.

Her time with the Kingsboroughs enlarged both her observation of society and her intellectual horizons, both her disgust at upper-class decadence and middle-class emulation and her increasing confidence in the power of her own 'mind'. She began to see herself as a 'genius' in the late eighteenth-century meaning of the word – not so much a transcendentally gifted individual as a uniquely gifted individual, distinct from others, for better or for worse – like Rousseau, whom Wollstonecraft was reading at this time, a 'solitary walker'. As a 'genius' her social alienation was transformed from social failure to intellectual and moral superiority, transcending merely fashionable or vulgar society and merely feminine women. The sense of being a 'genius' that she acquired from the Kingsborough period made possible her next advance in personal and professional life, to become a professional writer.

As she prepared to join the Kingsboroughs in the autumn of 1786 she felt anxious about her professional qualifications, about acceptance in elevated, aristocratic society, and about maintaining a separate, equal identity. The profession of governess was a woman's version of the most socially dependent professions available to men. Yet her new position would be considered a great opportunity within the patronage system that still dominated professional life. She also feared that in the Kingsborough household she would lack true domestic affections. As she wrote to George Blood:

> I by no means like the proposal of being a governess – I should be shut out from society – and be debarred the *imperfect* pleasures of friendship – as I should on every side be surrounded by *unequals* – To live only on terms of civility and common benevolence without any interchange of little acts of kindness and tenderness would be to me extremely irksome. (*Letters*, p. 110)

To her surprise she was received well and respectfully, as a 'gentlewoman'. The children quickly became fond of her, especially the eldest daughter Margaret. Wollstonecraft was accepted by the adults, her advice and help were sought, and she was asked to meet anyone of importance who came to visit. She could refuse to join in the Kingsboroughs' social life but when she did she held her own. She also enjoyed the attention of intellectual men such as the Kingsboroughs' friend George Ogle and her new friend the Reverend Henry Gabell. With the Kingsboroughs she experienced social inferiority yet social success and even independence. This success validated her self-conscious posture as social critic, detached from both the courtly upper-classes and those in other classes who emulated them.

But it was particularly as a woman that she defined her own social position against the upper-class women she saw, especially Lady Kingsborough. She became sharply critical of her, admitting that 'a fine Lady is a new species to me of animals'. By mid-November she wrote that Lady Kingsborough 'is a fine Lady

without fancy or sensibility' (pp. 126–7). By early March she found
her ladyship 'still more haughty and disagreeable', 'for she cannot
bear that any one should take notice of me', especially any of the
'gentlemen'. By May Wollstonecraft felt conscious moral and intellectual superiority to this merely courtly woman: 'She is devoid of
sensibility – of course, *vanity only* inspires her immoderate love of
praise – and *selfishness* her *traffick* of civility' (*Letters*, p. 151). In
public, social situations, however, Lady Kingsborough had power
Wollstonecraft could not challenge, and in June she complained
that she was still treated in public with less than her due: 'My spirit
rises and assumes its native dignity and feels itself superior to the
little souls clothed with adventitious' qualities such as rank and
wealth (p. 156).

In her encounter with intersecting conflicts of class and gender
she tended increasingly to see her personal experience in terms of
a general social critique. She found the social life at Mitchelstown
too courtly and ceremonial – 'the forms and parade of high life suit
not my mind' (*Letters*, p. 120). After a few months in Dublin she
thought the whole of Irish society vitiated by its courtly ruling class
and its emulative middle and lower ranks. In March 1787 she wrote
to Everina: 'I do not like Ireland. The family pride which reigns
here produces the worst effects – They are in general proud and
mean, the servile respect that is universally paid to people of
quality disgusts me, and the minute attention to propriety stops
the growth of virtue' (*Letters*, p. 141).

Generalizing her social situation and experience was one way
she dealt with internalized conflicts of class and gender. Hitherto
she had responded to these contradictions with pious resignation,
nervous debility, strenuous work, recourse to nature, cultivation
of the domestic affections and devotion to intellectual self-
improvement. But in Ireland she began to arrange these elements
of personal identity into the consciousness of a professional
middle-class revolutionary. Before going to Ireland she felt 'quite
alone in a crowd' and confessed that 'A whole train of nervous
disorders have taken possession of me – and they appear to arise
so much from the mind' (*Letters*, pp. 117–18). In spite of her
professional and social success she continued to feel 'gloom' and
longing 'for my eternal rest' (p. 126). But by December she had
acquired a philosophical interest in the relation of her mind and
body, writing to George Blood:

These disorders are particularly distressing as they seem intirely to arise from the mind – and that an exertion of the reasoning faculties would banish them and bring it to a proper tone – but slackened nerves are not to be braced by arguments[;] physical as well as mental causes have contributed to reduce me to my present weak state.   (p. 128)

She was learning to see herself and her experience in terms of Enlightenment materialism and the culture of Sensibility. She was more inclined to Sensibility because that movement was already a feminization of culture. She found that the merely fashionable women at Mitchelstown lacked 'sentiment': 'alas, poor sentiment it has no residence here – I almost wish the girls were novels [sic] readers and romantic, I declare false refinement is better than none at all' (Letters, p. 126). She was reading Rousseau, the master of Sensibility and bourgeois alienation from court culture. Like Rousseau, she refers to herself as 'alone in a crowd', 'a strange being' or 'an exile'. In February 1787 she boasted in Rousseauist vein, 'I commune with my own spirit – and am detached from the world' (Letters, p. 137). A few weeks later she was reading Rousseau's Émile and loved 'his paradoxes'. She even compared herself to Rousseau: 'he rambles into that chimerical [imaginary] world in which I have too often [wand]ered – and draws the usual conclusion that all is vanity and vexation of spirit'. She often used the last five words, from the Bible, to describe her view of life. In the same letter she refers to Rousseau's Confessions, the masterpiece of the Sentimental culture of subjectivity and writing the self.

Differences of class, gender and culture converged in her contest with Lady Kingsborough over George Ogle. In April 1787 she confessed to Everina that she had found her own Rousseau in Ogle: 'He is between forty and fifty – a genius, and unhappy – Such a man, you may suppose would catch your sister's eye.' But Lady Kingsborough had 'chosen him for her flirt'. Faced with a choice between a courtly coquette and a female 'genius', Ogle seems to have chosen the latter.[11] But Wollstonecraft later became disillusioned with both Ogle and Rousseau, discovering both to conceal courtly 'sensuality' in their 'sensibility'. During the 1790s she would come to see Sensibility as less a form of bourgeois revolutionary culture than an appropriation of courtly ideology by the bourgeois cultural revolution, especially in gender relations. This revaluation was central to her Revolutionary feminism, yet Sensibility provided her with a language of self and social relations during the 1780s, enabling her, and many other professional people, to construct an independent identity from the culture of the dominant classes.

Religious resignation played a continuing part in Wollstonecraft's self-identity, but here too there is a new, 'philosophical' attitude. For example, she uses religion to transcendentalize and thus legitimize the values and practices of her middle-class culture in her repeated and otherwise maudlin longing for death. Her materialist philosophy made her aware that socially conditioned mental distresses caused her bodily ills; thus the death of the body stands for the final liberation of the mind-self and the abolition of the social conditions of the mind-body's suffering. These social conditions include gender difference. In November 1786 she wrote to Everina, 'I struggle with myself – but I hope my Heavenly Father will not be extreme to mark my weakness . . . I almost wish my warfare was over' (*Letters*, p. 127). Such self-suppression was recommended in conduct books for women and is here presented in conduct-book language. The 'warfare' was her internalization of real divisions of class and gender, which she perceived as unalterable and intrinsic to the social system. If that system could not be changed, she could only await removal from it by death.

For the time being, religion remained a major compensation for social alienation and inward conflict. But by the spring of 1787 she wondered if religious resignation conflicted with critical consciousness. Replying to a letter from the Reverend Henry Dyson Gabell, who was a tutor in another Irish landed family, she argues that critical thought is not an obstacle but is essential to a moral life, especially for those like themselves, subject to an unjust and oppressive social system:

> Why have we implanted in us an irresistible desire to think – if thinking is not in some measure necessary to make us wise unto salvation. . . . Employing the understanding purifies the heart, gives dignity to the affections, by allowing the mind to analyze them. . . . How can the mind govern the body if it is not exercised. . . . refinement[,] genius – and those charming talents which my soul instinctively loves, produce misery in this world – abundantly more pain than pleasure. . . . My reason has been too far stretched, and tottered almost on the brink of madness –

no wonder then, if I humbly hope, that the ordeal trial answered some end, and that I have not suffered in vain. (pp. 149–50)

This argument remained Wollstonecraft's main integration of philosophy, religion and personal experience for the rest of her life, and was part of her feminism in the 1790s. The argument was also related to her professional work. While with the Kingsboroughs she developed her self-conscious professional identity and her professional principles and practice, and she used them to sustain herself in the face of her social superiors and their culture. Like many men of her time, she found that professional and personal experience were inseparable and, indeed, supported each other within a class-based culture. Her professional principles and practice were one with her general social critique, her version of the professional middle-class cultural revolution. Her profession required mastery of book culture, and books were another instrument of self-construction and a bridge between her personal experience, her 'philosophical' generalizing of that experience and her professional work. Many professional men found themselves in such a position, and Wollstonecraft grappled with men's book culture in order to achieve a detached social consciousness about that position. On the other hand, much of her reading was 'feminized' critical discourse in that it was a popularized , simplified or novelized form of men's book culture. Thus in constructing herself as a social critic through her reading Wollstonecraft encountered another area of culture divided by class and gender.

She was by now well-read in female conduct books and devotional literature. She refers to Rousseau's autobiographical writings and quotes from William Paley's *Principles of Moral and Political Philosophy* (1785), St Paul's epistles (a favourite source), La Rochefoucauld's maxims and Johnson's *Rambler* – Johnson remained one of her favourite authors. She refers to sermons by her friend the Reverend John Hewlett, Frances Burney's *Cecilia*, Cowper's moral-philosophical poems of domestic life, Madame de Genlis's *Letters on Education* (probably a translation of *Les Veillées du château*, 1784), the Baroness de Montolière's philosophical and Sentimental novel *Caroline of Lichtfield* and Charlotte Smith's widely read poems. She read 'Philosophy' and 'philosophical sermons', and Hugh Blair's *Lectures on Rhetoric and Belles Lettres*, the most comprehensive English summary of Enlightenment philosophy of discourse, which she found 'an intellectual feast' (*Letters*, p. 138). References to philosophical books and passages generalizing her own experience and social criticism increase in the letters of the last few months with the Kingsboroughs. Her life up to the summer of 1787 had given her a broad range of social and cultural experience for a woman of her time and class, with an acute sense of class and gender difference. In youth she felt that she belonged in a higher sphere, and her pursuit of professional identity and culture in adulthood replaced social status with nobility of 'mind' and cultural status. During the Kingsborough period she reconstructed herself as a professional and a 'noble soul' within overlapping discourses of Enlightenment and Sentimental culture, discourses that were mainly the cultural property of professional men in her time.

Having written herself as 'genius' and social critic in the letters of this period she took the next step, to become a professional writer. This was not only an advance in her career; it promised to solve her linked problems of social alienation from the hegemonic order and internalization of this alienation as psychological and physical dis-ease. Significantly, she refers to this step as a self-determination, writing to Joseph Johnson in September 1787:

> I often think of my new plan of life. . . . I am determined! – Your sex generally laugh at female determinations; but let me tell you, I never yet resolved to do, any thing of consequence, that I did not adhere resolutely to it, till I had accomplished my purpose. . . . In the course of near nine-and-twenty years, I have gathered some experience. . . . I long for a little peace and *independence*! (*Letters*, p. 159)

In her last months with the Kingsboroughs she completed a book that could be seen as her declaration of independence. Yet she chose the doubly oblique form of novelizing her personal experience and her reading. She wrote to Henry Gabell in September 1787 that in spite of her 'vexations' from living with the Kingsboroughs she had 'lately written, a fiction . . . ; it is a tale, to illustrate an opinion of mine, that a genius will educate itself. I have drawn from Nature' (*Letters*, p. 162). Though it bears its author's name in its title (if not on its title-page), *Mary: A Fiction* is more than an autobiographical novel; and though it belongs to the acceptably feminine genres of educational writing and the novel, it also advertises its author's grasp of Enlightenment philosophy and social criticism, the ethics and aesthetics of Sensibility and the social criticism of the professional middle-class cultural revolution.[12] *Mary* embodies Enlightenment-Sentimental culture by generalizing, politicizing and aestheticizing personal experience. At the same time, it shows Wollstonecraft's grasp of recent formal developments in the novel and her understanding of the novel's role in cultural reproduction, for better or worse, as understood at the time.

The form she chose was the *bildungsroman* – the novel of education and socialization, or self-construction, widely used by the bourgeois cultural revolution to represent and disseminate new ideology and practices of subjectivity. Her model here was Rousseau. As she had told Everina in March, 'He chuses a *common* capacity to educate – and gives as a reason, that a genius will educate itself' (p. 145). In the months between her letter to Everina and her letter to Gabell, Rousseau's view that 'a genius will educate itself' has become 'an opinion of mine'. Wollstonecraft saw herself through Rousseau the 'solitary walker' *and* social critic, the two identities creating and conditioning each other. Rousseau showed that the marginalized individual was perforce the authentic and unique individual, or 'genius', and thus in the best position to understand and to criticise the merely social domain. The connection between the subjective and the social was a major focus of Sensibility that appealed particularly to those who were socially marginalized. This appeal gave Sensibility a revolutionary potential recognized in the 1790s.[13] Reading herself through Rousseau also made her aware of the revolutionary potential of writing. Writing enabled Rousseau to represent his 'genius' and 'sensibility' and thus to disseminate his isolated and alienated self. Writing mediated the 'genius' into the social and cultural critic, showed the necessary relationship between the two and validated the social and cultural criticism by manifesting the 'genius' in writing. Writing empowered Rousseau culturally and socially in a way not available to him otherwise, an example that Wollstonecraft would turn toward feminism.

She considered female 'genius' and 'sensibility' in an early unfinished allegory, 'The Cave of Fancy', that may have been intended for her anthology *The Female Reader* (1788). Sagestus, a hermit in charge of educating the young orphan Sagesta, describes her sensibility in terms of Enlightenment materialist epistemology, basing mental faculties, abstract knowledge and moral and aesthetic 'taste' on physical sensation and sensitivity.[14] This is 'sensibility' as both refined bodily sense and uniquely cultivated moral and intellectual being, or 'genius'. But the form of 'The Cave of Fancy' is as important as its ideas. The philosophical tale was used by *philosophes* such as Voltaire and Rousseau and moralists such as Samuel Johnson, and would be apt for critical consideration of sensibility because its abstract and allegorical nature would seem anti-sentimental, a counter to kinds of fiction thought to celebrate and purvey sensibility to women of Wollstonecraft's own class, education and station.

Its form sets 'The Cave of Fancy' apart from Sentimental novels and tales, but in *Mary: A Fiction* Wollstonecraft takes on the form and themes of the Sentimental novel itself. This intention is evident in the subtitle. A 'fiction', according to Johnson's *Dictionary*, is merely something 'feigned or invented', and thus distinct from a 'novel', defined by Johnson as a 'small tale, generally of love'. The epigraph on the title page, from Rousseau's encyclopaedic novel of Sensibility, *La nouvelle Héloïse*, also suggests a didactic programme: *'L'exercice des plus sublimes vertus élève et nourrit le génie'* ('The exercise of the most sublime virtues raises and nourishes genius'). The 'Advertisement' or preface sets out this task in more detail – to create a heroine unlike those of Richardson's *Clarissa* and *Sir Charles Grandison* or Rousseau's *Émile*.[15] Such heroines represent woman constructed for man: the heroic feminine victim of the courtly rake and gallant, the virtuous feminine companion of the ideal professionalized gentleman, and the intellectually and erotically subservient companion of the ideal bourgeois man.

Wollstonecraft proposes to counter these false models by displaying her self, her 'genius': 'Those compositions only have power to delight, and carry us willing captives, where the soul of the author is exhibited, and animates the hidden springs.' Furthermore, as one of the 'chosen few, [who] wish to speak for themselves, and not to be an echo', she will not copy but create something original. She describes her objective:

In an artless tale, without episodes, the mind of a woman, who has thinking powers is displayed. The female organs have been thought too weak for this arduous employment; and experience seems to justify the assertion. Without arguing physically about *possibilities* – in a fiction, such a being may be allowed to exist;

whose grandeur is derived from the operations of its own faculties, not subjugated to opinion; but drawn by the individual from the original source.

This manifesto is polemical is every phrase. The words 'artless tale' reject the conventional novel as doubly 'artificial', concerned with fashionable life and affected in style, in contrast to the 'tale', which conventionally dealt with common life in a simple form and 'non-literary' style. 'Without episodes' means avoiding complex, numerous incidents for 'display' of 'the mind of a woman', or psychological realism. The statement that 'the female organs have been thought too weak' for the 'arduous employment' of thinking refers sarcastically to the Enlightenment materialist and determinist argument that women have weaker, more delicate sensory organs and mental powers than men and therefore are intellectually (and probably morally) weaker.[16] The distinction between philosophy's restriction to physical possibilities and fiction's licence to represent ideal potentialities suggests that fiction may be superior to philosophy in certain respects. This ideal transcends social categories of identity and worth, for though it may only be written and fictitious it has 'grandeur' (or sublimity) 'derived from the operation of its own faculties', or inner self, 'not subjugated to opinion' or merely social and conventional standards of value. This sublimity is drawn from and validated by the sublime 'original source' – God. By claiming that women may participate in this 'grandeur' through their 'thinking powers' she implies that the subordination of women is merely social, relative and contingent, and therefore may be subject to (revolutionary) change.

This manifesto would suggest to readers that the author aims to accomplish several tasks at once in her novel. She aims to advertise her own 'mind' – her intellectual and literary competence, her right to participate in the cultural revolution – and thus to authorize her argument that a woman may have 'thinking powers'. She aims to generalize her career into a critical representation of the social, economic and legal causes of women's subjection in contemporary society, thus transforming autobiography into a critique of false sensibility as court culture in disguise. More obviously, she aims to use the novel form itself to counter the conventional novel's representation and reproduction of women's moral and intellectual inferiority by means of this false sensibility. By purporting to represent its author's 'mind' in both the text at large and the 'mind' of the eponymous heroine, and by doing so within a critique of decadently Sentimental fiction, *Mary* aims to instruct its readers in the critical thought that will liberate them from the mind-forg'd manacles of the mere novel, and thus from subjection in real life.[17]

Mary uses what Patricia Meyer Spacks calls the female version of 'the picaresque novel of adolescence' in order to show how oppression may in fact produce the 'mind' of a 'genius', able to understand oppression and therefore counteract it.[18] Like many writers opposing a literary system they see as outmoded or purveying false ideology, Wollstonecraft claims superior 'authenticity' and 'realism' for her own work. Thus *Mary* aims to rewrite the conventional Sentimental novel by creating a more 'authentic' heroine, a more 'authentic' world for her to inhabit and a more significant political education for her in that world. Rather than describing scenes of fashionable life, *Mary* attacks fashionable life – and fashionable novels. Rather than scenes of genteelly sentimental distress, it presents its heroine's anguish at social misery. Rather than a 'romantically' attractive hero, it has one that is older, ugly and intellectual. Rather than advocate middle-class 'prudence' while toying with the sexual double standard, it asserts the right of women to passion and desire. Rather than have its heroine struggle toward marriage as the reward of virtue, it shows that marriage is a business deal between families and a prison for female desire. Rather than have a happy ending, the novel concludes that there is no such thing in mortal life for women. *Mary* rejects the conventional themes, settings and conclusions of Sentimental 'novels of the day' and shows that the world is unfit for 'genius', especially a female 'genius'. This is a favourite theme of Sensibility, but Sentimental novels usually accommodate bourgeois subjectivity to the dominant social order by depicting the heroine's nobility of soul and then marrying her to propertied nobility of rank. *Mary*'s plot refuses this accommodation.

Mary's critique of false sensibility is evident from comparing it with two Sentimental novels it singles out for condemnation. The first, *The History of Eliza Warwick* (1778), has an unfortunate heroine, noble lovers, charming rakes, seductions and betrayals, scenes of fashionable life and sentimental pathos, female jealousy and intrigue, coincidences, gloomy foreshadowing and displays of sentiment. But the sensibility here is merely fashionable and a mask for libertinism. The novel both gratifies and chastens its readers' interest in social climbing, for the apparent social success of the heroine in marrying Sir Charles Beaufort proves illusory. He is already married, and when his first wife reveals this, the heroine can only exclaim: 'when she declared to me *that I was robbed of virtue*, she had told me every thing that could strike horror into my soul'. The novel claims to defend moral propriety but flirts with courtly 'gallantry'. The heroine even accepts the sexual double standard, for when Sir Charles wishes to marry Eliza after his wife has conveniently died, she replies: 'never can I consent, even for your own credit's sake, to give you a wife whose innocence is stained, whose character is lost'. *Mary* defies this double standard in several ways. It replaces the hero of erotic desire with one of the 'mind'; it portrays a heroine with physical and moral courage who recognizes her own desire; it is set in common life; it values female friendship; and it avoids the gloomy foreshadowing that colours *Eliza Warwick*.

The second novel criticised in *Mary* is Mrs H. Cartwright's *The Platonic Marriage* (1787). Like *Mary*, it protests the conventional social and sexual destiny of upper- and middle-class women. It depicts a platonic (that is, unconsummated) yet happy and loving January–May marriage that rescues the penniless but 'sensible' Clara from predatory men without reducing her to sex-object or breeding-machine. But *Mary* goes a step further by contrasting two different kinds of 'platonic' marriage – the heroine's legal but unconsummated marriage with a conventional young gallant and her marriage of 'mind' with Henry, who is sickly and lacks conventional male attractions and amorous aggressiveness. Wollstonecraft also refuses to compromise on female sexuality. Clara is eventually united legally and sexually with a suitable man when her husband dies, but when Henry dies Mary faces the prospect of her husband's return to claim his conjugal rights. By refashioning the conclusion of *The Platonic Marriage* and combining it with an attack on the conventional, socially emulative sensibility of *Eliza Warwick* Wollstonecraft aims to construct a story at once more relevant to the experience of middle-class women she knew and more radical in criticizing the character and condition of women of her class.

Yet *Mary* may seem to lapse into sensibility of another kind. It claims mimetic truth and authority in creating a more authentic picture of 'things as they are' for women, but it seems unable to imagine how things might be better, in this life at least. Mary learns from her social and domestic experience only that earthly

life is all 'vanity and vexation of spirit' (p. 17) – one of Wollstonecraft's favourite biblical phrases (Ecclesiastes 2: 11) and also found
in *The Platonic Marriage*. Mary is left hoping for death and escape to
'that world *where there is neither marrying*, nor giving in marriage'
(p. 68) – another favourite biblical phrase describing life after the
resurrection and also found in *The Platonic Marriage*. These phrases
validate the argument of *Mary* by reference to a text of unques-
tioned authority – appropriately so, for the novel's plot seems to
carry its heroine through experience of gender oppression, to
understanding of it, to hope for resolution of it only in the transcendence of life after death.

This pessimistic conclusion of *Mary*'s plot does not cancel its
critique of conventional sensibility, however. For one thing, *Mary*'s
critique of conventional, 'fashionable' sensibility is reinforced by
its 'philosophical' treatment of its heroine's 'mind' within a comprehensive critique of class and gender relations. *Mary* illustrates
Enlightenment epistemology by showing how its heroine's knowledge and individuality are constructed by her material and social
circumstances. This philosophy informs *Thoughts on the Education of
Daughters* as well as Wollstonecraft's letters of the Kingsborough
period. But *Mary* also illustrates a theme of Sensibility – that some
minds are endowed with an 'instinct' or 'sensibility' that enables
them to become 'geniuses'. Thus Mary can educate herself:
'Neglected in every respect, and left to the operations of her own
mind, she considered every thing that came under her inspection,
and learned to think' (p. 4). She is further educated by Nature and
devises her own natural religion. Social alienation enforces self-
reflection, which shapes Mary as a 'genius' when her mother
rejects her confidences: 'In this manner was she left to reflect on
her own feelings; and so strengthened were they by being medi-
tated on, that her character early became singular and permanent'
(p. 7).

The natural and social worlds shape the 'mind' through the
body, but this moral and intellectual being is also inscribed on the
body and the social and ethical self. The novel uses the late
eighteenth-century system of physiognomy, by which the inward
self was thought to be legible in the features.[19] For example, Mary
is interested in Henry because he has 'strong lines of genius' in his
face. Yet the dynamic relation of mind and body is socially conditioned. The illness of Mary's friend Ann arose from disappointed
love, which in turn resulted from difference of social rank between

Ann and her suitor. Similarly, Henry is caught between the personal absolute of love for Mary and the social and legal prohibition against loving a married woman, and so he declines and dies. Social conflict is internalized, contributing to mental 'disorder' that is then externalized as a physical disorder that eventually destroys the self. This plot of dis-ease was at that time a common literary device for registering the personal cost of resistance to or transgression against the hegemonic order.

Mary requires psychological realism, then, to make its social critique convincing, and relies on the analytical use of conventional tropes, including a mechanical model of the mind, economies of contrary feelings and paradoxes of subjectivity. For example, Mary learns that Henry is near death, and as she walks home through the rain her absorbing mental turmoil gradually subsides, she becomes aware of her surroundings and she is able to reflect and then sleep and dream (p. 62). Several subjective economies are illustrated here, including countervailing force – strong feelings against 'the barrier of reason'. Another is the mind–body relationship: Mary is 'fatigued by the tumultuous emotions she had endured', but while her body can sleep, her 'fancy was still awake' producing dreams. Another principle is 'exercise', custom and habit: 'accustomed to think', Mary can detach part of her mind from the immediacy of her strong feelings, and thus eventually 'her softened heart heaved more regularly'. She even becomes aware of external sensations again – 'she felt the rain'. As the passage progresses Mary's mind advances from feeling to self-reflection, thereby exemplifying, as the novel's prefatory manifesto puts it, 'a [female] character different from those generally portrayed', that is 'a woman, who has thinking powers'.

Similarly, Wollstonecraft subordinates the sentimental love plot to representation of 'mind' within a broad social critique. Love was an established device for representing a personal absolute not governed by social categories. In the culture of Sensibility this device signifies inward, authentic identity inevitably in conflict with merely relative social identity, and often forced to transgress social conventions and structures dominated by other classes and therefore oppressive to the transgressor. But to Wollstonecraft such transgressive love does not have the same consequences for women and men. She now sees sentimental love as disguised courtly amorousness incorporating the sexual double standard, and women have more to lose than men in transgressing social conventions and laws for romantic love. For these reasons she gives love a 'philosophical' turn and draws it into her social critique. For example, in a long 'harangue' Mary contrasts her love for Henry with the feelings and conduct society requires of married women, and she sees human love as a divine and a personal absolute (pp. 40–1). The natural economy of love ('desires implanted in me') and the economy of self ('the internal monitor', 'my own esteem') are made congruent, validated by God and opposed to the merely social economy ('worldly wisdom', 'worldly prudence') that in turn rests on an economy of property and status ('riches and honours') perpetuated through marriage ('human ties', 'a vow'). Mary's self-vindication connects subjectivity to social critique by setting society against the self: 'the world . . . is ever hostile and armed against the feeling heart'.

In this way *Mary*'s treatment of subjectivity intersects with its treatment of the relation of class and gender. For example, Mary's upper-class parents, who are fashionable, extravagant and shallow, give her brother, the heir to the estate, an education, though Mary's is neglected. When her brother dies Mary becomes the heiress and is then educated in fashionable, showy 'accomplishments' to equip her for the marriage market. The family-based, class-based oppression of women is also illustrated by 'three fashionable females' who display a paradoxical combination of snobbish emulation and narrow 'propriety' characteristic of the middle station in society (p. 24). Class difference is inflected by gender and women reduced to 'noughts' by a specific class culture. The three women, kept in ignorance and lacking intellectual cultivation and self-awareness, are subjugated by upper-class culture; Mary, alienated from that culture by neglect and self-consciousness, or plenitude of self, learns resistance to it. Alienation and resistance produce authentic selfhood, or 'genius'. 'Genius' and resistance to the hegemonic order are one. In this case the 'stationing' or comparison and contrast of characters contributes to the novel's social critique.

This is also the case with the relationship between Mary and Henry, for nature and circumstance have also made him a social critic. By Sensibility's logic of sympathy Mary and Henry then fall in love. But even professionalized men such as Henry are vitiated by the hegemonic courtly culture, seen in his admission that he is charmed by wit and courtly coquettes and 'too fond' of genteel culture (p. 35). This triad of what Henry calls 'enchanting wit', 'the elegant arts' and 'woman – lovely woman' suggests that sexism is an inextricable part of court culture; it is represented even more clearly in the courtly gentleman whom Mary meets later (pp. 54–5). These characters show how the upper and middle classes have appropriated court culture, especially courtly libertinism and anti-feminism, and how even Sensibility, ostensibly a culture of middle-class subjectivity, domesticity and 'virtue', can take the form of courtliness.

Mary's portrayal of the lower classes reinforces the Sentimental social critique while characterizing the heroine. Mary's social sympathies are aroused early in life and she teaches herself 'the most rigid œconomy' in order to assist the poor. Later, when she returns to England from Portugal her observation of the lower classes furthers her sentimental education:

> she saw vulgarity, dirt, and vice – her soul sickened; this was the first time such complicated [complex] misery obtruded itself on her sight. – Forgetting her own griefs, she gave the world a much indebted tear; mourned for a world in ruins. (p. 48)

The lower classes' subjection to the hegemonic social order is strikingly pictured a few pages later, when Mary visits a starving family in 'the upper room in an old mansion-house, which had been once the abode of luxury' and 'the former scene of festivity' but is now 'crowded with inhabitants: some were scolding, others swearing, or singing indecent songs' (p. 50). The mansion-house, familiar symbol for the whole of society, represents the decadent and impoverished form of upper-class life adopted by the lower classes on the ruined and neglected site of former upper-class taste and luxury.

The point is to 'exercise' the heroine's sensibility; but she is also stirred to social action of the kind recommended by Sarah Trimmer in *The Œconomy of Charity*. The objects of Mary's care refuse to help themselves, however, and berate her when she suggests they do so. The moral is that 'the vicious poor . . . must ever grieve a benevolent contemplative mind' (p. 50). The background here is a problem that Wollstonecraft had pondered over several years, and one that recurs in her writings through the 1790s: the problem of evil, or the question of how a benevolent God could sanction the widespread personal and social misery apparent to any observer of the past and present. This problem was a major theme in eighteenth-century moral philosophy and it also preoccupied one of Wollstonecraft's favourite moral writers, Samuel Johnson.[20] In *Mary*, however, the problem is raised to invite sympathy with the heroine rather than with 'the vicious poor'; the lower classes hardly seem human, are emblematic of a fallen world and seem to exist for the moral and sentimental education of their betters. Like Sarah Trimmer, Wollstonecraft depicts them as pitiable but ignorant, insensitive, vulgar, improvident, emulative of the hegemonic upper classes and therefore requiring charity, moral re-education and ethical supervision by the middle classes, especially middle-class women. Wollstonecraft's critique of class converges with a critique of gender, expressing her version of the professional middle-class cultural revolution.

In opposition to false upper- and lower-class culture *Mary* presents a revised culture of Sensibility, transforming 'taste' from gentry-dominated connoisseurship, cosmopolitanism and patronage to a manifestation of the authentic inward self. 'Taste' is shown to be conventionally gendered, but this convention may be broken by the 'genius'. Taught by nature rather than art, Mary's taste is for the sublime, conventionally associated with male qualities. As a girl she retires to a cave she calls 'the Temple of Solitude' to read works of the descriptive, pathetic and epic sublime, such as Thomson's *Seasons*, Young's *Night Thoughts* and Milton's *Paradise Lost*. By contrast, her friend Ann is formed by society, is more feminine and prefers the beautiful and the refined (p. 8). Mary rejects decoration, the merely 'polite' (or polished) and the ornate – characteristics of decadent courtly culture – for expressiveness, the natural and the simple. Henry, her intellectual peer, resembles her, in contrast to the novel's courtly gallants and boorish squires. Sentimental taste such as Mary's and Henry's is unavailable to the lower classes and is produced by eluding hegemonic upper-class culture. Implicitly, then, it represents middle-class culture and exemplifies a class-based social critique.

Mary also exemplifies this critique in the heroine's social activism, which derives from Bluestocking feminism of the mid-century, set forth in novels such as Sarah Scott's *Millenium Hall* (1762). Bluestocking feminism aimed to feminize gentry capitalism by purging the gentry of court culture and modifying capitalist management of landed estates to provide better for the agrarian working class. In the 1780s this feminism was revised by Evangelicals such as Hannah More and Sarah Trimmer who advocated national reform through the *embourgeoisement* of society, to be carried out largely by the extra-domestic social work of middle-class women. At the end of *Mary* the heroine embarks on economic and social projects like those in *Millenium Hall*. 'She . . . retired to her house in the country, established manufactories, threw the estate into small farms. . . . She visited the sick, supported the old, and educated the young' (p. 67). Her estate thus contrasts with the image of society presented by the ruined, pauper-infested mansion-house described earlier in the novel. This mansion-house itself resembles Millenium Hall before it was bought and renovated by its feminist proprietors. Like Mary, the proprietors of Millenium Hall are the victims of a society divided by both class and gender and based on a property system that treats women as commodities, sexual objects or ways of transferring property and status from one man to another. But the proprietors of Millenium Hall have no object beyond their feminization of gentry capitalism, while Mary remains socially marginalized and alienated, with 'a heart', or subjective self, 'in which there was a void, that even benevolence and religion could not fill' (p. 68). If *Millenium Hall* offers a Utopian solution to the oppression of women, *Mary* seems to resolve the impasse of self and society with sentimental self-absorption and death.

In fact *Mary* also resolves this impasse through narrative structure, using 'free indirect discourse', the relatively new method of fusing third-person and first-person narration. This method was coming to dominate prose fiction, led by such novels as Frances Burney's *Cecilia* (1784), which Wollstonecraft had read. It combines an independent narrative voice guiding reader-response with immediacy and identification with a central subject consciousness. It answered to interest in subjectivity, psychological realism and writing the self. In *Mary* this narrative mode foregrounds the relationship between the narrator and the heroine, both of whom are characters in the novel. The narrator has the same 'voice' or style as the writer of the novel's prefatory manifesto, reinforcing the identification of narrator and author. The narrator appears capable of a range of descriptive styles, well informed on philosophical, cultural and social issues, and willing to pass moral judgement on the characters and events of the story, often in terms of a philosophical reflection or maxim. Thus she enjoys intellectual and perspectival superiority to characters in the story, including the heroine. But Mary resembles the narrator and this implicitly validates Mary's point of view.

The narrative style is established in the novel's first lines, where a personal and mildly ironic tone is occasionally sharpened to sarcasm with philosophical moral distinctions, such as that between 'opinions' and 'prejudices':

> Mary, the heroine of this fiction, was the daughter of Edward, who married Eliza, a gentle, fashionable girl, with a kind of indolence in her temper, which might be termed negative good-nature: her virtues, indeed, were all of that stamp. She carefully attended to the *shews* of things, and her opinions, I should have said prejudices, were such as the generality approved of.

As the narrative progresses the sarcasm is reserved for other merely fashionable ladies and emphasis shifts to representation of the heroine's consciousness through free indirect discourse.

For example, when Mary is watching by her father's death-bed, she seems to fall into reflections on mortality:

> Her father's unequal breathing alarmed her, when she heard a long drawn breath, she feared it was his last, and watching for another, a dreadful peal of thunder struck her ears. Considering the separation of the soul and body, this night seemed sadly solemn, and the hours long.
>
> Death is indeed a king of terrors when he attacks the vicious man! . . . No transporting greetings are anticipated, when the survivors also shall have finished their course; but all is black! – the grave may truly be said to receive the departed – this is the sting of death! (p. 18)

The passage moves from Mary's situation, to her feelings, to a reflection on death that could be a filtered version of Mary's feelings, with conventional typographical indicators of expressive feeling. But since the narrator moralizes in a similar vein elsewhere in the text (for example, on the previous page), the remarks on death could be the narrator's interjection. This ambiguity is deliberate, inviting the reader to perceive the narrator's and protagonist's minds as one.

This relationship is strengthened by characterizing the heroine almost entirely from within and by the narrator. There is little dialogue and Mary rarely enters it. When she does, her expressive, exclamatory speech contrasts with Henry's formality, the wittiness of the courtly gallants or the superficiality of the merely fashionable women. The novel also deploys a Sentimental economy of expressivity. When Mary confesses to Henry that she cannot '"conform to the maxims of worldly wisdom"' he is not convinced by her 'arguments', but 'her voice, her gestures were all persuasive' (p. 41). And if Mary speaks little she writes much. Like the narrator, Mary is a confessional-philosophical writer. She writes a 'fragment' on solitude, a devotional reflection on life and eternity, 'another fragment' on the struggle of reason and the passions, a 'rhapsody on sensibility' and 'a train of reflections' on a courtly gallant. These 'reflections received a tinge from her mind'. Her writing expresses her self in a way not possible in speaking or in letters, where she is constrained by social convention. Writing for herself is the only way she can express herself with freedom and authenticity; these are also occasions when Mary is available to the reader unmediated by the narrator.

Yet Mary as she writes herself turns out to be the same as Mary mediated by the narrator through psychological description, and similar to the narrator as she writes herself. But the differences between Mary and the narrator, like the differences between Mary and her friend Ann, follow gender differences in discourse. Mary's writing is personal, expressive, usually religious and devotional in character and occasionally critical of contemporary society. By contrast, the narrator writes Mary in a way that is more 'philosophical', within contemporary models of Lockean or materialist epistemology. Mary expresses her self in her writing; but the narrator both represents Mary's self and accounts for it. The narrator conducts a sociological and philosophical analysis of Mary and her social context while Mary is represented as only experiencing what the narrator analyzes. The disillusionment with society and mortal life reached by Mary at the end of the novel approaches the point of view of the narrator, but does not coincide with it. Furthermore, the narrator writes about Mary and her milieu in terms of Enlightenment philosophy of mind and sociology of culture, but these are terms of a discourse dominated by men. Mary writes about herself in the style of the Sentimental 'fragment', 'rhapsody' and detached 'reflections', which would be seen as a woman's discourse and thus lower down the hierachy of discourses than that practised by the narrator.

It is true that the name (and thus the sex) of the author is not indicated on the novel's title-page or elsewhere in the text. On the other hand, the novel's polemical preface denounces 'mere' women and the kind of fiction that keeps its readers 'mere' women; the narrator also has a sympathetic interest in the womanly character and experience of its heroine. These traits suggest a woman author and a narrator with a woman's outlook. Such a relationship of narrator and protagonist changes the import of the novel's plot. The conclusion to be drawn from Mary's adventures in themselves is that death alone can resolve the contradictions of self and society for women. But the character of the narrator exhibits a critical consciousness able to analyse Mary's situation in ways she herself cannot, and in the course of her adventures the heroine progresses toward this point of view. These features suggest a conclusion beyond the close of the novel, one in which Mary acquires the critical consciousness possessed by the (female) narrator from the outset.

The narrator writes woman in terms of a critical discourse that was, at the time, predominantly the cultural property of men. Yet the text is designed to show that woman can be written in terms of this discourse, and thus should be brought under that discourse or included in it. Enlightenment philosophy and social critique treated woman marginally, and as marginal; the literature of Sensibility, and especially the novel, treated women and their domain of the domestic and the quotidian as central. Just as Wollstonecraft writes a 'philosophical' novel, or appropriates serious intellectual discourse to the much-despised yet much-read novel, so she figures that appropriation in the central structural feature of her novel – the relationship between narrator and protagonist.

Wollstonecraft later came to be ashamed of her first novel. But for its time *Mary* was a very good novel indeed. She would have felt that it successfully transformed her personal and social experience into general social and cultural critique. She experimented with new fictional techniques within a broad social critique in order to engage seriously with central issues of gender and culture, gender and genre, in the professional middle-class cultural revolution. She attempted a bridge between the Bluestocking feminism of an older generation and the issues of the later movement of Sensibility in her own time, thus anticipating central concerns of Revolutionary feminism.

3

'The First of a New Genus'

Wollstonecraft was released by the Kingsboroughs in the summer of 1787; at Michaelmas she moved into London lodgings that Johnson had found for her south of the Thames. She revealed her plan to Everina:

> Mr Johnson whose uncommon kindness, I believe, has saved me from despair, and vexations I shrink back from – and *feared* to encounter; assures me that if I exert my talents in writing I may support myself in a comfortable way. I am then going to be the first of a new genus. . . . This project has *long* floated in my mind. You know I am not born to tread in the beaten track – the peculiar bent of my nature pushes me on. (*Letters*, pp. 164–5)

She was not of course the first woman to live on her writing; but the phrase indicates the way she always dramatized her situation. Yet professional women writers were rare enough and she had to lead a spartan life. She kept one servant – 'a relation of Mr Johnson's' – dealt with tradesmen herself, and when she ran out of housekeeping money had recourse to Johnson (*Letters*, p. 190). She received her sisters during the school vacation but preferred living alone.

She did not find it easy, confessing to George Blood in January 1788: 'I labor for tranquillity of mind – and that patient fortitude which will enable me to bear what I cannot ward off' (p. 169). By March 1788 there was recurrence of the physical ailments she had already learned to trace to mental and emotional stress. She told George Blood:

> I have lately been a little too studious, and the consequence is the return of some of my old nervous complaints. . . . I do not take sufficient exercise I know. . . . Even now I am suffering; a nervous head-ache torments me, and I am ready to throw down my pen. . . . Nature will sometimes prevail, 'spite of reason,

and the thick blood lagging in the veins, give melancholy power to harass the mind; or produce a listlessness which destroys every active purpose of the soul.   (p. 171)

By the following year such ailments had become chronic. She was often 'hurried' in her 'spirits' and suffered from loss of sleep. In another letter to Eliza she even suggested that she would not live long.

Her letters also reveal the harried and dedicated professional, who prefers working at night, has to use spectacles, complains about bad pens, keeps an indiarubber handy to correct and erase, needs more paper and worries about proper exercise and diet. She called on Johnson regularly at his lodgings over the bookshop in Paternoster Row for encouragement and consolation and the stimulation of his circle of intellectuals and writers. According to someone who knew Wollstonecraft, among the men of Johnson's circle 'whose friendship she held in high esteem' at this time were George Anderson, accountant to the Board of Control, the mathematician John Bonnycastle, the painter Henry Fuseli and Dr George Fordyce.[1] Much of her own writing would have been considered hack-work, the merely commercial side of professionalism. But as a self-supporting writer she was disciplined and constantly improving her professional skills, such as knowledge of modern languages. She acquired a reading knowledge of French, was willing to tackle an 'Italian MS' and even took on German. Her approach to translating seems to have been to fight her way through the original text with the aid of dictionary and grammar book, and then to polish or adapt her literal translation. She seems to have decided what translating she did, and regarded it as more than mere hack-work.

By 1789 and 1790 she was an established professional in the metropolis and found her advice being sought by others, such as the painter Joshua Cristall. She advised study and self-improvement, to be ready for whatever 'happy concurrence of circumstances' might arise. The failures of her family and friends had shown her that, without relentless self-discipline and self-improvement, opportunity or patronage would not guarantee success. Her own success induced a sharper sense of social differences and conscious superiority to 'mere' women of her class. In September 1787 she rejected George Blood's plan for a school in Dublin partly because she saw the place as narrowly middle-class. Her disgust for the commercial bourgeoisie, developed in the 1770s and early 1780s, now became disdain. Going to visit her sister in September 1787 she had to share a coach with 'three opulent tradesmen' and wrote to Johnson that 'their conversation was not calculated to beguile the way'. 'I listened to the tricks of trade – and shrunk away, without wishing to grow rich . . . though one of them imagined I should be a useful partner in a good *firm*' (p. 162).

As well as enhancing her sense of being superior to what she called the 'vulgar' bourgeoisie, her increasing identification with the professional middle class also made her more critical of merely domestic women. In the early 1780s her observations of couples she knew had made her critical of physical demonstrativeness, which she saw as an appropriation of courtly amorousness and 'gallantry' into middle-class domestic life, diminishing the dignity of women. She now saw conjugality of any kind as incompatible with her identity as a professional. In March 1788 she wrote to George Blood describing the physical and intellectual decline of the wife of the painter James Sowerby, which Wollstonecraft saw as resulting from the demands of childbearing and conjugal life when unsupported by moral and intellectual cultivation.

In the summer of 1790, however, Wollstonecraft visited the Reverend Henry Gabell and his wife and to her surprise found herself approving of their conjugal life, comparing it to that 'of which Milton has given a description, when he speaks of the first pair' (*Letters*, p. 192). Nevertheless, she caught herself wishing for her own 'little room' in London, 'and a ramble to St Paul's Church-yard' – Johnson's place. As the visit wore on she became more fixed in her preference for professional life over even the paradisal 'domestic felicity' she saw in the Gabells. She wrote to Everina that Milton's description of Adam and Eve in Paradise filled her 'with benevolent satisfaction'; yet she viewed 'the first pair' as her 'inferiors because they could find happiness in a world like this – A feeling of the same kind frequently intrudes on me here – Tell me, does it arise from mistaken pride or conscious dignity which whispering me that my soul is immortal & should have a nobler ambition leads me to cherish it?' (p. 195).

By the summer of 1790 her ability to imagine a superior conjugality to that of the Gabells or even Milton's Adam and Eve was also due to a personal and intellectual relationship she had recently formed. After returning to London from the Gabells she wrote to Eliza mentioning a 'friend' who was 'so peculiarly circumstanced'

that she could not enjoy his 'society' (p. 199). The 'friend' was
Henry Fuseli, then preparing an illustrated edition of Milton, and
who was in the 'peculiar circumstance' of being married. Yet her
relationship with Fuseli would help her to break out of the domain
of acceptably feminine hack-writing in which she had worked from
1787 to 1790.

Nevertheless, this early work was professionally successful and
laid the basis for the Revolutionary feminism of the 1790s. Her first
book as a professional writer placed her in the same class as A. L.
Barbauld and Sarah Trimmer. *Original Stories* was published
anonymously by Johnson in 1788, and was revised for a second
edition in 1791 with the author's name on the title-page and plates
by Joseph Johnson's occasional protégé, William Blake. It was
reprinted several times, finally in an elegant edition of 1820. This
last edition, however, reflects a fear that such elegance and the
name of the author of *A Vindication of the Rights of Woman* were
incompatible: Wollstonecraft's name does not appear on the title-
page or elsewhere in the text. The usefulness and saleability of her
work outlasted her own reputation.

Original Stories was successful partly because it combined a new
kind of educational practice with a new form of literature for
children, in both of which women were leading the way.[2] Writing
on educational practice was acceptably feminine, an extension of
women's domestic authority, but it was sub-literary, merely practical or useful rather than theoretical or learned; yet it enabled many
women to appropriate 'major' kinds of writing, such as social
criticism and learned discourse. It also gave women a role in the
bourgeois cultural revolution promoting defence of middle-class
youth from corruption by court culture and contamination by
lower-class culture. At the same time, new kinds of writing for
children were designed to supplant a traditional repertory of print.
Historically, children had learned to read with Bible stories, chapbooks and 'fairy stories'. But chapbooks were seen as the print
form of lower-class culture, and many 'fairy stories' were known to
be courtly appropriations of popular culture.[3] The chapbook repertory had remained unchanged for over a century and 'progressive'
social critics saw it as a repository of 'superstition' and outmoded
cultural values. In the later eighteenth century sharpening class
differences led middle-class educators to warn against chapbooks

and even against the lower-class oral culture of tales and ballads. Fiction and narrative in themselves were seen as childish, primitive or vulgar. Thus there was an increasing market for books purveying the 'right' sort of values, even if these books still had to be in the form of fictitious narrative in order to supplant the dangerous chapbooks.

Traditional chapbook literature embodies a lottery mentality of *carpe diem*, belief in fortune, wish for lucky gifts (such as great strength, cleverness or beauty), a view of time as cyclical or repetitive and avid interest in predicting the future. This was the culture of subjugated social groups in a subsistence economy, with little opportunity or hope of improving their lot. The new writing for children, by contrast, embodies an investment mentality. This meant saving for the future, 'proper' distribution of personal resources, avoiding extravagance, conceiving of time and one's own life as cumulative and progressive, and valuing self-discipline and personal development for a better future under one's own control. This was the mentality of a progressive or revolutionary class. They aimed to instil it in their own children and make it the mentality of all classes by using the professional class's technology – print. Women such as Anna Laetitia Barbauld, Dorothy Kilner and Sarah Trimmer, followed by Wollstonecraft, became leaders in this kind of educational writing in the 1770s and 1780s.

Barbauld was the daughter of a major figure in the English Nonconformist Enlightenment and her *Lessons for Children* (1778, 1779) were published by Joseph Johnson. They represent women teaching the young to verbalize, describe and reflect in the setting of domestic affections and quotidian experience, constructing the critical consciousness necessary to the professional middle class and their cultural revolution. Kilner's *The Life and Perambulation of a Mouse* (1783–4) uses animal characters like those in chapbook fables and fairy tales, but to promote a bourgeois social vision and the critical consciousness modelled in Barbauld's *Lessons*. Portraying the human world through animals defamiliarizes that world and opens it to critical reflection in didactic analyses and dialogues. *Perambulation* also promotes quietism to make the subjugated (children, women, the lower classes) accept their lot and prize personal merit over social status. As mouse Nimble notes, *'virtue* and a desire to be *useful* to others, afford far greater satisfaction and peace of mind, than any riches and grandeur can possibly supply'. Trimmer's *Fabulous Histories* (1786), better known as *The History of the Robins*, uses animals – birds rather than mice – in the same way. Because the critical viewpoint is displaced from humans to animals, it seems authentic and 'natural' rather than class-based. The critique is validated by the robins' survival, which is due to practising the bourgeois investment economy. The critique is also validated through the mediating, authoritative figure of Mrs Benson, one of many such characters found in children's books of the time. Her name (benson = benison, God's blessing) signals her mission as divinely inspired interpreter of the natural quotidian world and authoritative validator of a particular order – that prescribed by the professional middle-class cultural revolution.

Wollstonecraft's *Original Stories* was indebted generally to Barbauld and Kilner, but particularly to Trimmer's *Fabulous Histories* and *Easy Introduction to the Knowledge of Nature* (1780), both of which were published by Joseph Johnson with other booksellers. Wollstonecraft, like Trimmer, uses a frame narrative and dialogues arising from commonplace, everyday domestic events to educate children in the full range of professional middle-class beliefs, values and practices. But in its own right *Original Stories* is an important contribution to the new field of fictionalized educational writing for children. It was a step forward from *Thoughts on the Education of Daughters*, presenting more clearly Wollstonecraft's synthesis of Enlightenment philosophy, Sentimental culture and liberal Nonconformist ethical theology, focusing on the condition of women, especially in relation to the moral and intellectual culture of professional men. It is also more complex formally than *Thoughts*, enabling Wollstonecraft to extend her command of 'feminine' discourse.

The scope of the book's social, cultural and literary critique is indicated in its full title: *Original Stories, from Real Life; with Conversations, Calculated to Regulate the Affections, and Form the Mind to Truth and Goodness*. The first part of the title indicates that the 'stories' are not merely fictitious but have a factual basis in domestic, quotidian life, though readers would understand 'from real life' to mean 'based on' or 'adapted from real life', and not necessarily 'representation of actual events'. The 'stories' are 'original' because narratives for children should start afresh in order to avoid continued ideological contamination from vulgar chapbooks or courtly 'fairy tales'. The phrase 'real life' strengthens 'original', excluding both the artificial and the fictional or imaginary. 'Conversations' suggests familiar, familial discourse rather than formal moralizing. 'Calculated' suggests a programme rationally determined. These 'conversations' and 'stories' are also to construct the youthful self in a particular way, by regulating 'the affections' or emotional self and forming 'the mind' or rational and moral self 'to truth and goodness' – understood in terms of professional middle-class culture.

The book's reformative project is stated in the 'Preface': 'These dialogues and tales are accommodated to the present state of society; the author attempts to cure those faults by reason, which ought never to have taken root in the infant mind' (p. v). Parents lack the professional expertise to accomplish this task themselves as it 'requires more judgment' than generally falls to the lot of parents (pp. v–vi). Appropriate style is necessary to avoid passing on courtly values: 'In writing the following work', Wollstonecraft declares, 'I aim at perspicuity and simplicity of style; and try to avoid those unmeaning compliments' that educators use to flatter the parents of their pupils (p. vi). Tales rather than direct argument are used because 'example directly addresses the senses, the first inlet to the heart, the object education should have constantly in view, and over which we have most power' (p. vii). The 'heart' stands for the emotional, sympathetic, imaginative, subjective self; but it is also a moral self. Furthermore, reason has validated the tales, and may be referred to once the moral has reached the heart: 'the Tales, which were written to illustrate the moral, may recall it, when the mind has gained sufficient strength to discuss the argument from which it was deduced' (p. x). This is a manifesto for the new movement in writing for children.

The main text comprises the frame narrative, the inset tales and the conversations that explicate the tales, plotted to enact the reform that the 'Preface' outlines. This text novelizes the principles of the 'Preface' and aims to achieve in the real world what its protagonist, Mrs Mason, does in the story: change the world through education. For *Original Stories* insists that women receive the kind of moral and intellectual training given to men preparing for professional life. It shows this in the re-education of two girls, Mary and Caroline, by their 'near relation', Mrs Mason. She does not rely on classroom instruction and textbooks but takes the girls on excursions, using the characters and events that occur to question her charges, reveal their ignorance and prejudices (the result of their earlier mis-education) and correct these by moralizing, telling tales and recounting her own experience. The book's

'Preface' advises adapting this material to the reader's own situation and the children the reader may be educating, thus making
Original Stories a novelized conduct book.

Like other such books, *Original Stories* mounts a comprehensive
social and cultural critique in the modest guise of didactic fiction;
but it also anticipates Wollstonecraft's Revolutionary feminist reconstruction of the relation of class and gender within the bourgeois cultural revolution. *Original Stories* sees the role of women as
mainly domestic, but argues that women, too, must be given a
professional critical consciousness, consisting of 'reason' and
'virtue'. As Mrs Mason puts it, 'it is reason which exalts a man
above a brute . . . for wisdom is only another name for virtue'.[4]
'Man' here is no mere general noun; Wollstonecraft and her readers knew that reason was conventionally seen as an attribute of
men, not women. 'Virtue' was more likely to be expected of
females, but Wollstonecraft rejects 'virtue' as sexual purity and
uses the term for the disciplined self produced by reason, in
control of the appetites, passions or desire for the social other, and
thus independent of the merely social, especially social emulation
and the patronage system. This remasculinizing of virtue is affirmed in the definition she offers in her own translation from
Rousseau's *Émile*: 'The term virtue, comes from a word signifying
strength. Fortitude of mind is, therefore, the basis of each virtue,
and virtue belongs to a being, that is weak in his nature, and
strong only in will and resolution' (p. 153).

Reason and virtue not only make one independent of society's
relativities and inequalities, they re-establish social hierarchy on
inward merit rather than ascribed status. Mrs Mason tells Mary:
'children are inferior to servants' because servants can reason
whereas 'children must be governed and directed'; 'it is the proper
exercise of our reason that makes us in any degree independent'
(p. 99). 'Exercise', another of Wollstonecraft's key terms, is the
process of self-construction, which she calls 'improvement' or
'habit', and it results in the independence that should be the
product of education. 'When life advances', Mrs Mason says, 'if
the heart has been capable of receiving early impressions, and the
head of reasoning and retaining the conclusions which were
drawn from them; we have acquired a stock of knowledge, a mine
which we can occasionally recur to, independent of outward circumstances' (p. 107). Such self-construction is the professional
middle-class version of the investment economy: the moral and

intellectual self is life-capital, to be conserved against moral or intellectual extravagance, indulgence of the 'passions' or investment in the merely immediate and contingent.

The economy of self-construction is represented in terms of class. In Chapter 23 Mrs Mason tells of a tradesman ruined by his upper-class customers' inability to pay their bills because they wasted money on personal luxuries or impulsive, merely sentimental acts of charity (pp. 165–6). Mrs Mason criticizes the luxury economy of the upper classes and the lottery economy of the lower classes in favour of a middle-class investment economy. She accepts the class system itself as divinely ordained while affirming the superiority of moral and intellectual merit to merely social categories and hierarchies: 'Before the greatest earthly beings I should not be awed, they are my fellow servants; and, though superior in rank, which, like personal beauty, only dazzles the vulgar; yet I may possess more knowledge and virtue' (p. 101). Mrs Mason situates herself between 'the greatest earthly beings' and 'the vulgar', who are linked by the 'dazzle' of courtly display; and since she is not dazzled, she is implicitly superior to both. Later she gives her moral and intellectual class system a divine validation, transcending the merely social, when she observes we are God's 'children' if we are convinced that 'the vain distinctions of mortals will fade away, and their pompous escutcheons moulder with more vulgar dust!' (p. 139).

This critique of the class system is presented in several inset tales and in the relationship of the main characters, Mrs Mason and her two charges. Mary and Caroline are the daughters of wealthy parents but they have been spoiled by servants and other 'ignorant' people. Mary has an unfounded sense of her own superiority, expressed in a turn for ridicule, and Caroline has been made vain by the flattery of servants. These may seem minor points, but they indicate that the girls have internalized the ideology of both the decadent upper class and the degenerate lower class. Mrs Mason's task as an educator is to purge this false consciousness and to instill the values of the professional middle class in her pupils. The plot of *Original Stories* traces her success in carrying out this task.

Thus Mrs Mason is not only, as Mitzi Myers says, the 'vital center' of *Original Stories*, she is also its key, in several senses.[5] She may have been named after one of the assistants at Wollstonecraft's short-lived school at Newington Green,[6] and she may be a version of her author, but her name indicates her role as a social

builder and thus her status as a rhetorical figure in the text. She is
the key to *Original Stories* because she embodies the principles of
the text; she is the agent of those principles in reforming the
vitiated girls put in her charge; she is the explicator of the principles illustrated in the tales and in the sights she encounters
with the girls; and she is the example of what Mary and Caroline
may become if they follow her precepts through to womanhood.
Mrs Mason is not only the voice of the text's social critique, she
embodies Wollstonecraft's vision, at this point in her career, of the
relation of class and gender in the bourgeois cultural revolution.

Mrs Mason prefigures the 'female philosopher' who would be
Wollstonecraft's representation of herself in her Revolutionary
feminist texts of the 1790s. In the first place, Mrs Mason is a figure
of moral and intellectual authority. She is a surrogate mother to
Mary and Caroline and thus has authority over them; but she also
has authoritative knowledge, as 'reason'. Like the mentors in
contemporary novels of education, she effects the moral re-
education of her pupils by manipulating everyday experiences so
that they discover their errors before she has to explain them. She
supplements direct experience by tales and conversations rather
than dry moralizing. She validates many of her lessons with
illustrations from her own experience and that of her acquaintances. She has the authoritative style of the philosopher of everyday life, seen especially in her use of maxims to cap a story or
introduce one. When a quarrel between the girls over who should
feed a bird results in the bird's death, Mrs Mason observes: 'It is
easy to conquer another; but noble to subdue ones-self' (p. 28). In
the conversations she acts as a catechist leading the pupil forward
from one point to the next.

She is also the character who displays plenitude of self. When
tears start from her eyes at a moonlit scene she explains:

> I have been very unfortunate, my young friends; but my griefs
> are now of a placid kind. Misfortunes have obscured the sun I
> gazed at when first I entered life . . . but I am not enveloped in a
> thick fog. – My state of mind rather resembles the scene before
> you, it is quiet – I am weaned from the world, but not disgusted
> – for I can do good – and in futurity a sun will rise to cheer my
> heart – beyond the night of death, I hail the dawn of an eternal
> day! (pp. 118–19)

She then describes the economy of transcendence, validated by her own experience of sublime anticipations of a better world. Her evident possession of this experience and of a complex, authentic self validates her judgements of this world. Paradoxically, her disappointments and losses in life qualify her as an authority on life. She exemplifies the economy of transcendence through worldly failure, an economy for those marginalized and oppressed by the dominant class and culture.

This could be the economy of a group such as the professional bourgeoisie, denied opportunity and the rewards of merit by a courtly patronage system. It could also be the economy of women, denied opportunity and the rewards of merit by an unjust, patriarchal system within the professional bourgeoisie. Mrs Mason's philosophy encompasses both class and gender difference. But women of the professional middle class are at a double disadvantage, so Mrs Mason's re-education of Mary and Caroline must prepare them for female destinies in a world where they will be doubly disadvantaged. This was the central point and problem of the conduct literature for girls and women, especially by the late decades of the eighteenth century. Compromise was achieved by allowing the same moral training for both boys and girls but allotting girls a different intellectual training – as companions for professional men.

Mrs Mason does not herself occupy this role. It is represented by Mrs B., who is cultivated for both domestic and social life and says: 'Mr B. has a taste for the fine arts; I wish in every thing to be his companion. – His conversation has improved my judgment, and the affection an intimate knowledge of his virtues has inspired, increases my love to the whole human race' (pp. 147–8). Her cultivation is for home and family; her benevolence is for mankind. Mrs Mason has Mrs B.'s 'mind' but not her career, for she is neither wife nor mother. In the eighteenth century the title 'Mrs' was conferred on any woman of a certain age, regardless of her marital status. If Mrs B. represents the normal place of a properly educated woman in the professional class – applying her professional values and her feminine version of professional culture within marriage – then Mrs Mason is both an alternative to that norm and a failure to realize it. Though Mrs Mason knows how to educate (or re-educate), she is not a *professional* teacher. She *is* qualified morally and intellectually, by 'tenderness and discernment', but her principal qualification is domestic – she is 'a near relation' to Mary and Caroline (p. xi).

On the other hand, both Mrs Mason and Mrs B. represent the specifically ideological and cultural aspects of the professional class. Because they have professional culture but do not work as professionals, they represent professional culture as an end in itself, re-sited in the home and disseminated through the domestic affections. Nevertheless, the differences between the two women are significant. In her contented, companionate conjugality Mrs B. represents the normal or ideal destiny for women of the professional middle class. By contrast, Mrs Mason is 'quiet' and 'weaned from the world', looking forward to death and 'the dawn of an eternal day'. In terms of the domestic ideal, Mrs Mason is at best marginal, at worst a failure – through no fault of her own or of society. Yet the text foregrounds Mrs Mason, the alternative to professionalized domestic woman, and not Mrs B.

Mrs Mason is foregrounded by the way she is characterized, by her position as master of all discourse within the text and by the plot. Not only does she have intra-textual authority conferred on her by the author in the 'Introduction', she is also the most fully realized character in the text, with a wide range of experience and full subjectivity. She is master of discourse through controlling the events, tales and conversations that re-educate Mary and Caroline. She is also the *mistress* of discourse because what she arranges and the way she teaches could be seen as female philosophizing. Her plan of education is applied rather than theoretical, set in quotidian domestic life rather than a classroom. She reasons in a practical, concrete way, using analogies, contrasts, fables, emblems and anecdotes, drawn from everyday life and personal experience, rather than syllogisms, theses, deduction, authority or philosophical tradition. In that time her methods of argument would seem to be the philosophic discourse resorted to by women or anyone without training in abstract thought or forensic argument.

Finally, Mrs Mason is foregrounded by the plot of the ideological and cultural re-education of Mary and Caroline, dramatizing the role of education in the social reproduction of a class and the remaking of society in that class's image. This revolutionary transformation may be effected by girls and women because the professional middle-class cultural revolution made woman the moral and cultural animating spirit of the 'house' (as both home and family) and arbiter of the household economy. In this capacity she determined the local moral, social and material economy by setting a moral example, supervising domestic education, regulating and instructing the domestic servants, encouraging practice of the arts and high culture in the home and local community, and discriminating proper objects locally for receipt of her nurturing, charitable care. It was from such local economies that the nation itself was to be constituted.

Yet the example of Mrs Mason may also suggest that a woman can be a cultural revolutionary without being a wife and mother. Significantly, Mrs Mason, like Wollstonecraft, is an author: at the end of *Original Stories* she gives Mary and Caroline her own book – an account of their conversations as a permanent record and reinforcing reminder of her reformative presence in their lives. To this extent *Original Stories* offers an alternative to the exclusively domestic role of woman within professional middle-class culture. It dramatizes social and cultural reproduction as a key role for women, a role extended beyond, though not far beyond, the family. Mrs Mason operates as a social revolutionary in a marginal, ambiguous space between the family and full professional life. When Wollstonecraft wrote *Original Stories*, as a newly fledged professional still working in acceptably feminine kinds of writing, she was herself in such an ambiguous space.

The paradox of the woman writer was again implicit in her next project – *The Female Reader; or, Miscellaneous Pieces in Prose and Verse: Selected from the Best Writers, and Disposed under Proper Heads; for the Improvement of Young Women*. It was published in April 1789, ascribed on the title page to 'Mr. Cresswick, Teacher of Elocution', but Johnson later affirmed that it was Wollstonecraft's work.[7] As she acknowledged, it is modelled on William Enfield's *The Speaker*, a work first published by Johnson in 1774 and reprinted well into the nineteenth century. Enfield was lecturer on the *belles-lettres* at Warrington Dissenting Academy, one of the centres of the English provincial and Nonconformist Enlightenment, and thus a centre of the middle-class cultural revolution.[8] *The Female Reader* and *The Speaker* look similar but they are quite different, due to the different social and professional destinies in store for the readers of the two books.

The Speaker is for young men going into professional life, and gives method, system and exercise to the necessary professional skills of reading aloud and speaking in public. It transforms public speaking from the avocation of gentlemen, able to command attention by their superior rank, into a professionalized skill manifesting the speaker's moral and intellectual merit, whether in private company or professional office. Wollstonecraft's title might suggest acceptance that men use their skill as readers in public whereas women only read privately. But the 'female reader' also reads aloud, though as Wollstonecraft would know, a woman had no public, professional outlet for such a skill. Thus Wollstonecraft's defence of the skill seems feeble: 'if it be allowed to be a breach of modesty for a woman to obtrude her person or her talents on the public when necessity does not justify and spur her on, yet to be able to read with propriety is certainly a very desirable attainment'.[9] Skill in reading aloud will refine women's domestic conversation, whereas it will help men in both their public, professional work and the social conversation that was adjunct to such work. Nevertheless, such a skill is 'very desirable' because it requires a woman to be well-informed and capable of critical thought; that is, trained intellectually in the same way (if not to the same extent) as men intended for the professions.

Both *The Speaker* and *The Female Reader* belong to the elocution movement, which aimed to 'improve' spoken English, or rather the pronunciation of what was emerging as 'standard' English. This dialect was to provide a single form of spoken English throughout Britain. It was in turn based on standard written English, completed in the late eighteenth century as a form of the language suitable for all professions, made the basis of their education and controlled by them.[10] Standardized pronunciation based on standard written English was emphasized by the leader of the elocution movement, Thomas Sheridan, and by William Enfield.[11] These 'standards' concealed the particular regional and class origins of professional people, and made them the general or national class; 'standard' language still performs these functions today. Thus emergent standard English was class property, an instrument of the professional middle-class cultural revolution.

Wollstonecraft aims to make this instrument available to women. She instructs girls to memorize passages from *The Female Reader*, to say them aloud and then to write them out. By this means 'the pupil will express herself both in speaking and writing, provided she has a tolerable capacity, with a degree of propriety that will astonish those that have not adopted the same plan'

(p. xiii). This plan will secure the pupil against vulgar speech and incorrect writing as well as emulation of false and artificial upper-class language: 'She will understand English, and express her sentiments in her native tongue; instead of which our young ladies of fashion write a mixture of French and Italian, and speak the same jargon' (p. xiii). Speaking and writing standard English is almost a patriotic duty. But women will not use the standard language as men do: 'females are not educated to become public speakers' (p. v) and standard English has solely private and domestic use for them.

For this reason Wollstonecraft treats the *Reader* as an extension of the conduct book, to train girls for moral and intellectual independence and for the duties and vicissitudes of domestic life. Drawing on a commonplace philosophical association of morals and aesthetics, she argues that reading aloud achieves moral education by means of aesthetic training: 'The main object of this work is to imprint some useful lessons on the mind, and cultivate the taste at the same time – to infuse a relish for a pure and simple style. . . . Simplicity and sincerity generally go hand in hand, as both proceed from a love of truth' (p. iv). Reading aloud 'with propriety' requires both trained understanding and cultivated taste, a point made by all writers of the elocution movement, whereas 'the ignorant', who are only 'made wise by the experience of others' and not by their own reason, 'never read with propriety' (p. v).

Wollstonecraft designs the educational programme of the *Reader* for the two major phases in the life of a woman in the well-to-do middle classes – before marriage and after it. Hence she is more concerned to warn women against seduction by court culture than to protest their subordination within the middle classes. For example, she argues that a 'cultivated mind' is the best source of the outward attractions that make a woman desirable for marriage: 'Exterior accomplishments are not to be obtained by imitation, they must result from the mind.' Accordingly, she redefines the woman's education as intellectual and moral training rather than social polish: 'the improvement of her mind and heart – that is the business of her whole life' (p. xiv). The purpose of this kind of education is not to obtain a profession, as it is with men, but to obtain 'that happiness of which we can form no conception in our present state' (p. xv), that is, salvation.

For like most writers on women's education, Wollstonecraft assumes that women can have no lasting pleasure or fulfilment in this life. The 'female reader' is simply better trained to support women's lot without protest. For this reason the *Reader* includes devotional readings not found in Enfield's *Speaker*. Referring to John Gregory's *A Father's Legacy to His Daughters*, Wollstonecraft observes that women do not have the recourse of professional life or social dissipation 'when oppressed by sorrow, or harassed by worldly cares'; therefore they must rely on religion. She then quotes the leading woman writer of the Nonconformist Enlightenment, Anna Laetitia Barbauld, on the superior value of religion over philosophy (p. x). Philosophy was seen as a discourse practised by men whereas religious devotion was regarded as a feminine practice. Thus *The Female Reader* is a feminization rather than a feminist appropriation of the male-oriented goals of the elocution movement and such readers as Enfield's *The Speaker*.

The Female Reader, like *The Speaker*, promotes not only the language culture of the professional middle class but also their literary culture and social criticism. But again, the *Reader* gives these functions a feminine inflection. Both *The Speaker* and the *Reader* have sections of maxims, narratives, didactic pieces, dialogues, pathetic pieces and descriptions. *The Speaker* alone has sections of argumentative pieces, orations and harangues appropriate for young men intended for public, professional life. By contrast, the *Reader* alone has a selection of allegorical pieces of the kind recommended by conduct books for the moral instruction of females; a selection of conversations and fables for the same purpose; and a section of devotional pieces. The same kind of difference is found in the two books' range of sources. Both include numerous passages from the accepted canon of English literature, from Shakespeare and Milton to Young and Cowper. Both include numerous periodical essays, which combine genteel belletrism with bourgeois moral, cultural and social values. Both include extracts from a few sermons, though as moral rather than religious writing.

But differences in the sources of *The Speaker* and *The Female Reader* show how writing was gendered at the time. Enfield includes a wider range of poets and more moralistic poets than Wollstonecraft does, and he emphasizes the *belles-lettres* more, aiming to develop a discriminating literary taste as part of the culture of a gentrified professional man. The moral and ethical emphases of the two anthologies also differ. Both books open with a section of moral and ethical maxims, but Enfield's maxims deal with conduct in the 'world' whereas Wollstonecraft's stress the moral and intellectual character and domestic duties of women. This emphasis is reinforced by Wollstonecraft's numerous quotations from the Bible – Enfield has none – and her section of devotional pieces. Enfield's selections emphasize public and political life, ethical correctness and social success; Wollstonecraft's emphasize private and domestic life, moral self-discipline and acceptance of one's lot. Both anthologies include a broad range of social criticism, but the *Reader* orients this criticism toward the particular situation of women, their domestic roles and interests.

The *Reader* claims to follow the 'methodical order' of *The Speaker* so as to impress 'habits of order on the expanding mind' (p. iv). To this end, each section has a certain thematic consistency and generic diversity. In the *Reader's* Book I, 'Narrative Pieces', for example, the story of La Roche and his daughter, from Henry Mackenzie's *Mirror*, illustrates the sustaining power of religion in life's vicissitudes, as well as the value of paternal and filial love. It is followed by part of the story of Joseph from the Bible, illustrating filial and fraternal love, in spite of trials and even betrayals. Three short extracts then illustrate further aspects of filial virtue. The much-reprinted story of Inkle and Yarico from the *Spectator* and Cowper's verses on Crazy Kate show the power of a woman's love and the cruelty of betrayal and loss. The next four extracts show the negative rather than the positive side of woman's character, especially in women of the courtly and emulative classes. Book I closes by turning from fictitious narrative in verse and prose to two examples of historical narrative: Voltaire's account of the discovery of the New World and William Robertson's one-paragraph summary of the contact of decadent and barbaric cultures in late antiquity, resulting in the Dark Ages that were only enlightened eventually by 'liberty and independence' (p. 51). Thus Book I contains a considerable variety of forms of narrative organized around a few major themes, most of which touch on the condition of women, and it spans human experience from the personal and domestic in common life to general and historical movements affecting millions over a span of millenniums.

But structural differences between *The Female Reader* and *The Speaker* further reveal the gendered nature of discourse and culture. For example, Book II of the *Reader*, 'Didactic and Moral Pieces', focuses sharply on the condition of women, in contrast to the corresponding Book, 'Didactic Pieces', in *The Speaker*. Enfield's extracts delineate general virtues and vices, such as modesty, honour, indolence, taste and the pleasures of the imagination. Wollstonecraft includes some of these topics but also deals with favourite conduct-book themes such as 'Female Passion for Dress and Show', 'Government of the Temper' and criticism of courtly women and their middle-class emulators.

Similarly, the *Reader*'s third and longest Book, 'Allegories and Pathetic Pieces', is only partly matched by Enfield's Book VIII, 'Pathetic Pieces'. 'Pathetic' means reflecting, arousing or appealing to the feelings. For male readers these pieces would provide practice in expressing sympathy and pathos on appropriate public or professional occasions, and Enfield includes such passages as 'Antony's Funeral Oration over Caesar's Body' from Shakespeare's *Julius Caesar*. The *Reader*'s emphasis is different. Because women were supposed to be given to pathos, or strong feelings of sympathetic association for the suffering, oppressed and downtrodden, Wollstonecraft includes extracts such as the reconciliation of King Lear and Cordelia. Book IV of the *Reader*, 'Dialogues, Conversations, and Fables', corresponds in part to *The Speaker*'s Book VI, 'Dialogues'. The dialogues in both books are mostly from well-known plays, but again Enfield's selections exhibit a broad critique of court culture and social emulation and deal with political questions and 'affairs of state', whereas Wollstonecraft's selections deal with the particular role of woman in this critique and avoid expressly political speeches.

Wollstonecraft's Book V and Enfield's Book VII are both titled 'Descriptive Pieces'. But Enfield is again more interested in the public, political and social sphere, and in showing how that sphere is vitiated and corrupt in contrast to the idealized domain of 'Domestic Love and Happiness' and 'The Pleasures of Retirement' (two of Enfield's selections from James Thomson). Wollstonecraft, too, is interested in the public, political sphere, but shows it as a sphere in which women are at a disadvantage and which they enter at their peril. This is the moral of Wollstonecraft's first two descriptive pieces, 'The Character of Queen Elizabeth' from David Hume's history of Britain and 'The Character of Mary Queen of Scots' from William Robertson's history of Scotland. Other public and political topics in the *Reader* are of conventionally feminine kinds, supposed to appeal to women's sympathetic nature and domestic feelings, such as the plight of slaves, the deserving poor and animals.

Wollstonecraft's sixth and last Book, 'Devotional Pieces, and

Reflections on Religious Subjects', has no counterpart in Enfield. If there is one, it would be Book v, 'Orations and Harangues', which includes passages from classical authors and eighteenth-century Parliamentary speeches. These passages would be trebly inappropriate for females as pertaining to politics, public speaking and classical studies. Significantly, too, Wollstonecraft's last Book is the one that contains most of her original contributions. There is a religious theme in *The Speaker*, but it is predominantly ethical rather than devotional. Wollstonecraft feminizes religion in accordance with the conduct books; at the same time, her emphasis on the intellectual, moral and aesthetic aspects of religion makes public and social manifestations of religion, such as the institutional and the ethical, seem secondary. In certain ways, then, Wollstonecraft does turn the gendering of discourse and culture against itself, thereby implying a feminist critique of it.

Though *The Female Reader* contains little of Wollstonecraft's own writing, its selections contain many images, compositional schemes and rhetorical figures that recur in her later work through the 1790s. The desultory and yet associative structure of the *Reader* is characteristic of all of Wollstonecraft's non-fiction writings. Many selections in the *Reader* rely on argumentative figures favoured in her other writings, especially analogy and simile (drawn from common life rather than from learned discourse), association, contrast, the maxim, the personal witness or anecdote and redefinition of commonplace terms. These schemata are grouped around certain central themes, such as contrast of outer and inner, social and personal. The *Reader* also contains metaphors used often in her polemical works, such as dress and drapery, 'tinsel' and ornaments, 'display' and 'parade', to stand for what she sees as the superficial, specious, 'dazzling' character of court culture, especially as related to women in that culture.

The Female Reader is hack-work, but it assembles a wide range of themes from the middle-class cultural revolution, it indicates what Wollstonecraft was reading, and it reveals her pre-Revolutionary way of reading. On one hand she chooses extracts that seem to support the ideal of domestic woman as well as the feminization of culture. But when contrasted to *The Speaker*, the *Reader* shows Wollstonecraft working on the paradoxes and contradictions of woman as constructed by and for the professional middle-class cultural revolution. Moreover, the structure of the *Reader* and its recurring images, figures and devices could be read as a woman's form, especially in relation to the gendered order of discourse in Wollstonecraft's time.

Wollstonecraft's translations were also hack-work. Johnson, with his wide circle of intellectual friends and good contacts in the book trade, could put such work her way. She found it difficult and irksome, but she did it in her own way, adapting rather than translating, and choosing works that were not only on acceptably feminine topics of education and religion but also popularizations of the bourgeois cultural revolution.

Her first translation was Jacques Necker's *De l'importance des opinions religieuses*, recently published in Paris. Necker was a Swiss Protestant from Geneva who had been a banker and director of the French treasury. He would be seen in England, and especially in Johnson's circle, as a bourgeois revolutionary stymied and victimized by the court system. Wollstonecraft's translation appeared late in 1788; through it she could approach the public, political sphere indirectly, as a mere translator, and her name did not appear in the book. Yet she did the work in her own way, noting in her prefatory 'Advertisement' that 'some Liberties have been taken by the Translator, which seemed necessary to preserve the Spirit of the Original'. This was not unusual for the time, and as Ralph Wardle puts it, 'though she usually translated accurately and idiomatically, she sometimes perpetrated . . . clumsy phrases' or even unintelligible ones, but 'often improved on her original'.[12]

Necker insists on the importance of 'religious opinions' to both private morality and public order. By 'religious opinions' he seems to mean a religious form of professional bourgeois ideology as a force pervading the whole of society and the state, and supplanting both court and plebeian ideology. He argues that religion alone can console the thinking and feeling person for the inevitable disappointments of a social world unresponsive to individual worth – that is, a world divided by class, operating by courtly favouritism and patronage, and in which power, property and talents are unequally distributed. Religion enjoins the individual to continual self-improvement, guarantees the domestic affections, restrains court government and reconciles the lower classes to their lot and to public order. In short, Necker addresses the major topics of the cultural revolution in Britain; but he does so in a struggle for leadership within the cultural revolution, against the atheism and materialism of certain French *philosophes*. He claims that these 'philosophers' attack religion out of 'vanity' and a desire for social eminence and a fashionable following; he accuses them of 'libertinism' and other courtly vices; and he portrays them as courtiers engaged in a conspiracy to suppress 'religious opinions' merely to serve their own advancement at court.

By translating Necker Wollstonecraft was able to translate herself into a political writer without appearing to do so. By translating him critically she also learned that she might be at least the intellectual equal of such a 'great' man and public figure. Shortly after her translation was published she reviewed the book herself in the *Analytical Review* and was somewhat critical of Necker (vol. 3, January 1789, pp. 47–8); in her *Historical and Moral View . . . of the French Revolution* (1794) she would be even more so (pp. 61–2).

She next translated a book resembling her own *Original Stories* – *Young Grandison: A Series of Letters from Young Persons to Their Friends: Translated from the Dutch of Madame de Cambon, with Alterations and Improvements* (2 vols, 1790). The book's title notwithstanding, Wollstonecraft worked from a literal English translation which, according to Johnson, 'she almost re-wrote'.[13] An 'Advertisement' notifies readers that the translation is loose, and that some incidents have been thrown out and others added according to her belief that the mind of the young reader ought not to be brought forward 'prematurely'. Once again Wollstonecraft's name did not appear on the title-page or elsewhere, for hers was not yet a name to sell books.

Young Grandison, like Necker's *Religious Opinions*, expresses leading themes of the bourgeois cultural revolution, as a European and not just a British movement. It capitalizes on the European popularity of Samuel Richardson, whose *Sir Charles Grandison* (1754) portrays the fusion of gentry and professional bourgeoisie in the character of its hero. De Cambon retains Richardson's epistolary form and central characters, but inscribes Richardson's novel within feminine writing by the theme of education and the form of the fictionalized conduct book. Wollstonecraft re-Anglicizes de Cambon's *De kleine Grandison* and her prefatory 'Advertisement' claims to revise it in accordance with her own educational principles, while acknowledging the low cultural status but utilitarian value of her work. Significantly, she renamed some of the characters after members of her own family. For example, the bad boy of the book has the same name as her detested older brother. In her

preface she also notes the importance of the book's 'hints relative
to natural philosophy; which, while they tend to awaken curiosity,
lead to reflections calculated to expand the heart'. Such study of
'the book of nature' was recommended because, along with Scripture, it was supposed to furnish evidence of God's being that was
suited for even the simplest understandings, such as those of
children, the lower classes and women.

Young Grandison resembles contemporary English children's
books in several respects. It describes various adventures of several children, contrasting the good with the bad, as in Thomas
Day's *Sandford and Merton* (1785), which Wollstonecraft knew. The
emphasis is on the domestic setting of education as training in
self-discipline and social criticism rather than the mere acquisition
of 'useful' knowledge. This is social reproduction through the
family based on domestic affections rather than property and rank.
The children's adventures are moralized by several adults, including Dr Bartlett, the model professional man and a character in
Richardson's novel, and Sir Charles Grandison, the professionalized gentleman. Thus the book is a loose arrangement of episodes
each of which makes some point in the book's social vision, often
through dialogue. Such an apparently desultory form domesticates
and softens the social criticism.

As in Richardson's novel, the social critique of *Young Grandison*
mediates the culture of the landed gentry and the 'learned' professions as 'reason' and 'virtue', the domestic affections of family and
friendship, social 'duty' (especially toward those lower down the
social scale) and rejection of court culture. *Young Grandison's* social
vision is shown in Charles's account of the difference between
artists and 'mechanics' (that is, manual labourers): 'Those employments, in which the mind is exercised more than the body, tend to
cultivate the understanding, the noblest kind of superiority' (vol.
1, p. 263). The economy of work produces intellectual differences
that subvert the structure of social class, basing status not on rank
and wealth but on inward merit and social usefulness, degrading
the courtly upper class below even the labouring class. In fact
'those employments, in which the mind is exercised more than the
body' are the class property of the professional bourgeoisie. Within
this class-based culture, gender difference is secondary and treated
in the usual way: girls receive a purely domestic version of the
education given to boys so they may be the rewards of virtue and

the domestic companions of professionalized gentlemen (Emilia Grandison marries William at the end of the book).

Wollstonecraft's next and last translation was published late in 1790 and early in 1791 as *Elements of Morality, for the Use of Children: with an Introductory Address to Parents.*[14] It was taken from Christian Gotthilf Salzmann's *Moralisches elementarbuch* (1782) and embellished with engravings by another of Johnson's protégés, William Blake. Again, Wollstonecraft's name was not on the title-page, though it was affixed to the prefatory 'Advertisement' which claims that she has made the book 'an English story' and added to or altered 'many parts of it', while attempting to catch the 'simplicity' of her original. She also claims that 'all the pictures are drawn from real life', refers to her own *Original Stories* and notes that she has added 'a little tale to lead children to consider the Indians as their brothers'.

Elements of Morality is a fictionalized conduct book, but Salzmann supplies an analytical outline of the book, arranged according to topics as in a philosophical treatise. This outline is supported by a philosophical 'Introductory Address to Parents', a manual recommending that the appropriate tale from the book be applied to particular occasions in domestic life. Here women have a unique role assigned by biological destiny: 'Your sex has undeniably more tenderness than ours; the female voice is, in general, more persuasive and soft, and more easily insinuates itself into the hearts of children.' Furthermore, 'your abilities, and the domestic ties, which so firmly attach your children to you', are 'hints from God, that the first formation of their character devolves on you' (vol. 1, pp. xx–xxi). Appeal to imagination and personal ties of domestic affection will best achieve the ideological construction of the subject. Thus the feminine is better fitted to internalize the state in the individual than are the law and command of patriarchy. Social reproduction through the mother will reinforce authentic social relations – the domestic affections – and inculcate 'a taste for the sweetest of all enjoyments which God has sent us – a taste for domestic pleasures'.

Wollstonecraft adapts the book to her own experience, again renaming central characters for members of her own family and the Bloods. As Ralph Wardle points out, she made minor changes such as reducing the number of times characters weep, kiss or embrace, adding explanations and moral observations of her own, criticizing the health hazards of factory work and reducing Salzmann's admiring remarks on the upper class.[15] She retains Salzmann's moralizing maxims highlighted in italics. _Elements_ advances the social vision of the bourgeois cultural revolution, though it promotes the values and the practices of the mercantile middle class more than those of the professionals. Mr Jones is the exemplary character here, providing factory work for lower-class women and children and enforcing good conduct among his employees. The redeemable upper-class characters emulate such self-discipline and social responsibility, while the admirable lower-class characters emulate middle-class virtues and are contented in their sphere.

Apart from providing income, close work with foreign languages and the confidence gained from completing irksome and difficult work, these translations from three different parts of Europe were assimilable to the English cultural revolution and must have enhanced Wollstonecraft's sense of being a cultural revolutionary in a European context. Her translations were also increasingly fine as publications, reflecting Johnson's growing confidence in her work, and each one was more successful commercially than its predecessor.

But her professional mainstay in the years from 1787 to 1790 was her work for the _Analytical Review_. Joseph Johnson was planning the _Analytical_ by the summer of 1787, and he set Wollstonecraft up as a writer that autumn so she could help when it got going; she wrote for it almost from its beginning in May 1788. This work brought a steady income, broadened her intellectual horizons, developed her professional confidence and ensured regular contact with Johnson's 'Academy' of intellectuals, writers and artists. More important, as Mitzi Myers points out, Wollstonecraft's reviews 'provide an instructive example of a woman writer's struggle' to define what Virginia Woolf calls her 'difference of view', and to evade what Roland Barthes calls the 'already-written'.[16]

The _Analytical_ was one of an increasing number of magazines, newspapers and periodicals that manifested and stimulated the 'rise of the reading public'. They served professional men as a digest of current print culture and a guide to social, political, cultural and literary issues. The _Analytical_ was designed by its conductors, Johnson and Thomas Christie, to provide such a service, as its title-page for May 1788 indicates: *The Analytical Review; or, History of Literature, Domestic and Foreign, on an Enlarged Plan; Containing Scientific Abstracts of Important and Interesting Works, Published in English; A General Account of Such as Are of Less Consequence, with Short Characters; Notices, or Reviews of Valuable Foreign Books; Criticisms on New Pieces of Music and Works of Art; and the Literary Intelligence of Europe, &c.*[17] 'Analytical' here means a 'scientific abstract' or methodical outline, and suggests that the journal will be 'objective' and avoid judgements of value.

It was widely believed that reviews promoted particular political, social, cultural and religious values and covertly advertised their publishers' own books with 'puffs', or extravagant false praise. Wollstonecraft expressed this belief and an intellectual's self-conscious disdain for the 'reading public' when she wrote to Johnson late in 1788 condemning the rival *Critical Review* as 'a timid, mean production', and declaring its success was 'a reflection on the taste and judgment of the public'. She thought even less of the *Monthly*, which she found 'tame, and eager to pay court to established fame' (*Letters*, pp. 179–80). The *Monthly* (founded 1749) and *Critical* (founded 1756) were the major reviews of the second half of the century. They first developed the 'analytical' style of reviewing and then in the 1780s turned to a more evaluative style.[18] The *Analytical* professed to return to its earlier style but in fact compromised with evaluative reviewing. Like the *Monthly* and *Critical*, the *Analytical* also expressed particular political and cultural views. Though the *Analytical* denied it was a 'party' magazine it was founded during the Nonconformist campaign for full civil rights and most of its contributors came from the Nonconformist and provincial Enlightenments.[19]

This staff made the *Analytical* a major cultural force during its eleven years of existence, though it had a print run of only 1500 copies in the 1790s, compared to 4550 for the *Gentleman's Magazine*, a miscellany, and 3500 for the *British Critic*.[20] Like other reviews, the *Analytical* mainly covered books of interest to professional men. Christie told the publisher John Nichols that reviews rightly served 'persons who have much leisure', but 'it is also proper that some regard should be paid to the ease of men engaged in active life and professional business', who are 'too much involved in the necessary duties of their stations, to find leisure to peruse volumes in quarto and folio'.[21] Christie could have added that books were very expensive. Accordingly, the *Analytical* for July 1788, in which

Wollstonecraft first appeared for certain, covered 'Theology; Philosophy; History of Philosophy, Arts, etc.; Bibliography; History of Academies, Antiquities; Law; Natural History; Botany, Chemistry, Mineralogy; Medicine, Anatomy, Surgery; Mathematical Sciences; Poetry; Theatre; Music; Romances [that is, novels]; Agriculture; Voyages and Travels; Paintings and Engravings'. The list of departments indicates not only their order of precedence but also their relative cultural status. *Belles-lettres* and especially novels were a minor department and received little space in any of the periodicals. This was the department which Wollstonecraft helped to manage and in which she did most of her reviewing.

It was also her least-known work, since reviews in the *Analytical* were signed only with initials. Originally Christie intended that reviews be signed, in line with the policy of openness and objectivity; but as Gerald Tyson points out: 'The anonymity of the contributor became established not as a protection against an action for libel but because contributions to periodicals were considered beneath the dignity of most writers.'[22] Reviews signed 'M.' are almost certainly by Wollstonecraft, and those signed 'W.' may also be hers; she may have used other signatures as well.[23] When Johnson set Wollstonecraft up as a writer in the autumn of 1787 he intended that she would earn a steady income by reviewing, for in May 1788, when the first issue of the *Analytical* appeared, she wrote jubilantly to George Blood that she expected to earn 'above two hundred pounds this year' (*Letters*, p. 174). This was a fair professional income for any man, and reviewing would have provided much of it.

In spite of her jubilation when the *Analytical* first began, her attitude a few months later was one of grim professional determination. Early in the summer of 1788 she wrote to Johnson:

> I send you *all* the books I had to review except Dr. J[ohnson]'s Sermons, which I have begun. If you wish me to look over any more trash this month – you must send it directly. . . . I am trying to brace my nerves that I may be industrious.   (*Letters*, pp. 178–9)

Wollstonecraft was assigned a good deal of *belles-lettres* written by women, especially novels, and from the outset she approached books of all kinds in terms of their ideological and cultural import, though not noticeably more so than other reviewers of similar material. Her critical remarks are often energetic and incisive, though most of her reviews are 'analytical' rather than evaluative. For example, her first major review, of Charlotte Smith's *Emmeline* (July 1788; signed 'M.'), follows the usual form of plot summary with long extracts, concluded by a brief critical overview – a conventional condemnation of novels for inculcating false values in young women. Through the next year 'M.' reviewed novels, books on education and other topics of interest to Wollstonecraft, such as the 'science' of physiognomy and the characters in Shakespeare's plays. 'W.' reviewed poetry, two anthologies of Rousseau's writings, novels, the autobiography of the slave Equiano, a conduct book for women in 'the lower ranks of middle life', and the mystic Emanuel Swedenborg's *On Marriages in Heaven: and on the Nature of Heavenly Conjugal Love*; the last review comments sarcastically on the possibility of 'conjugal pleasures' in heaven (April 1789).

By mid-1789 Wollstonecraft's reviews were more prominent and dealt with more diverse topics. 'W.' continued to review poetry and poetry criticism and 'M.' to review novels, but 'M.' also had the second and third articles in the June *Analytical*, substantial reviews of Alexander Jardine's *Letters from Barbary, France, Spain, Portugal, &c.* and Hester (Thrale) Piozzi's *Observations and Reflections Made in the Course of a Journey through France, Italy, and Germany*. These travel books develop Enlightenment sociology of culture, including the role and condition of women in society. 'M.' notes Jardine's argument that 'the subject of female education, consequent manners, and station in society' is 'of the greatest consequence in a system of civilization, or progress toward improvement', and his denunciation of 'the present mode of polishing and indulging women, till they become weak and helpless beings, equally unnerved in body and mind' (p. 142). In August 'W.' had the fourth article, reviewing the biography of a notorious French royal minister in the early eighteenth century. The review roundly condemns court government of political and sexual intrigue (pp. 406–7). These reviews together anticipate major themes of Wollstonecraft's *Vindication of the Rights of Woman*.

Through the autumn and winter of 1789 and 1790 she continued to expand the range of her cultural criticism while staying close to acceptably feminine subjects. 'M.' reviewed books on arts such as music and architecture, plays, sermons and devotional writing, while 'W.' reviewed poems and books on aesthetics and education. 'M.'

also reviewed two important novels: John Moore's *Zeluco* (September) and Charlotte Smith's *Ethelinda* (December). *Zeluco* was a vehicle for Scottish Enlightenment sociology of culture, depicting the growth of a vicious character under the decadent court governments and culture of Italy. 'M.' praises its social and moral critique but deplores its lack of psychological realism. By contrast, she praises *Ethelinda* for its psychological realism and discrimination of characters but deplores its relentless series of misfortunes and its lack of 'general views'.

Wollstonecraft's growing confidence as a cultural critic is shown in two reviews of books on music. Her first lead article, 'M.'s' long review of Charles Burney's *General History of Music* (February 1790), adopts Rousseau's musical criteria – simplicity, expressiveness and passion – and sees music's cultural role in religious and philosophical terms: 'it affords the contemplative mind the most exalted intellectual pleasure, and becomes the food of [religious] devotion' (p. 130). 'M.'s' review of André Grétry's *Mémoires; ou, essai sur la musique* expresses a major theme in Wollstonecraft's rhetorical theory by applying the same criteria to the author's style:

> It is true that this essay abounds with what some may term egotism, which might, perhaps, with more propriety be styled individuality; yet, so much heart appears in the memoirs, that it is impossible not to love a man, who thus ventures to appear in his true colours.   (May 1790, pp. 23–4)[24]

Wollstonecraft's increasing interest in the popularisation of 'philosophy' as professional social and cultural critique is seen in 'M.'s' praise of Georg Joachim Zollikofer's *Moral and Philosophical Estimates of the State and Faculties of Man*:

> the author seems never to have forgotten that the greater number of men have not been accustomed to think, and therefore must be instructed in a manner adapted to their languid unexercised faculties. There is a manly plainness running through the style of the original, which must excite respect, whilst, in many passages, a sudden glow of eloquence fastens on the affections, and sinks the instruction deeper than dry arguments ever can. Every where, indeed, appears that degree of earnest sincerity, which gives a commanding dignity to the simplest language, seldom to be found in more laboured compositions, when a more ignoble pursuit animates the abilities of the writer, or

attempts at elegance absorb the mind, and render the sentiments coldly correct.   (July, 1790, pp. 289–90)

By contrast, 'M.' condemns J. Hassell's *Tour in the Isle of Wight* for its 'affected' phrases, 'continual display of extatic feelings', 'redundancy of adjectives' and excessive use of the word 'sentimental'. Worse still, 'This is a book that will probably fall into the hands of females; and we are sorry to find that it is written in an artificial style, calculated to pamper the imagination and leave the understanding to starve' (August, p. 393). Wollstonecraft would make the same charges against Edmund Burke three months later in her *Vindication of the Rights of Men*.

For November 1790 saw the turning point in Wollstonecraft's career, as a reviewer and as a woman writer. 'M.'s' review of Catharine Macaulay Graham's *Letters on Education, with Observations on Religious and Metaphysical Subjects* was the first article in that month's *Analytical*, testimony to the importance of both the reviewer and the book reviewed. An educational book would seem acceptably feminine, but Macaulay aims to revolutionize the conduct book by considering education in general and philosophical terms. 'M.' confirms the centrality of education (p. 241) and approves of the way 'this masculine and fervid writer' relates it to the entire system of government and social structure and then to 'religious' and 'metaphysical' questions of the nature of evil and divine benevolence, free will and 'necessity'. 'M.' also confirms points such as Macaulay's view that girls should have the same education as boys, for there is 'no characteristic difference in sex'. She closes by observing that Macaulay's book 'displays a degree of sound reason and profound thought which either through defective organs, or a mistaken education, seldom appears in female productions' (p. 254).

Letters on Education showed Wollstonecraft what could be done with a 'woman's' subject such as education and how it could be related to the largest political and philosophical questions of the day; it also showed her how women's education should be treated as central to the largest questions of political and cultural reform at the time. It was precisely the kind of book to read and consider just before the publication of Edmund Burke's *Reflections on the Revolution in France* on 1 November 1790 provided the occasion for Wollstonecraft to draw together all the literary and political ideas developed over three years of professional work.

4

From the Rights of Men to Revolutionary Feminism

A Vindication of the Rights of Men was published at the end of November 1790 and transformed Wollstonecraft from a successful – for a woman, very successful – but obscure hack-writer to a social critic and public figure. Yet she may not have written the *Vindication* but for Henry Fuseli and Joseph Johnson. Fuseli had the broad classical, literary and artistic knowledge to inform her break from women's writing into political polemics, and Johnson shamed her into completing the work when she was ready to give it up halfway through.[1]

Fuseli was the leading representative in England of the anti-court, nationalistic German *Sturm und Drang* and the *enfant terrible* of the art world. He was one of those producing art for the professional cultural revolution, combining classical simplicity of style with classical heroism, reinspired with bourgeois values of self-discipline, duty and self-sacrifice to family and the state. He also led artists using the cult of subjectivity and professionalization to promote their work and social status and to control their careers. He created striking paintings, such as 'The Nightmare', exhibited at the Royal Academy in 1782, and cashed in by controlling engraved versions of the painting. He chose subjects of emotional crisis and incorporated the supernatural, macabre or erotic, composed in striking ways, with simplified outlines and exaggerated features, rendered in subdued colours to suggest universal values. He preferred subjects from literature to those from history, and called his work 'poetical painting' to distinguish it from the history painting that headed the official hierarchy of pictorial genres at that time. He also participated in such commercializations of bourgeois classicism as the Shakespeare Gallery of the 1780s, a project by the businessman and politician Boydell to have famous artists paint scenes from Shakespeare which would be exhibited to the public for an admission fee and which would also be sold as engraved reproductions. Later, in the summer of 1790, Fuseli planned a similar project, the Milton Gallery.

When Wollstonecraft met him he was the star of Johnson's weekly dinners because of his wide-ranging knowledge, charismatic personality and energetic manner. He was also married, to a former artists' model who was younger and socially and intellectually inferior (she was probably illiterate). But by the autumn of 1790 Wollstonecraft was fascinated and perhaps in love with him. According to Fuseli's friend and biographer John Knowles, it was a shared enthusiasm for the French Revolution which 'brought about a closer intimacy' between them.[2] At that moment Edmund Burke's *Reflections on the Revolution in France* was published.

Reflections shocked many in Britain, especially those in Johnson's circle. Burke had promoted political reforms to reduce the political influence of the court – a cause supported by Nonconformists in their push for full civil rights. At a meeting of the Revolution Society (named for the Glorious Revolution of 1688) in November 1789 Wollstonecraft's mentor Richard Price praised the Revolution in France as an extension of the Glorious Revolution and therefore a model for reforms that would emancipate the Nonconformists in England. Many thought Burke too would welcome the French Revolution as the overthrow of court government in France and thus an example for Britain. But throughout 1790 he distanced himself from the Revolution and its British supporters, and when he published *Reflections* he condemned it and them, singling out Richard Price and the Revolution Society.

Burke's position was in fact consistent with his earlier politics. As a 'new man' who had made it from the professions to the landed gentry he had always represented the interests of the gentry against the Crown, court and aristocratic magnates, while acknowledging the importance of the professional and other middle-class men.[3] In *Reflections* Burke equates the national interest with that of the capitalist gentry, who are defined by ownership of landed property, a particular culture (a combination of 'antient chivalry', classical humanism and Christianity) and conduct conformable to that culture and that class's interests. *Reflections* argues that the Revolutionaries in France and those in Britain represented by the Revolution Society are disqualified on the first two counts. Certain aristocrats in France and Whig opposition aristocrats in Britain were betraying their class interest and so were disqualified on the third count.

To display his own qualifications to speak for the 'gentlemen',

Burke follows his long-established rhetorical strategy. In part this is based on the classical rhetoric of *ethos*, according to which the known character of the speaker, embodied in his style, is the most persuasive form of argument. Following Cicero, who represented the *equites* or 'gentry' of ancient Rome, Burke chooses the 'middle style', avoiding both grandiloquence, or speaking above the subject and the audience, and vulgarity, or demeaning the subject and himself. He chooses the form of the public letter addressed to a particular person – seen as the written equivalent to the personal yet public address of the Roman Senate or the British Parliament. He aims to be personal yet argumentative, suitably learned (for a landed gentleman) yet familiar. He exhibits the classical humanist culture that was the common educational training and cultural heritage of men of both the landed class and the upper bourgeoisie – the source of 'new men' who were supposed to make Britain's society uniquely open and 'progressive'. Yet he exhibits knowledge of 'business' – economics and management of both the individual landed estate and the larger estate that is the nation. In short, he exhibits the 'mind' qualified for membership in the 'political nation' and thus for authoritative public 'reflections' on the national interest, in contrast to the disqualifications of the Revolutionaries and their British supporters.

But Burke's rhetoric also participates in the culture of Sensibility. In the late eighteenth century the rhetoric of *ethos* was adapted to the expressive, individualistic rhetorical aesthetics of Sensibility made commonplace in handbooks such as Blair's *Lectures on Rhetoric and Belles Lettres*, which Wollstonecraft read in 1787. In Burke's speeches and writings he combined the rhetoric of *ethos* with a Sentimental poetics of 'genius' in order to emphasize his individualism and thus to acknowledge and capitalize on the well-known fact that he was a 'new man' who had risen by his merits, or individual qualities, to membership in the 'political nation'. He did not always maintain this delicate balance, and his peers were divided in their opinions of his 'eloquence'.[4] Nevertheless, the content and style of *Reflections* were consistent with Burke's entire political career. But in late 1790 many could not see this, and many who had thought of Burke as fellow traveller, including those in Johnson's circle, felt betrayed. Stories circulated that, like opposition politicians and 'reformers' before him, he had been bribed by the Government or Crown to betray the causes he had once supported.

Wollstonecraft followed this line, finding in Burke's style and arguments the evidence for his corruption by court culture. In taking this line she could rely on her own understanding of the poetics of Sensibility and Fuseli's unrivalled knowledge of rhetorical theory and history. The association of different kinds of rhetorical style with different political structures and cultures was a well-established topic in eighteenth-century political debate.[5] One classical source of this debate was Tacitus's *Dialogus de oratoribus* (in the eighteenth-century thought to be by Quintilian). Available in translation and known to Fuseli, it provides an explanation for what Wollstonecraft and others saw as Burke's sell-out. Set in the early imperial period of Rome, the *Dialogus* debates the use of rhetoric under an authoritarian government, where the arts of persuasion can have no public scope but are used only to curry favour by flattering the court or denouncing its 'enemies'. In contrast to the ideal orator, or *vir bonus dicendi peritus* (honest man skilled in speaking) of Cicero and Quintilian, is the *delator*, or man who uses his rhetorical skill in extravagant denunciations of innocent citizens in order to share their property as a reward from a grateful ruler.

In *A Vindication of the Rights of Men* Wollstonecraft represents Burke as the *delator* and herself as the *vir bonus dicendi peritus*. She claims that Burke's extravagant denunciations and purple passages are designed to play up to the court and privileged orders for personal ambition and gain. She claims that his attempts at the rhetoric of *ethos* are tricks of 'the head' masquerading as effusions of 'the heart', resulting in 'declamation', the *delator*'s inverted form of ethical rhetoric. Taking this line requires her to adopt the rhetorical strategy of 'turning the tables', outdoing Burke at his own game – the rhetoric of *ethos* adapted to the poetics of Sensibility. This was doubly risky for her. To validate arguments by exhibiting personal character and 'sentiments' in style and composition might be very well for a man who was an established figure in public, political life. Even then this stylistic option was often condemned as effeminate. Such a strategy could be immediately disabling for a woman, especially when she left 'feminine' kinds of writing for the masculine domain of politics and public affairs. Not surprisingly, Wollstonecraft kept her name off her title-page, at least for the first edition of *A Vindication of the Rights of Men*.

She aims to turn the tables on Burke in several ways. She gives

her own version of the main issues in *Reflections* – the character of
the Revolution; the nature of 'rights'; the economic basis of the
state; the question of religious establishments and church lands;
the nature and evolution of the British constitution; the qualifications and character of the ruling class; the condition of the poor;
and the conduct of the Revolution's English supporters. Like
Burke, she relates her arguments on these topics to broad issues of
the time: the nature and relationship of reason and imagination;
whether or not 'civilization' means progress; divine validation of
social and political organization; and conflict of 'rights' and 'duties'
– but she interprets these issues in her own way, to show equal
mastery of them. She uses Burke's own aesthetics, enunciated in
his early treatise on the sublime and beautiful, against him. Like
Burke, she claims to be writing from her feelings, in response to a
particular situation, but she claims to temper these feelings with
'reason' and 'virtue', unlike Burke.[6] Like Burke, she avoids the
formal, forensic, detached style of a treatise for a style that is
immediate and occasional (that is, addressed to a particular occasion); but whereas he does so to avoid the style of Revolutionary
'philosophers' and theorists, she does so to counter Burke's discourse. Another, covert, reason is that women writers were not
supposed to write philosophical treatises. To conduct her argument she, like Burke, uses the epistolary form, personal address, a
desultory and associative method of argument and certain key
rhetorical figures – some, such as architectural metaphors, taken
over from Burke and turned against him – but she claims to do so
with a sincerity Burke can only feign.

   She also aims to turn the tables on Burke by deliberately neglecting or downplaying certain elements of his material and style. For
example, she does not meet his detailed accounts of economics,
currency and legislation, and she gives much briefer consideration
to constitutional history, the events of the Revolution and the
actions of its English supporters. Burke argues that government
and politics are complicated and consequently only for the few
who have leisure and means to pursue them; by treating only
Burke's 'grand points' Wollstonecraft implies that this argument
and its discursive manifestation, in the length and variousness of
Reflections, are false. Secondly, and as a consequence, she claims to
reject some of Burke's rhetorical methods, principally 'wit', condescending sarcasm, rhetorical extravagance or 'declamation',
elaborate and copious style and 'paradoxes'. She represents these

discursive traits as symptoms of a vitiated mind, dominated by 'imagination' rather than 'reason', serving 'ambition' and 'vanity', desiring specious objects. Against this she claims to assert 'basic principles' in a 'simple' style, expressive of her own rational mind, controlling her righteous indignation, addressing 'reality' rather than appearances. By exemplifying the mind and social vision of the professional middle-class revolution in her own method and style she would expose Burke's method and style as those of one who has betrayed that revolution and gone over to court government and culture.

As Mitzi Myers notes, then: 'The lack of organization imputed to Wollstonecraft's essay by some critics is greatly overestimated.'[7] Both *A Vindication of the Rights of Men* and *Reflections* claim to be desultory, occasional and *ad hoc* in order to claim authenticity of polemical feeling; but both are well-organized according to contemporary conventions of polemical writing and the occasions they address. Wollstonecraft's prefatory 'Advertisement' states that she began reading *Reflections* 'more for amusement than information', but found her 'indignation was roused by the sophistical arguments . . . in the questionable shape of natural feelings and common sense'. Thus 'many pages of the following letter were the effusions of the moment', which eventually swelled to a considerable size. Then 'the idea was suggested of publishing a short vindication of *the Rights of Men*'. The italicized phrase strikes at Burke's argument that the representative Revolutionary event was not the Declaration of the Rights of Man and Citizen in August 1789 but rather the Paris mob's attack on Versailles in October. (Tom Paine's *Rights of Man* follows Wollstonecraft on this point.) Wollstonecraft concludes her 'Advertisement' by stating that she has confined her 'strictures . . . to the grand principles at which [Burke] has levelled many ingenious arguments in a very specious garb'. 'Garb' was a favourite metaphor of Wollstonecraft's for representing the merely external, superficial or specious; but Burke also uses images of dress to represent the 'dignity' of 'polished', 'civilized' humanity in contrast to the theory of the Revolutionary 'philosophers'. From the outset, then, Wollstonecraft emphasizes the stylistic, discursive character of Burke's text, and establishes her strategy as turning the tables.

The main text, which has the title 'A Letter to the Right Honourable Edmund Burke', continues this emphasis. It opens by attacking Burke's style and contrasting it with that Wollstonecraft herself

proposes to use, associating different styles with different political
cultures. To his 'courtly insincerity', 'equivocal idiom of politeness', twisted 'periods' (or sentences), disguised sentiments,
culled words, invidious phrases, 'flimsy ridicule' and 'lively fancy'
she will oppose emphatic indignation, sublime 'truth', beautiful
simplicity', the 'liberty of reason' and a 'manly definition' of truth.
Thus she turns against him his own well-known treatise on the
sublime and the beautiful, with its separation of aesthetic, intellectual and moral categories into the 'manly' and feminine.

She goes on to a sociological explanation for Burke's mind and
style: he is 'though a vain, yet a good man', but had to rise in the
court system by merit, or rather by the very 'eloquence' she puts
on trial here (pp. 3–4).[8] His naturally 'lively imagination' made him
ambitious, eagerly cultivating the wit and eloquence that enabled
him to shine. But according to the economy of 'mind', imagination
and wit are cultivated at the expense of profundity and reason. The
wit is like the courtly coquette, she suggests, thus associating
Burke with such a woman. But the 'Ladies' repeat his 'sprightly
sallies' and 'pathetic exclamations' because 'Sensibility is the *manie*
of the day' (p. 5): Burke feminized politics by sentimentalizing
them, according to mere fashions followed by upper-class women
('Ladies') and possibly of alien origin, as suggested by the French
word *manie*. There is another suggestion in *manie*: in English the
word is mania, and signifies not only a fad but mental derange-
ment; Burke's 'eloquence' is made of extremes – wit and sentimen-
tality – symptomatic of madness. By contrast, she exhorts Burke:
'let us, Sir, reason together'. The patronizing tone implies that
when it comes to reasoning she will have to lead the way. This
concludes the opening section of *A Vindication*.

Like Burke, she uses transitions by association to articulate each
stage of her argument with the next. Having established her
rhetorical ground and invited Burke to 'reason' with her, she
proceeds to reason by asserting her 'grand principles', defining
'the birthright of man' as 'such a degree of liberty, civil and
religious, as is compatible with the liberty of the other individuals
whom he is united with in a social compact' (p. 7). For tactical
reasons she speaks of 'man' here and uses masculine pronouns
throughout, nowhere indicating that she is a woman or that the
masculine gender assumed for humanity by such language is an
issue for her. Her main aim is rather to establish a doctrine of
rights. There were different forms of the compact theory of rights

in the eighteenth century, but Wollstonecraft's version of it derives from the political philosophy of the eighteenth-century 'Commonwealthmen'. This philosophy looked back to the seventeenth-century Commonwealth, and to the anti-court, anti-monarchic politics of republican antiquity; it was strong in the English Nonconformist Enlightenment and such writers as James Burgh and especially Richard Price, both of whose works Wollstonecraft knew.[9]

Throughout the *Vindication* she uses this philosophy against Burke, thus vindicating Price whom Burke singles out for attack. She argues that humanity is denatured because 'the demon of property has ever been at hand to encroach on the sacred rights of men' (p. 8). To Burke property is qualification for membership in the 'political nation' – those with a vested interest in government of the state – and thus the guarantor of liberty. But to Wollstonecraft property is the enemy of liberty, especially property as institutionalized by the landed classes – a family trust passed down by male primogeniture. Property and the institutions built on it vitiate the individual and yet are perpetuated through the generations by what she calls education and 'custom'. Hereditary property and honours cause an imbalance of power in society, creating a 'partial' civilization and a merely social culture of emulation. This in turn 'benumbs' the faculties of the propertied class, whose 'superior' rank misleads them into seeing social relations and happiness as the exchange of 'homage' for 'charity'. In fact, she argues, social culture should be based on 'morals' (or inward merit), rooted in the subjective self. 'True happiness' is in the domestic affections, and these can only 'be enjoyed by equals' in 'an intercourse of good offices and mutual benefits'.

Having attacked Burke's argument for a constitution based on property, Wollstonecraft then attacks his grounding of that constitution in history, custom and tradition, by showing how the civilization and the constitution he celebrates arose from mediaeval 'barbarism'. She rereads the history of the British constitution as a history of struggle between the landed classes and the monarchy, leading to the supremacy of the former, embodied in the state as Parliament and the established Church – the two institutions Burke defends in *Reflections*. The result of this struggle, she argues, was the subordination of the poor. She insists that rights depend on reason and God, not history. She then asks Burke if he is not a friend of property rather than liberty because he receives a state pension. This looks like a merely personal attack, but her points are, first, that Burke is a beneficiary of the constitution he defends and, secondly, that such pensions reveal the constitution to be a structure for exercising power through patronage. She also asks how Burke can use history to reject reform of the constitution yet accept the Protestant Reformation, or even the coming of Christ, for they too effected revolutions in the established order. If history is prescriptive, she asks, how could Burke have defended American independence, and how could negro slaves ever hope for emancipation.

From this point she makes another transition, to the condition of the poor, a subject treated at some length in *Reflections*, which concludes that the consolation of the poor would be in life after death.[10] She accuses Burke of defending the security of property, but only for the rich. The labourer's property is his liberty and that is sacrificed, through such practices as pressing into the navy, in order to defend the property of the rich, while there are savage penalties for petty theft and violation of the game laws, though self-preservation is the first law of nature. She suggests that as a '*gentleman*' Burke has a 'sensibility' made so delicate by luxury, and an 'imagination' and 'taste' so vitiated by art, that he cannot sympathize with a mere '*man*' and with misery as it really is.

> Misery, to reach your heart, I perceive, must have its cap and bells; your tears are reserved, very *naturally* considering your character, for the declamation of the theatre, or for the downfall of queens, whose rank throws a graceful veil over vices that degrade humanity; but the distress of many industrious mothers, whose *helpmates* have been torn from them, and the hungry cry of helpless babes, were vulgar sorrows that could not move your commiseration, though they might extort an alms. 'The tears that are shed for fictitious sorrow are admirably adapted,' says Rousseau, 'to make us proud of all the virtues which we do not possess.' (pp. 25–6)

Apart from the pointed play on 'misery' and 'commiseration', Wollstonecraft here turns several of Burke's own points against him: his dismissal of the Revolutionaries as merely theatrical; his claim that the glamour of the French court had expiated its vices; his dismissing the poor to Providence and the charity of the wealthy; and his attack on Rousseau as a prophet of Sensibility but indifferent to the sufferings of his own children.

Effecting another transition, she goes on to say that Burke's contempt for the poor resembles his contempt for Richard Price and to contrast Burke with Price, who was well-known for his practical schemes to improve the lot of the poor, by, for example, applying his considerable mathematical knowledge to insurance schemes for them. By contrast, Burke's arithmetic in *Reflections* is devoted to such issues as state revenue and the value of Revolutionary paper currency secured on confiscated church lands. Wollstonecraft also contrasts Price's joy at the dawn of liberty in France with Burke's fascination for the glance of the French Queen. Furthermore, while Burke denounces the Nonconformists for intruding religion into politics, she argues that Price stood for the toleration that enables free discussion of religion and politics – the only way to reveal truth. Wollstonecraft also contrasts Burke and Price as interpreters of the British constitution and system of government. She turns the tables on Burke by taking up another authority he cites, the legal commentator Blackstone, claiming that Blackstone agrees with Price that the succession of the crown depends on the will of the people. She then applies the point to Burke again, insisting that as a Member of Parliament he must know how the constitution really works – by bribery, corruption, and patronage (p. 41). This challenge is appropriate because Burke presumes his experience as an MP gives him a knowledge of government and the constitution that people such as Price cannot have. Furthermore, Burke was himself a 'man of merit' risen from the professions and had opposed those very devices of taxation, patronage and bribery that she lists here as the salient characteristics of the constitution he defends in *Reflections*.

This constitution, as Burke himself points out, defends property, and so Wollstonecraft makes another transition, repeating her point that property obstructs liberty, and goes on to argue that property also denatures family and social relations. Here she does consider the condition of women, while discussing the social and cultural effects of property as a family trust perpetuated through primogeniture, confining 'benevolence' to the 'narrow circle' of the family itself, producing a 'brutal attachment to children' as the means of perpetuating property, and forcing children 'to do violence to a natural impulse, and run into legal prostitution' or arranged marriages (p. 43). This system is especially harmful to females, because they are 'sacrificed to family convenience' and forced to practise selfishness and coquetry in self-defence.

Property also affects social relations and culture by inspiring emulation and conspicuous consumption:

> It would be an arduous task to trace all the vice and misery that arises in society from the middle class of people apeing the manners of the great. The grand concern of three parts out of four is to contrive to live above their equals, to appear to be richer than they are; and how much domestic comfort and private satisfaction is sacrificed to this irrational ambition! It is a destructive mildew that blights the fairest virtues; benevolence, friendship, generosity, and all those endearing charities which bind human hearts together, and the pursuits which raise the mind to higher contemplations . . . are crushed by the iron hand of property!   (p. 47)

The 'feudal' system of property not only denatures domestic affections, it also produces false social relations based on 'an unmanly servility', reproduced throughout society by courtliness and patronage. 'Men of some abilities play on the follies of the rich; and mounting to fortune as they degrade themselves, they stand in the way of men of superior talents, who cannot advance in such dirty steps, or wade through the filth *they* never boggle at' (p. 48).

Wollstonecraft herself proposes a property system based on intellectual and moral capital ('talents' and 'virtue'): 'The only security of property that nature authorises and reason sanctions is, the right a man has to enjoy the acquisitions which his talents or industry have acquired' (p. 48). There would be several benefits from making property 'fluctuate', or circulate according to talents and virtue. There would be 'no other road to wealth or honour'. Family pride would not favour blood over merit. The landed class itself would not degenerate through luxury, idleness and uncontested social supremacy, and in their degeneracy corrupt the rest of society. 'Virtuous ambition' would replace the aristocratic vice of gambling. The domestic affections would replace social relations of power and exploitation. Romantic 'love' would replace the courtly 'gallantry' which Burke, 'with knightly fealty', venerates. As a result, wives and mothers would carry out their domestic functions rather than coquetting in high life.

Wollstonecraft describes two different societies and cultures, based on two different institutions of property: the entailed family trust passed down through the male line and the reward of merit. This critique of landed property is the core of the *Vindication*'s political economy, already enunciated by the professional middle-class cultural revolution and anticipating the utilitarian political economy of the early nineteenth century. But Wollstonecraft's emphasis is less on landed property than on the social evils arising from it. From these vices she then turns to Burke's exculpation of them – one of the most notorious passages in *Reflections*. According to Burke, such vice is palliated by the elegance of the vicious – it 'loses half its evil by losing all its grossness' – and he argues that without the luxurious culture of the upper classes 'a king is but a man; a queen is but a woman; a woman is but an animal, and an animal not of the highest order'. Wollstonecraft argues that, on the contrary, the kind of false homage Burke would pay to women 'vitiates them, prevents their endeavouring to obtain solid personal merit; and, in short, makes those beings vain inconsiderate dolls, who ought to be prudent mothers and useful members of society' (p. 51). In both Burke and Wollstonecraft the condition of women represents the values of an entire society and culture; here is the basis of *A Vindication of the Rights of Woman*.

Wollstonecraft makes another transition, moving from Burke's sentimental treatment of the French royal family to his behaviour toward the British royal family. Burke laments the National Assembly's 'humiliation' of the French King, but during the regency crisis in Britain Burke himself tried to subordinate the King to the Commons so that the Prince of Wales and his own party could assume power. She argues that Burke exaggerates the distresses of the French royal family when threatened by the Paris mob at Versailles in October 1789, but he ignored the distress of the British royal family during the King's madness – 'A father torn from his children, – a husband from an affectionate wife, – a man from himself!' (p. 54). She herself gives an energetic and sympathetic portrait of madness, but she also refers to the 'proverbial observation, that a very thin partition divides wit and madness' (p. 60). Since she has already characterized Burke as a 'wit', the suggestion is that he himself may be close to madness, or at least that form of madness caused by ambition and passions ruling reason.

She then seems to digress into a consideration of 'genius' and the 'romantic' (as 'false, or rather artificial, feelings'). Drawing on her poetry reviews for the *Analytical*, she relates Burke's style of affected 'sensibility' and 'sentimental jargon' to his defence of irrational principles of conduct, such as 'instinct' and fear of God. Against this she restates her view of the improvement of the mind and society by God-given, divinely validated reason, proven by self-reflection and confirming her belief in the rights of men: 'I reverence the rights of men. – Sacred rights! for which I acquire a more profound respect, the more I look into my own mind; and, professing these heterodox opinions, I still preserve my bowels [compassion]; my heart is human, beats quick with human sympathies – and I FEAR God!' (pp. 73–4). This is the central passage in the *Vindication*. Here Wollstonecraft opposes Burke's assertion that the social order is legitimized for the individual by non-rational impulses within and by the external authority of history and tradition, both sanctioned by God, and thus cause 'to fear Him'.

She is then able to consider a major thematic complex in *Reflections*: the role of the clergy and the relation of church and state. She continues the previous topic as well as broaching a new one, focusing on the way landed property and primogeniture vitiate a major body of professionals, the clergy. 'It is a well-known fact, that when *we*, the people of England, have a son whom we scarcely know what to do with – *we* make a clergyman of him' (p. 77). The phrase '*we*, the people of England' is another sarcastic echo of Burke, who uses the expression to suggest that he could speak for the nation but the English supporters of the Revolution could not. Burke claims that a national religious establishment sanctifies state politics; Wollstonecraft sarcastically notes the debauchery and corruption of election-time. He claims the people respect the national church; she says this 'respect' is expressed in outbursts of religious bigotry such as the Gordon Riots of 1780. He claims that 'our education' (that is, the education of young gentlemen) is almost wholly in the hands of clergymen; she insists that tutors and chaplains are too often treated with disrespect in great families (pp. 86–7).

Reflection and understanding, not property, guarantee religion, she argues, and thereby makes a transition to Burke's views of the French National Assembly and the British Parliament. Burke condemns the National Assembly for lacking the weight of property and noble families, and he praises Parliament for possessing them. She replies that the rich and titled have no cause to exercise their talents, for 'talents are only to be unfolded by industry', as Burke himself will know – 'you are an exception; you have raised yourself by the exertion of abilities, and thrown the automatons of rank into the back ground'. But, she argues, his 'popularity' has waned, making him envious of new political heroes, such as Richard Price. This was the genesis of *Reflections*. 'You were the Cicero of one side of the house [of Commons] for several years; and then to sink into oblivion . . . was enough to rouse all that was human in you – and, producing these impassioned *Reflections*, has been a glorious re-vivification' (pp. 100–1).

She concludes that Burke may have imagination and sensibility but he lacks countervailing moral and intellectual stability, and thus he is like the mere women he describes in his treatise on the sublime and the beautiful. She suggests that Burke is effeminate rather than possessing the feminine virtues of sympathy and sensibility he claims, for like the women he describes in his treatise his aim is to be loved, so he counterfeits 'weakness' and 'littleness', neglecting the 'manly morals' of 'truth, fortitude, and humanity' necessary to 'any preparation for a more exalted state' (pp. 106, 108). The point comes from her review of Macaulay's *Letters on Education* and would be central to *A Vindication of the Rights of Woman*, which she anticipates here by opposing Burke's 'libertine imagination' and gendered morals and aesthetics: 'should experience prove that there is a beauty in virtue, a charm in order, which necessarily implies exertion, a depraved sensual taste may give way to a more manly one'. But 'such a glorious change can only be produced by liberty', for 'inequality of rank' – be it social class or gender – 'must ever impede the growth of virtue, by vitiating the mind that submits or domineers' (pp. 109–10).

From these evils of 'inequality of rank' and property Wollstonecraft makes a transition to the last movement of her polemic: consideration of the propertyless poor in relation to her general theme, the French Declaration of the Rights of Man and Burke's condemnation of it. She comes full circle from her opening argument that the institution of landed property is contrary to liberty, 'the birthright of man', necessary for salvation. Returning to the debate on the problem of evil, which had long preoccupied her, she agrees with Burke that poverty must be part of the divine plan and that divine justice will operate in the life hereafter, but she insists that misery is educative only in the individual life, not in society as a whole. God would not make some miserable merely to give the charitable rich opportunities for salvation. This realization, she says, was behind the French Declaration of the Rights of Man and the abolition of feudal privileges and religious establishments. Yet, she claims, Burke exercises his wit and imagination not only on this Revolution but also on its principal beneficiaries, the poor.

She then argues that Burke's witty contempt for the Revolution and the poor evince lack of judgement and hence an unbalanced mind: 'Judgment is sublime, wit beautiful; and, according to your own theory, they cannot exist together without impairing each other's power (p. 134). Burke characterizes the sublime as masculine and the beautiful as feminine, and since, she claims, wit predominates in *Reflections*, it must be a feminine text; but a 'feminine' text by a man would be effeminate. Thus she claims that Burke's rhetoric is condemned by his own aesthetic theory and reveals his vitiated mind and sensibility.

She then illustrates this vitiated sensibility by taking Burke's favourite metaphor for the state, the gentleman's country estate, as indeed an Arcadia of 'art and taste', though one where everything 'is cherished but man'. She then describes her version of Arcadia:

> if, instead of sweeping pleasure-grounds, obelisks, temples, and elegant cottages, as *objects* for the eye, the heart was allowed to beat true to nature, decent farms would be scattered over the estate, and plenty smile around. Instead of the poor being subject to the griping hand of an avaricious steward, they would be watched over with fatherly solicitude, by the man whose duty and pleasure it was to guard their happiness, and shield from rapacity the beings who exalted him, by the sweat of their brow, above his fellows. . . . It is not in squandering alms that the poor can be relieved, or improved – it is the fostering sun of kindness, the wisdom that finds them employments calculated to give them habits of virtue, that meliorates their condition. (pp. 138–9)

This is less a Revolutionary social vision than an echo of the Bluestocking feminists' amelioration of gentry capitalism or the Evangelicals' programme of social reform.

Her point is, however, that in unrevolutionized Britain 'the polished vices of the rich, their insincerity, want of natural affections, with all the specious train that luxury introduces' have reduced the poor to beings 'scarcely above the brutes' (p. 143). She then asks, 'What were the outrages of a day' (6 October 1789) compared to the 'continual miseries' of such brutalized beings:

> Such misery demands more than tears – I pause to recollect myself; and smother the contempt I feel rising for your rhetorical flourishes and infantine sensibility.
> — — — — — — — — —
> — — — — — — — — (p. 145)

According to Sentimental textual convention, the dashes represent authentic feelings beyond words, her silence in place of Burke's 'rhetorical flourishes', but presumably more eloquent.

She resumes, but the remaining half-dozen pages introduce no important new theme, and that is the point. Like the text it attacks, the *Vindication* is open, circular, repetitive and associative rather than linear, cumulative and syllogistic, thus suggesting that its argument could be taken up or left off anywhere. It ends, rather than closes, with the observation that if Burke's 'system' holds true, 'the gods, as Shakespeare makes a frantic wretch exclaim, seem to kill us for their sport, as men do flies' (p. 150). This quotation from King Lear in his tragic torment is characteristic of Wollstonecraft's shrewd use of quotation and allusion – as shrewd, though in a different way, as Burke's. The allusion strikes at Burke's picture of the sufferings of the King (and Queen), suggesting that his portrayal is pathos rather than tragedy. The allusion also strikes at Burke's use of theatrical analogies to revolution, and suggests that the *Vindication's* author can outdo Burke in such tropes. Finally, the allusion recollects her earlier suggestions that Burke himself may be mad, though by her account his madness lacks the tragic grandeur of Lear's.

Effective as this ending is, Wollstonecraft may have felt it was too pessimistic, for she added another long paragraph to the second edition of the *Vindication*, published only three weeks after the first. She says that Burke at least deserves praise for his 'consistency in avowing a veneration for rank and riches'. By contrast, 'some of the *enlightened* philosophers, who talk most vehemently of the native rights of men', in fact 'bow down to rank', property and reputation. 'But', she concludes, 'neither open enmity nor hollow homage destroys the intrinsic value of those principles which rest on an eternal foundation, and revert for a standard to the immutable attributes of God.' This inscribes her principles under the 'standard' of God, as she has done throughout. It is a necessary ending because, with her name now on the title-page, she too could be seen to be without the 'adventitious drapery' of 'rank', 'property' or a 'sounding name'. As a 'mere' woman author writing on politics she had need to invoke divine validation.

Nevertheless, *A Vindication of the Rights of Men* is a considerable achievement. Not only did Wollstonecraft take on the most celebrated political orator and writer of the day, and the man who set the terms for the British debate on the French Revolution, but she engaged with both the central themes and the rhetorical strategy of the *Reflections*. She was one of the first to reply to Burke, and if she did not demolish Burke's defence of the gentry, as he understood it, she competently, clearly and cogently put her case against the gentry property system and the culture built on that system, against what she saw as the political structure of court government and the economic structure of patronage that together secured the gentry's power. Furthermore, she did this with considerable rhetorical skill and subtlety, turning Burke's own rhetorical strategy, general aesthetic and political principles and even particular figures and tropes against him. At the same time, she emphasized the major role of gender in the struggle of class and culture. This may explain why she added her name to the second edition of *A Vindication of the Rights of Men* – to capitalize more fully on the way she, as a woman, had turned the tables on Burke in terms of a gendering of 'mind' and culture advanced by Burke himself.

An early, informal reaction to the book confirmed her success as a woman defending the wing of the professional middle-class cultural revolution attacked by *Reflections*. Her book was published at the end of November and she sent a copy to Richard Price; he replied from Hackney on 17 December:

> Dr Price presents his complim^{ts} to Miss Wolstonecraft, and returns his best thanks for sending him her Vindication of the rights of men in answer to Mr Burke, and for the pleasure he has derived from the perusal of it. He has not been surprised to find that a composition which he has heard ascribed to some of our ablest writers, appears to come from Miss Wolstonecraft. He is particularly happy in having such an advocate; and he requests her acceptance of his gratitude for the very kind and handsome manner in which she has mentioned him.[11]

This is one of the few letters to her that Wollstonecraft bothered to preserve. It is recognition by one of the leaders of the English Nonconformist Enlightenment and a leading contributor to the French Revolution debate, 'happy' to have 'such an advocate'. 'Happy' here means both 'fortunate' and 'appropriate', and 'such an advocate' could mean 'an advocate with Wollstonecraft's qualifications', including the qualification of gender. The letter also states that before her authorship became public her book was ascribed 'to some of our ablest writers'; Price was not likely to invent or exaggerate such a fact.

Other readers, however, attacked her for transgressing gender boundaries of discourse. The second edition of the *Vindication* was published the day after Price wrote to her. This was the edition reviewed in the magazines, and by identifying herself as the author she made it possible for the book to be treated as the work of a mere woman. The *Analytical's* review (signed 'O.') should have been favourable but it was tepid, noting the 'irony' in Burke, the self-professed knight of chivalry, finding two of his boldest adversaries to be women (Wollstonecraft and Macaulay Graham). It found 'many agreeable and interesting digressions', 'just sentiments, and lively and animated remarks, expressed in elegant and nervous language' (December 1790, pp. 418–19). This is hardly praise for a book replying to one of the leading political writers of the time and intervening in the most important political debate of the day.

The pro-Government *Critical Review* considered the book in December 1790 along with several other replies to Burke and, not surprisingly, condemns Wollstonecraft for 'too nearly approaching to the levelling principles of the present times' (vol. 70, p. 695). 'Levelling' here means democratic or even revolutionary. The reviewer also criticizes the book's style and organization. But at least *A Vindication* is treated seriously. Significantly, however, the reviewer admits to having read the first edition of *A Vindication*, refers to its author as 'he' and adds a note:

> It has been observed in an old play, that minds have no sex; and in truth we did not discover this Defender of the Rights of Man to be a Woman. The second edition, however, which often reveals secrets, has attributed this pamphlet to Mrs. Woolstonecraft, and if she assumes the disguise of a man, she must not be surprised that she is not treated with the civility and respect that

she would have received in her own person. As the article was written before we saw this second edition, we have preserved [preferred] an acknowledgement of this kind to the necessary alterations. It would not have been sufficient to have corrected merely verbal errors [the masculine pronouns]: a lady should have been addressed with more respect.   (p. 694)

This combination of sarcasm and gallantry was a familiar response by men of letters and public affairs to women 'trespassing' on their literary or political terrain. But Wollstonecraft, who had already offered the view that 'minds have no sex' in her earlier works, would remember the phrase and the distinction between a 'woman' and a 'lady' in her next *Vindication*.

The *Gentleman's Magazine*, long a vehicle for gentrification of the professional bourgeoisie, also reviewed the second edition, and found the book good enough to doubt whether the author 'be a real and not a fictitious lady', that is, a man writing under a woman's name. Otherwise, the reviewer was hostile and condescending:

The *rights of men* asserted by a fair lady! The age of chivalry cannot be over, or the sexes have changed their ground. We should be sorry to raise a horse-laugh against a fair lady; but we were always taught to suppose that the *rights of women* were the proper theme of the female sex; and that, while the Romans governed the world, the women governed the Romans.
(vol. 61 (February 1791) p. 151)

Wollstonecraft would soon turn her full attention to the 'proper theme' of 'the rights of women' and the role of women in the state, without giving up the political themes that many found inappropriate for a woman writer.

After the publication of *A Vindication of the Rights of Men* Wollstonecraft wished more than ever to use her new advantages as an established professional to improve the social position of herself, her family and friends. Joseph Johnson later sketched these efforts:

Her brothers and sisters were occasionally with her, when they were unsettled it was their home, & she took every method to

improve & prepare them for respectable situations. . . . Much of
the instructions which all of them obtained were obtained under
her own roof, & most if not all the situations which her sisters
had were procured by her own exertions. . . .

In a part of this period, which certainly was the most active of
her life, she had the care of her fathers estate, which was
attended with no little trouble to both of us. She could not
during this time I think expend less than £200 upon her brothers
& sisters.[12]

Johnson knew of these matters because he helped Wollstonecraft
with them.

Her oldest brother Edward became insolvent, apparently from
trying, like his father before him, to live in a grander style than his
means would allow. Her father had remarried but was again in
desperate financial straits and by early 1792 she was afraid she
might become responsible for his support. Wollstonecraft also took
in a young girl of nine or ten years old named Ann, apparently a
niece of Hugh Skeys's second wife and reported to be 'an orphan
Girl, which the dying mother of the Child . . . gave her to bring
up & w^c she is educat^g she says a Child of nature'.[13] By the autumn
of 1790 Eliza and Everina were teaching at a school in Putney. In
1791 Everina went as governess to an Irish gentleman's family and
Eliza to a similar position in Wales. Wollstonecraft felt that they
were 'settled very comfortably', but their letters show that they
were often desperately unhappy, felt helplessly dependent on
their older sister and resented her sense of superiority.

She sent her brother Charles to Ireland for a start in professional
life, tried to get him a place in the 'East India service', and later in
1791 asked her new friend, the Liverpool lawyer and banker
William Roscoe, to get him a place in a counting-house. But she
turned down one opportunity Roscoe offered because she doubted
Charles's 'professional knowledge' (*Letters*, p. 206). Finally, her
new American friends Joel and Ruth Barlow encouraged Charles to
go out to the United States with them, and she paid for his stay at a
farm near Leatherhead to learn farming. To advance her brother
James's naval career she sent him to study navigational mathemat-
ics with John Bonnycastle, a friend of Johnson's and collaborator in
the *Analytical*. James felt good connections and patronage would
do more for him than merit, however, and he 'threw some money
away to dance after preferment, when the fleet last paraded at

Portsmouth', but found he had to condescend 'to take the command of a trading vessel' on 'a voyage of speculation' (*Letters*,
p. 203). Meanwhile, George Blood proposed marriage to Everina
early in 1791; it was Wollstonecraft who had to let him down, but
she continued to help him on in a career, and to arrange Caroline
Blood's maintenance at a workhouse (p. 205). Not surprisingly,
though, Wollstonecraft saw in her father, brothers and George
Blood men too easily diverted from professional self-discipline by
false social emulation.

Reviewing for the *Analytical* continued to support her and her
family patronage system, while her reviews often picked up issues
that would be developed in her next book, on the rights of women.
For example, 'M.' praises Elizabeth Inchbald's novel *A Simple Story*
(May 1791), a powerful critique of the socialization of women to
decadent court culture, though complaining it did not go far enough:

> Why do all female writers even when they display their abilities,
> always give a sanction to the libertine reveries of men? Why do
> they poison the minds of their own sex, by strengthening a male
> prejudice that makes women systematically weak?[14]

In the second half of 1791 'M.'s' review of a book on French court
life and politics confirmed Wollstonecraft's dim view of the *ancien
régime*. By contrast, she praises a book on the United States by the
French Revolutionary Brissot for its depiction of open class-
relations and especially 'the innocent frankness that characterizes
the American women, and the consequent *friendly* intercourse that
subsists between the sexes, when gallantry and coquetry are equally
out of the question':

> Indeed, there cannot be a clearer proof of the purity of morals,
> that still prevails in America, than the easy, unreserved behav-
> iour of the women. Men and women mix together like social
> beings; and, respecting the marriage vow, mutually improve
> their understandings by discussing subjects that interest the
> whole race; whilst in Europe the conversations that pass be-
> tween *gentlemen* and *ladies*, in general, consist of idle compli-
> ments and lively sallies; – the frothy food of vanity. (September
> 1791, p. 38)

When she wrote these words Wollstonecraft was planning her
own revolutionary call to transform British society by rejecting the
gender differences of court society.

Meanwhile, she was trying to revolutionize her personal and professional life by combining domestic affections and moral-intellectual identity in a philosophical passion for Henry Fuseli. Having publicly transgressed the gendered canons of writing with *A Vindication of the Rights of Men*, she tried to transform that transgression into an unconventional relationship with the man who helped make her transgression possible. Rather than a contradiction of her new public identity as the author of *A Vindication of the Rights of Men*, her passion for Fuseli grew out of the book and the new identity. Rather than a contradiction of her attack on courtly amorous culture in *A Vindication of the Rights of Woman*, her obsession with Fuseli was another form of those arguments.

John Knowles affirms that Wollstonecraft's attraction to Fuseli was intellectual and cultural: 'previously to her acquaintance with Mr. Fuseli, she had never known any man "possessed of those noble qualities, that grandeur of soul, that quickness of comprehension, and lively sympathy"' – the words Knowles quotes here, as elsewhere, are from one of Wollstonecraft's letters to Fuseli.[15] Not surprisingly, 'she imagined' that such traits 'would be essential to her happiness, if she entered into the marriage state' (p. 163). Fuseli, however, was already married and, according to Knowles, 'to a woman whom he loved'; yet Wollstonecraft 'expressed to some of her intimate friends, that although Mrs. Fuseli had a right to the person of her husband, she, Mrs. Wollstonecraft, might claim, and, for congeniality of sentiments and talents, hold a place in his heart; for "she hoped," she said, "to unite herself to his mind"' (p. 165). Wollstonecraft's use of 'mind' here was not casual, for the term was central to her argument that 'mind has no sex' and should not be gendered in educational, cultural or social practice. According to Knowles, Wollstonecraft's 'delusion' that she could unite herself to Fuseli's 'mind' did not last long. 'From an admiration of his talents she became an admirer of his person, and then, wishing to create similar feelings in Fuseli, moulded herself upon what she thought would be most agreeable to him' (pp. 165–6).

In her professional self-dedication she had hitherto lived a spartan life, which now became politically correct as well: 'The notions of privation which some of the revolutionists in France were now endeavouring to inculcate, rather encreased than diminished this tendency in Mrs. Wollstonecraft, and Fuseli found in her (what he most disliked in a woman) a philosophical sloven.' The last phrase means that Wollstonecraft neglected appearance on 'philosophical' principle, 'her usual dress being a habit of coarse cloth, such as is now worn by milk-women, black worsted stockings, and a beaver hat, with her hair hanging lank about her shoulders' (p. 164). A portrait of her just after the publication of *A Vindication of the Rights of Men* shows her in this habit, with the defiant look of the vanguardist. But during 1791 her growing 'attachment' to Fuseli made her wish 'to create similar feelings' in him: 'she now paid more than ordinary attention to her person, dressed fashionably, and introduced furniture somewhat elegant into commodious apartments, which she took for that purpose' (p. 166). This self-transformation was complete by October 1791, when William Roscoe had her portrait painted in her new guise of elegant dame and she moved from George Street to Store Street. By no accident, in the same month she was also engaged on a book merging her personal, professional and political identities, and she told Roscoe that if he did not like the picture of her, 'I will send you a more faithful sketch – a book that I am now writing, in which *I* myself . . . shall certainly appear, head and heart' (*Letters*, p. 203).

5

'A Revolution in Female Manners'

A Vindication of the Rights of Woman, like most of Wollstonecraft's work, was conceived and written quickly. She had it in mind by June 1791, began writing in the autumn, gave the manuscript to the printer as she wrote and corrected final proofs in early January 1792. Not surprisingly, she told William Roscoe: 'I am dissatisfied with myself for not having done justice to the subject', and complained that had she more time she 'could have written a better book, in every sense of the word'; but, she adds, those who must write for pay have no choice but to write in haste, unlike 'gentlemen authors' such as Roscoe (*Letters*, p. 205). The book's 'Advertisement' claims that a sequel will include 'a full discussion of the arguments which . . . rise naturally from a few simple principles', 'the laws relative to women' and 'the consideration of their peculiar duties', but admits that 'fresh illustrations' occurred as she wrote, so that 'only the first part' is now presented to the public.

The book calls for 'a revolution in female manners' and it is characteristic of its author's work in rising from a broad view but addressing a particular historical moment. The moment was Talleyrand's report to the French National Assembly in 1791, proposing a national system of education but one that directed girls to domestic duties only. Her title also suggests a larger context, echoing her first *Vindication* and Tom Paine's *Rights of Man*, as well as the French Declaration of the Rights of Man and Citizen of August 1789, which uses 'man' as a general noun, though only 'men' were to enjoy the rights it set forth. After the Declaration there was a debate on the civic and educational rights of women, including Olympe de Gouges's *A Declaration of the Rights of Woman* and Condorcet's *Memoirs on Public Instruction* (1790).[1] Nevertheless, *A Vindication of the Rights of Woman* is addressed to the cultural revolution in Britain rather than to the Revolution in France. It is a critique of 'woman' constructed for court culture and appropriated by the professional middle-class cultural revolution through education in the broad sense, including socialization and culture.

The problem again was in finding the right form for such an address. If she were to write on such a subject in a conventionally feminine mode she would be implicitly accepting the existing subordination of women in writing, culture and society. If she were to write in a 'man's' mode she might be discounted as that rare being, a woman of 'masculine mind'. Accordingly, *A Vindication* had to be an experiment in feminist writing for its time – a revolution in discourse to support and to exemplify 'a revolution in female manners'. Wollstonecraft argues for women's liberation, starting with education, leading to full participation in the professional middle-class cultural revolution, resulting in social usefulness and warranting legal and civic equality. She would gain authority for this argument by arguing as a woman – by constructing a textual persona as one who knows whereof she writes and who exemplifies, in the way she writes, the rights of women to full moral, intellectual, social and civic being. In other words, she again adopts the argument from *ethos*.

Her rhetorical strategy was again to 'turn the tables' on a number of writers who in turn represent sexist 'prejudice' in society and the systematization of that prejudice in social relations, the gendering of culture (including writing), education and laws of property and marriage. She aims to 'turn the tables' on the oppression of women that produces their inferiority, an inferiority that is then used to justify their continued oppression. In order to do this she not only attacks oppression directly but also exemplifies in the way she makes her attack how women may convert the conditions of their inferiority and subordination into means for emancipation. For there was no neutral, ungendered discourse, style or genre available to her. All forms of writing were already strongly associated with either 'masculine' or 'feminine' culture, or would become primarily gendered discourse as soon as she applied them to a topic such as 'the rights of woman'. Thus she avoids an objective, detached, learned, syllogistic or sarcastic and sharply polemical style that could be considered as that which a man would use. That could 'unsex' her, undermining her rhetorical authority. But she also avoids what would be considered as a woman's belletristic, domestic, personal style and relative lack of formal argument. That could undermine her claim that women given the same education, culture and rights as men would be able to take an equal if different role in culture and society with men.

She defined her strategy in relation to those of her women contemporaries. In *Letters on Education* Catharine Macaulay Graham writes in a fairly detached and 'philosophical' style but feminizes men's intellectual discourse by treating it in terms of education, especially female education. In contrast was Helen Maria Williams's *Letters Written in France* (1790), which the *Analytical* reviewer (who may have been Wollstonecraft) described as 'truly feminine' (December 1790, p. 431).[2] Williams treats the Revolution in terms of acceptably feminine spheres of interest, especially 'sensibility' and the domestic affections, just as she had feminized such issues as slavery, imperial exploitation and the American Revolution in her poems of the 1780s. Furthermore, as the *Analytical* reviewer points out, Williams also adopts the appropriately feminine form of the familiar letter, and she writes in a personal, expressive, often lyrical, figurative and apostrophizing style.

From these examples and her own experience with *A Vindication of the Rights of Men* Wollstonecraft determined to compose a quasi-treatise, a discourse that would be seen to have attributes of both 'men's' and 'women's' writing – not an 'androgynous' form but one that converts the conventional limitations of women's education, 'mind' and writing into techniques for advancing and exemplifying women's claim to minds and careers equal to if different from those of men.[3] In order to carry out this rhetorical task Wollstonecraft feminizes 'philosophy', polemics and the politics of a particular moment in the evolution of the French Revolutionary state and the British cultural revolution's debate on the French Revolution. She incorporates the themes of earlier conduct books and educational writing but resituates them in the context of the Revolutionary decade and a feminism for such a decade. By means of a relentless sociological analysis she relates this feminism to the major themes of contemporary social and cultural criticism and to the major political issues of the day.

The text has several traits of a 'philosophical' work. Wollstonecraft calls it 'a treatise', describes the 'three parts' she plans to write, divides it into chapters in an orderly sequence, refers to her 'arguments' and 'principles', and uses terms found in philosophical argument, such as 'hence', 'inference' and 'therefore'. There are even footnotes. On the other hand, the title suggests a combative, 'engaged' and perhaps personal work. The chapters vary greatly in breadth, particularity and length, and often have polemical titles. The footnotes are not so much citations of sources and evidence as asides and exclamations. For example one note, to a quotation from Rousseau, reads simply, 'What nonsense!'[4] These traits suggest something other than a treatise – some discursive 'other' exemplifying the book's argument that domestic woman is the 'other' to patriarchy in law, society, culture and writing. The text moves from chapter to chapter in an orderly and progressive way, though the order is not rigid and the progression is not emphasized. The argument proceeds by incremental repetition, recurring to certain topics, themes and images, restating them in a different form and in relation to different topics.

The style is personal in several ways. First-person singular pronouns are much in evidence. There are many passages of direct second-person address, used to indicate immediacy, expressivity and intensity. Sometimes these expressive moments are reinforced by conventional typographical devices – dashes, exclamations and other visible signs of an individual 'voice'. There are many lyrical passages, signalling textualized authorial presence, and personal observations and autobiographical references. Such devices are found in other polemics, including Burke's *Reflections*, but they were also seen as features of much women's writing. Thus the argument has elements of rational, general, abstract and 'philosophical' method, but is formulated in terms of 'women's sphere' of common, quotidian, domestic life, and expressed in what would be seen by many readers as a 'woman's voice'. This imbrication or overlapping of 'philosophy' and the personal exhibits what could be seen as the only resources available to a woman in a society that systematically denies her intellectual equality, and therefore moral, professional and civic equality. By arguing against women's oppression with discursive materials that betoken that oppression, she indicates how the discursive order reproducing oppression can be broken.

This order should be broken by women themselves, or rather by a few 'geniuses' who lead the way. Christine Battersby argues that 'genius' was a gendered category in the eighteenth century.[5] Nevertheless this identity had interested Wollstonecraft since the late 1780s, when she tried to assume it as a way out of the limitations of femininity in her class and time. But nowhere is her assumption of this identity more important rhetorically than in *A Vindication*. For the personal style of *A Vindication* is also that ascribed in rhetoric handbooks to the 'genius' or unique individual. Yet Wollstonecraft's 'genius' is properly female, according to the code of domestic woman that she partially accepts. This is not a transcendent genius but one in touch with quotidian, domestic 'reality', theorizing from the materials of her own experience and observation. Thus the 'author', a character constructed in and by the text, exemplifies the ability of some women to achieve the moral autonomy and intellectual authority that she claims for all women, and to achieve it without any sign (in her text) of having been blessed or denatured by a man's education or having become one of those 'masculine women' decried by men (p. 8).

This 'turning the tables' on the supposed limitations of women's 'mind', education and style of writing is reinforced by Wollstone-craft's critical use of language, renovative use of figurative devices and bricolage, or improvisation, on 'women's' genres and discourses. Women were widely supposed to lack full competence in the domain of writing. They were thought to be more oriented to speech than to writing – to gossip, chat, fashionable phrases and the informality of face-to-face speech. Correspondingly, they were thought to have a weak grasp of grammar, spelling, lexicon and semantic precision in standard written English – seen in such familiar literary characters as Mrs Malaprop in Sheridan's play *The Rivals* (1775). They were thought incapable of discriminating appropriate registers and levels of language and unskilled in established decorums of style, genre and discourse. They were thought to have limited originality or energy, and to be imitative and hackneyed in use of language. Conduct books, for example, warned females against appearing 'witty' or 'original' – qualities associated with courtly women. As Wollstonecraft sarcastically points out, Rousseau claimed that a girl would rather look pretty than learn to write (p. 42 and note). Finally, women were thought incapable of the highest, noblest, sublime genres and uses of language.

Wollstonecraft aims to turn the tables on these ways of subordinating women within language and writing. She exhibits a vigorous, various, 'nervous' style, thought at the time to be characteristic of genius, and engages in flights of the elevated and sublime. She draws attention to the issue of gender and language from the outset, in her 'Introduction' expressly rejecting 'those pretty feminine phrases, which the men condescendingly use to soften our slavish dependence'. She takes the 'unoriginality' of women's language, supposedly arising from their lack of 'mind', or full critical awareness, and renews it in several ways. She enlivens dead metaphors and revivifies hackneyed similes. She redefines words that she claims divide and oppress, and then uses these words for her own emancipatory purpose. She takes some words in their root sense, a technique favoured by Fuseli, following Milton, to suggest a radical clearing-away of time-encrusted obfuscations of 'original' meaning. She uses paradox and oxymoron to seize attention and challenge received ideas. This critical use of language is also an expressive device, characterizing the 'mind' and thus validating the intellectual authority of the author. Her use of language and rhetorical figures is designed to exemplify critical thought at work – not critical thought of a learned, professionally trained (man's) mind but that of a mind forced to rely on a woman's education, yet capable of protesting against such education.

This use of language parallels Wollstonecraft's use of 'women's' genres, including the conduct book, the 'rhapsody', the anecdote (personal, confessional and domestic), the familiar letter, the maxim, devotional prose, the familiar essay and prose fiction. She had already assembled such genres into a curriculum of self-formation for women in the *Female Reader*, and *A Vindication* could be seen as another 'Female Reader', but using a bricolage of sub-literary 'women's' writing to emancipate its readers from the intellectual and cultural subordination usually associated with and reproduced by such writing. For example, *A Vindication* incorporates elements of the conduct book but is itself a meta-conduct book – a commentary and critique on conduct books as instruments in the construction of woman for oppression. Reading *A Vindication* should mean that conventional conduct books could never be read the same way again. *A Vindication* aims to revolutionize the conduct book and thereby revolutionize the professional middle-class cultural revolution.

A Vindication makes different use of 'rhapsody', in the sense of short, lyrical passages, including apostrophes, personal anecdotes, confessions and devotions. Such passages help give *A Vindication* its distinctive personal voice and authority. *A Vindication* could also be seen as a 'rhapsody' in the sense of a mixed or diverse composition, often used pejoratively to mean a medley or confused work; Wollstonecraft herself used the term disapprovingly of Burke's *Reflections*. But such characteristics could also validate the rhapsody as authentic, natural, original, eccentric, the work of 'genius', and thus more truthful than the polished, finished work conforming to an 'objective' or social standard. Rhapsodic writing could advertise an intent to be original, avant-garde, experimental and consequently subversive of the established order of discourse. Rhapsody could be associated with women's writing because it lacked characteristics of writing by the well-trained, classically educated, disciplined and self-critical mind. Wollstonecraft inverts these associations, suggesting that rhapsody is the form that the female 'genius' uses to transgress the discursive order and thus break out of that order's oppression of women.

Another form of writing associated with this oppression is the maxim. Situated between the courtly epigram and the plebeian proverb, the late eighteenth-century maxim was associated with middle-class culture and used to inculcate middle-class morality; courtly maxims such as those of La Rochefoucauld (quoted in *A Vindication*) had been appropriated by the bourgeois critique of courtliness. Maxims were recommended for women because they were supposed to instil moral principles in those not fitted by nature or education to acquire such principles for themselves: philosophy for men, maxims for women. Wollstonecraft uses the maxim in the usual way, to generalize common experience and thereby speak immediately to experience, without recourse to analysis or logic. But the maxim's pithy and 'nervous' form was also seen as characteristic of the style of 'genius', overleaping the reasoning required by lesser minds. Thus Wollstonecraft converts the maxim from an emblem of women's inferior 'mind' to a characteristic of 'female philosophy'. She does so by using the maxim to anchor a passage of personal, polemical or rhapsodic prose, in contrast to the short pithy statement that might conclude a passage of forensic, syllogistic reasoning.

The familiar essay, another brief form, was often recommended to women as more suited to their limited education and intellectual capacities than the formal discourses practised by and for men. Such essays were seen as a legitimate way to popularize philosophy and learned writing. When a philosopher such as David Hume wished to make the philosophical arguments of his treatise more accessible, for example, he put them in the form of essays. Furthermore, essays such as those anthologized in the *Female Reader* were used to popularize a gentrified literary and social culture for the rising professional bourgeoisie, the new 'reading public'. These essays often use personal tone, informal style, settings in contemporary daily life, illustrative anecdotes, the letter form and dialogue, traits associated with women's writing. *A Vindication* is more like a series of such essays than a 'treatise'. Each chapter forms a separate essay, though the essays are linked and some chapters fall into shorter essays. Thus *A Vindication* is like a collection of essays on different, related topics enunciating the same moral, cultural and social vision. In the process it revolutionizes the essay by transforming it from emblem of women's inferior 'mind' into instrument of women's emancipation.

A Vindication less obviously incorporates the epistle or 'familiar letter'. This was, again, the kind of informal, unlearned, personal, domestic, desultory, brief writing for which women were thought to be suited by nature and education. In everyday life women – even a professional woman such as Wollstonecraft – would use the letter to sustain a personal, familial network; in women's published work the letter often converts personal, private, familial relationships and communication into public issues. In *A Vindication* Wollstonecraft uses the dedicatory epistle to Talleyrand to claim participation in men's public discourse, and though she abandons the epistolary form in her main text, she retains its informality, personal tone, direct address and desultory progression.

Similarly, *A Vindication* purposefully approximates novelistic discourse – not so much the novel form itself as what that form does to the discursive order of its time. The novel was closely associated with women and accordingly had low literary status. But it had a wide readership because it embodied a variety of cultural and social discourses in a form accessible to a diverse reading public, 'novelizing' the cultural revolution. More than any other form of print but the newspaper, the novel brought the public sphere 'home' to its readers. If Wollstonecraft's later *Maria; or, The Wrongs of Woman* is a polemical novel, *A Vindication* is a novelized polemic. For example, it appropriates traits of the novels of manners, sentiment and emulation reviewed by Wollstonecraft in the *Analytical*. Such novels represent social, cultural, political and economic issues in terms of individual moral and ethical choices made in the context of familial, social and institutional constraints.[6] In such novels individual experience validates and generalizes the conclusions to be drawn from experience of 'things as they are', as in *A Vindication*. Furthermore, like many novels of social protest in the 1790s, *A Vindication* uses the confessional, first-person mode to create a self-validating text addressed to the reader as an equal, thereby calling the 'reading public' into being as a political collective made up of individuals with common traits based on common social experience – in fact, the experience of the professional bourgeoisie. In these uses of novelistic discourse *A Vindication* again converts a sub-literary kind of writing strongly associated with women into an instrument of women's 'vindication' and emancipation.

A Vindication is 'novelized' polemic in another sense. Mikhail Bakhtin argues that the novel is 'dialogical' in that it incorporates the many diverse 'voices' (or heteroglossia) of a society, thereby relativizing the hierarchical power structure within a language at any particular time. The novel also appropriates other literary and non-literary discourses, relativizing them, too. It does this by intertextuality, showing that particular texts, genres and styles are defined not by their intrinsic 'nature' but by their 'dialogical' relationship with each other. The novel can even represent within itself an entire culture's order of discourses or cultural practices, 'novelizing' this order and thereby relativizing, subverting or revolutionizing it.[7] *A Vindication* 'novelizes' the discursive order of professional middle-class culture in order to show that this order is hierarchically gendered. It then revolutionizes this order by showing that women's discourses – rhapsody, maxims, the essay and so on – can represent the equality in difference of women's discourses to men's, and therefore can represent the equality in difference of women to men. Because of writing's status in professional middle-class culture and the power of writing and print to create a class consciousness throughout the nation, *A Vindication* aims to revolutionize that class by novelizing its written discourse. In doing so it aims to effect 'a revolution in female manners' by means of a reading revolution. Wollstonecraft's manifesto for this revolution is stated at the outset, in the dedication of *A Vindication* to Talleyrand. She claims to be 'disinterested', pleading 'for my sex – not for myself'. She is able to do so because she is 'independent' and thus able to express herself 'with freedom', unlike most women. Implicitly, this independence must rest on her professional career as a writer, but she aims to obtain it for all women, so ensuring 'the progress of those glorious principles that give a substance to morality' – the principles of the French Revolution as enunciated in the Declaration of the Rights of Man and Citizen.

Contending for the rights of woman, my main argument is built on this simple principle, that if she be not prepared by education to become the companion of man, she will stop the progress of knowledge and virtue; for truth must be common to all, or it will be inefficacious with respect to its influence on general practice. (p. 4)

She argues that the denial of such freedom to women is characteristic of court government, producing 'the system of duplicity' that has spread through the whole of French society. Yet, she argues, much of this system is preserved in the Revolutionary order, including Talleyrand's proposal for a national system of education, which perpetuates patriarchy by relegating women to an inferior education and a merely domestic role. But the patriarchal family parallels the patriarchal state, and each reinforces and reproduces the other. 'In this style, argue tyrants of every denomination, from the weak king to the weak father of a family; they are all eager to crush reason; yet always assert that they usurp its throne only to be useful' (p. 5). Wollstonecraft does not oppose the domestic role of women altogether, but insists that such a role must be the free, rational choice of women themselves.

They cannot choose freely, however, because they are admired as sexual objects, not rational beings (p. 4), and they are educated to seek such idolizing through merely 'personal accomplishments' designed for the marriage market. Such an 'education' is counterproductive, for 'whilst [women] are only made to acquire personal accomplishments, men will seek for pleasure in variety', and by an ethical economy 'faithless husbands will make faithless wives' (p. 6). Therefore men attempt to control women by depriving them of civic and property rights; but women who are 'not taught to respect public good, nor allowed any civil rights' will 'attempt to do themselves justice by retaliation', and use 'coquetry' and 'cunning' to obtain 'indirectly a little of that power of which they are unjustly denied a share: for, if women are not permitted to enjoy legitimate rights, they will render both men and themselves vicious, to obtain illicit privileges' (p. 6).

The main text of *A Vindication* sets forth the same argument in more detail. The opening paragraph of the 'Introduction' establishes the central themes of the book, its rhetorical posture, stylistic register and argumentative method:

After considering the historic page, and viewing the living world with anxious solicitude, the most melancholy emotions of sorrowful indignation have depressed my spirits, and I have sighed when obliged to confess, that either nature has made a great difference between man and man, or that the civilization which has hitherto taken place in the world has been very partial. I have turned over various books written on the subject of education, and patiently observed the conduct of parents and the management of schools; but what has been the result? – a profound conviction that the neglected education of my fellow creatures is the grand source of the misery I deplore; and that women, in particular, are rendered weak and wretched by a variety of concurring causes, originating from one hasty conclusion. The conduct and manners of women, in fact, evidently prove that their minds are not in a healthy state; for, like the flowers which are planted in too rich a soil, strength and usefulness are sacrificed to beauty; and the flaunting leaves, after having pleased a fastidious eye, fade, disregarded on the stalk, long before the season when they ought to have arrived at maturity. – One cause of this barren blooming I attribute to a false system of education, gathered from the books written on this subject by men who, considering females rather as women than human creatures, have been more anxious to make them alluring mistresses than affectionate wives and rational mothers; and the understanding of the sex has been so bubbled by this specious homage, that the civilized women of the present century, with a few exceptions, are only anxious to inspire love, when they ought to cherish a nobler ambition, and by their abilities and virtues exact respect.   (p. 7)

The personal voice and tone are evident, though not excessive – four uses of 'I'. Self-reference is seen in 'melancholy emotions', 'depressed my spirits', 'I have sighed'. Such recourse to feeling may seem an unphilosophical, merely 'feminine' response to the human scene, both past ('the historic page') and present ('the living world'). But this response is part of an argumentative scheme used often – from observation ('considering', 'viewing'), to feeling ('melancholy emotions'), to a reasoned conclusion – meant to represent a woman's way of reasoning and arguing, relative to men's argumentative discourse of that time.

Wollstonecraft often uses simile and metaphor in a similar way. The figure used here is characteristic: an extended comparison, drawn from nature, of women and flowers 'planted in too rich a

soil'. The simile suggests that women's preoccupation with outward beauty rather than inward merit is not their fault but due to
the circumstances of their 'growth', a 'natural' consequence of
their miseducation. The simile is complex, for the language used to
build it has strong overtones of the luxury ('too rich a soil'), display
('flaunting') and over-refinement ('a fastidious eye') of decadent
court culture, thus keeping her polemic against court culture in
view. Furthermore, in Western amorous culture women are associated with flowers to symbolize their delicacy and desirability.
Wollstonecraft turns the tables on these associations, playing on
the realities of sexuality and subordination. In the late eighteenth
century the study of botany by women was often frowned upon
because it would entail study of sexual reproduction – knowledge
thought to be unfeminine and perhaps morally dangerous for
women. But in her flower simile Wollstonecraft emphasizes sexual
reproduction, turned into an ironic comment on the reduction of
women to sexual objects, thereby disqualifying them for responsible execution of their role in domestic and social reproduction, as
'affectionate wives and rational mothers'.

Another characteristic argumentative method is her use of paradox, especially oxymoron, seen in the phrase 'barren blooming'.
This is a logical contradiction but effective: it continues the simile
of women as flowers, it suggests the particular age ('blooming') at
which women are most attractive to those for whom they have
been 'grown', it suggests that the bloom conceals moral and
intellectual barrenness, and it suggests the fruitless – in more ways
than one – future of such merely 'flaunting' flowers.

The paragraph closes with yet another characteristic device –
pairing and contrasting words and ideas. Often these contrasting
pairs are strung out in a series, as here – 'women' rather than
'human creatures', 'alluring mistresses' rather than 'affectionate
wives and rational mothers', and so on. There is also a characteristic play on words in the phrase 'so bubbled by this specious
homage'. Throughout her writings Wollstonecraft uses a variety of
words and figures suggesting emptiness and fair-seeming in her
critique of the mere outwardness, display and alluring but decep-
tive appearance of court culture, in contrast to the inwardness,
authenticity, plenitude of meaning and value of what she herself
stands for – a version of professional middle-class culture. In this
passage 'specious' reinforces 'bubbled', in the then common sense
of cheated or deceived, from the empty but attractive appearance

of a bubble, to suggest that the 'false system' of educating women not only subordinates them in an empty and specious culture but does so by constructing them as empty and specious.

She continues these associations when she turns to the major issue of biological determinism. She accepts natural physical inequality between the sexes, evidenced by animal sexual behaviour:

> In the government of the physical world it is observable that the female in point of strength is, in general, inferior to the male. This is the law of nature; and it does not appear to be suspended or abrogated in favour of woman. A degree of physical superiority cannot, therefore, be denied – and it is a noble prerogative! But not content with this natural pre-eminence, men endeavour to sink us still lower, merely to render us alluring objects for a moment . . . . (p. 8)[8]

The implication in her admission, however, is that the physical and sexual are inferior to the intellectual and moral as the animal is inferior to the human. She agrees with criticism of 'masculine women' if that means women who pursue men's vices, but not if it means 'the imitation of manly virtues, or, more properly speaking, the attainment of those talents and virtues, the exercise of which ennobles the human character, and which raise females in the scale of animal being, when they are comprehensively termed mankind; – all those who view them with a philosophic eye must, I should think, wish with me, that they may every day grow more and more masculine'.

She intends to 'consider women in the grand light of human creatures, who, in common with men, are placed on this earth to unfold their faculties'. Nevertheless, class difference must be taken into account, 'for the instruction which has hitherto been addressed to women, has rather been applicable to *ladies'*, or upper-class women and their emulators; by contrast, she will 'pay particular attention to those in the middle class, because they appear to be in the most natural state' (p. 9). She must adopt an appropriate language for this task and eschew courtly language:

> Dismissing then those pretty feminine phrases, which the men condescendingly use to soften our slavish dependence, and despising that weak elegancy of mind, exquisite sensibility, and sweet docility of manners, supposed to be the

sexual characteristics of the weaker vessel, I wish to shew that elegance is inferior to virtue, that the first object of laudable ambition is to obtain a character as a human being, regardless of the distinction of sex.

In a series of phrases that echo the first *Vindication*'s denunciation of Burke's style, she continues:

Animated by this important object, I shall disdain to cull my phrases or polish my style; – I aim at being useful, and sincerity will render me unaffected; for, wishing rather to persuade by the force of my arguments, than dazzle by the elegance of my language, I shall not waste my time in rounding periods, or in fabricating the turgid bombast of artifical feelings, which, coming from the head, never reach the heart. – I shall be employed about things, not words! – and, anxious to render my sex more respectable members of society, I shall try to avoid that flowery diction which has slided from essays into novels, and from novels into familiar letters and conversation.

These pretty superlatives, dropping glibly from the tongue, vitiate the taste, and create a kind of sickly delicacy that turns away from simple unadorned truth; and a deluge of false sentiments and overstretched feelings, stifling the natural emotions of the heart, render the domestic pleasures insipid, that ought to sweeten the exercise of those severe duties, which educate a rational and immortal being for a nobler field of action.   (p. 10)

Courtly language, style and discourse are responsible for the courtization of women, reproducing their moral and intellectual inferiority and thus perpetuating court hegemony. Therefore Wollstonecraft must reject such language and style; she refers particularly to kinds of discourse – 'essays', 'novels', 'familiar letters' and 'conversation' – that she herself appropriates in *A Vindication* so as to revolutionize them, breaking their power to reproduce court hegemony and making them serve Revolutionary feminism.

The 'Introduction' to *A Vindication* asserts that women should be the moral and intellectual equals of men but are in fact degraded by the values and practices of court society, mistakenly perpetuated by the French Revolution and by the cultural revolution in Britain. Chapter 1, 'The Rights and Involved Duties of Mankind Considered', goes on to show how this false gender culture arises from false distinctions of class. Wollstonecraft begins by flourishing treatise-like terms, declaring that she will 'go back to first principles in search of the most simple truths', ask 'some plain questions' and get answers 'as unequivocal as the axioms on which reasoning is built' (p. 11). She then builds up a connected set of such 'axioms'. First, 'man's pre-eminence over the brute creation' consists 'in Reason'. Secondly, the 'acquirement' that 'exalts one [human] being' over another is 'Virtue'. Thirdly, the passions were implanted so that 'man by struggling with them might attain a degree of knowledge denied to the brutes'. She concludes: 'Consequently the perfection of our nature and capability of happiness, must be estimated by the degree of reason, virtue, and knowledge, that distinguish the individual, and direct the laws which bind society' (p. 12). Here is the same triad of traits constituting 'mind' in professional culture.

After this display of 'philosophical' method she turns to reason's enemy, 'prejudice', which is based on 'partial' experience. There is a philosophic play on words here: partial or incomplete experience produces partiality or selfish prejudice, and parties or self-serving social and political groups. The root of this comprehensive system of 'prejudice' is that denounced in A Vindication of the Rights of Men: 'hereditary honours, riches, and monarchy', or court government, called 'civilization'. So extensive is 'the wretchedness that has flowed' from this system that 'men of lively sensibility have almost uttered blasphemy' to explain how a benevolent deity could allow it to exist. She refers here to Rousseau's well-known rejection of such 'civilization' for a state of nature, and concludes, 'Rousseau exerts himself to prove that all was right originally: a crowd of authors that all is now right: and I, that all will be right' (p. 15). She justifies her conclusion from mainstream Anglican theology and Richard Price's rationalism, referring again to the debate on the purpose of evil under a supposedly benign God: 'that wise Being who created us and placed us here' willed 'that the passions should unfold our reason, because he could see that present evil would produce future good' (p. 14). The rest of Chapter 1 presents her argument against a 'partial' society and 'civilization', or society and culture based on class.

Chapters 2 and 3, 'The Prevailing Opinion of a Sexual Character Discussed', consider gender difference in relation to social structure and culture. Chapter 2 analyzes three related accounts of the origin and nature of woman: the Book of Genesis, Milton's *Paradise Lost* and Rousseau's *Émile*. The chapter opens with an attack on Milton's 'true Mahometan strain' in seeming to deprive women of souls, and turns the tables on Milton by quoting his Adam: 'Among unequals what society / Can sort, what harmony or true delight?' Women can achieve the ideal of equality and fellowship only if educated to be morally and intellectually 'independent' (p. 21), but such an education requires a social revolution, because 'Men and women must be educated, in a great degree, by the opinions and manners of the society they live in'.

'The opinions and manners' of 'the present corrupt state of society, contribute to enslave women by cramping their understandings and sharpening their senses', depriving them of the principles and habits necessary to the professional man. They lack 'order' or intellectual discipline and method:

> To do every thing in an orderly manner, is a most important precept, which women, who, generally speaking, receive only a disorderly kind of education, seldom attend to with that degree of exactness that men, who from their infancy are broken into method, observe.

Therefore women are incapable of abstract thinking and intellectual generalization and consequently of progressive critical thought, or improvement – intellectual operations necessary in professional work. Women's 'negligent kind of guess-work . . . prevents their generalizing matters of fact – so they do to-day, what they did yesterday, merely because they did it yesterday' (p. 22).

The knowledge women do acquire is limited by their domestic circumstances:

> [It is] of a more desultory kind than the knowledge of men, and it is acquired more by sheer observations on real life, than from comparing what has been individually observed with the results of experience generalized by speculation. Led by their dependent situation and domestic employments more into society, what they learn is rather by snatches . . . . In the education of women, the cultivation of the understanding is always subordinate to the acquirement of some corporeal accomplishment . . . . They dwell

on effects, and modifications, without tracing them back to causes. (p. 23)

Women's knowledge is local rather than general, particular rather than abstract, quotidian and 'real' rather than universal and speculative, social rather than intellectual, immediate rather than detached, interested rather than objective, and concerned with details rather than connections and relations. Though Wollstonecraft considers such knowledge inferior, her strategy in *A Vindication* is to show how it can be the basis for a woman's kind of philosophizing and thus the basis for women's liberation from the limitations of their knowledge.

She immediately gives a paradoxical turn to her point by comparing women's knowledge to that of soldiers. Women and soldiers would seem to be very different, in terms of gender difference; yet 'military men', like women, are 'sent into the world before their minds have been stored with knowledge or fortified by principles'. Then they 'acquire a little superficial knowledge' and 'what is termed a knowledge of the world'. 'Where is then the sexual difference', she asks, 'when the education has been the same?' (p. 23). Such analogies give striking illustration to Wollstonecraft's argument and show that the trivialization of women's minds is only one aspect of the cultural politics of court-dominated societies.

This trivialization is based more particularly on the politics of family property. 'Riches and hereditary honours have made cyphers of women to give consequence to the numerical figure' – that is, women in a family are made 'cyphers' or nothings, and are also left a cypher, or nothing, in order to make them the means of increasing the size of the family estate, its 'numerical figure'. The resulting 'idleness' or lack of useful social roles for women introduces 'a mixture of gallantry and despotism', or courtly social practice, into society, inducing 'the very men who are the slaves of their mistresses to tyrannize over their sisters, wives, and daughters'. Not only is courtly love based on a sexual double standard, it produces domestic tyranny. This economy of gender relations resembles that of court government: 'as blind obedience is ever sought for by power, tyrants and sensualists are in the right when they endeavour to keep women in the dark', because tyrants 'only want slaves' and sensualists only want 'a play-thing' (p. 24).

Accordingly, she turns to consider Rousseau as a major appropriator of courtly woman into bourgeois culture.[9] He argues that women are 'so weak that they must be entirely subjected to the superior faculties of men' (p. 25). But he shows his courtly values when he concludes that this weakness shows women are made for love. Wollstonecraft replies that love 'should not be allowed to dethrone superior powers, or to usurp the sceptre which the understanding should ever cooly wield' (p. 27). Women's 'natural' weakness is also supposed to make them gentle, forbearing and long-suffering. These may be sublime virtues, Wollstonecraft agrees, but not if they are tokens of dependence. Historically men have dominated women and women have simply responded like courtiers, devising 'amiable weaknesses' to enslave their 'masters' (p. 37). The comparison to court government again underlines the central role of women's oppression in such governments' structures of power.

Chapter 3, 'The Same Subject Continued', has two sections. First, Wollstonecraft considers more fully women's inferiority to men, wrongly extrapolated from the physical to the moral and intellectual plane. Such inferiority is supposed to attract men and thereby give women power they would not otherwise have. Wollstonecraft replies that this leaves women imprisoned by the body, and she argues that such physical weakness should be reformed by exercise, making bodily strength the basis of moral and intellectual strength and resiting women's attractiveness in their moral and intellectual being. She authenticates this *embourgeoisement* of the body from her own observation. 'I have, probably, had an opportunity of observing more girls in their infancy than J. J. Rousseau', she claims (p. 43), countering his male fantasies and theories with her experience in everyday life and echoing her comment in the previous chapter that the 'knowledge which women of strong minds attain . . . is acquired more by sheer observations on real life' than from 'speculation'. The figure 'I have seen' undermines the supposed intellectual authority of men's abstract, general, speculative thinking which Rousseau claims is beyond the capacity of women.

What is required, Wollstonecraft argues, is Revolutionary feminism as part of a general revolution: 'It is time to effect a revolution in female manners – time to restore to them their lost dignity – and make them, as a part of the human species, labour by reforming themselves to reform the world' (p. 45). She then describes such an ideal woman and her 'heroism' in domestic life, as wife, mother and widow, validated in death by God (pp. 50–1). She closes the chapter by restating her revolutionary plan to create such women through education in the same qualities of 'mind' required by professional men, thus enabling women of the 'middle ranks' to carry out their mainly domestic roles. If these women are denied this kind of 'mind' and treated like women in court society, they will reproduce court ideology and culture in themselves, their children and their domestic sphere, thus corrupting their own class and society at large.

Chapter 4, 'Observations on the State of Degradation to Which Woman Is Reduced by Various Circumstances', describes this courtization of women as the denial of 'reason', or the critical thought necessary to both professional intellectual work and regulation of professional discourses: 'The power of generalizing ideas, of drawing comprehensive conclusions from individual observations, is the only acquirement, for an immortal being, that really deserves the name of knowledge.' Knowledge so defined is power, and though Wollstonecraft means a mental power, on this power all others depend. Yet conduct writers insist that it is 'inconsistent' with women's 'sexual character', and women are excluded from it by 'the very constitution of civil governments' (p. 54). In consequence, women are forced to rely on coquetry, neglecting their 'understanding'. This makes them unstable, impulsive, sensual, unreflective and improvident, qualities seen at the time as characteristic of the lower classes, primitive peoples and children. Not surprisingly, then, men oppose educating women in the same way they 'argue against instructing the poor' (p. 62).

The rest of Chapter 4 considers Enlightenment philosophers' arguments, supposedly 'deduced from nature', that 'degrade' women 'morally and physically' by constructing them around their sexual, amorous role (p. 69). These include claims that women have weaker understandings because they arrive at physical maturity sooner than men, that polygamy is natural in certain societies and climates and other 'scientific' justifications for a sexual double standard. Wollstonecraft argues that women educated only for love will be unqualified for domestic duties and disappointed by the inevitable decline of conjugal passion. Consequently the best basis for marriage is 'friendship', 'the most sublime of all affections, because it is founded on principle, and cemented by time' (p. 73). This argument has led later feminists to conclude that Wollstonecraft collaborated in the denial to women of sexual equality and subjective fulness, as 'desiring subjects' – a denial now seen as one cause of women's subjection. In fact, Wollstonecraft is warning not against women's sexuality but against the construction of women around sexuality within court culture, or appropriations of that culture by the middle classes.

Having considered society's prevailing views of women she turns in her fifth and longest chapter to particular writers responsible for or representing such views, in 'Animadversions on Some of the Writers Who Have Rendered Women Objects of Pity, Bordering on Contempt'. The first of five sections attacks Rousseau's appropriation of courtly woman to the bourgeois domestic ideal. Wollstonecraft argues that this error 'arose from sensibility': when Rousseau 'should have reasoned he became impassioned, and reflection inflamed his imagination instead of enlightening his understanding' (p. 90). In the first *Vindication* she made the same charge against Burke and his chivalrous defence of the French court's mistress, Marie Antoinette. This creates an unstated intertextual irony, for the counter-Revolutionary and the father of the Revolution both trivialize women.

The second and third sections broaden her critique, turning to the most frequently reprinted English conduct books by men – Fordyce's *Sermons to Young Women* (1765) and Dr John Gregory's *A Father's Legacy to His Daughters* (1774). Fordyce, like Burke and Rousseau, uses mere rhetoric to hide empty concepts, and like a courtly gallant he employs 'the lover-like phrases of pumped up passion' (p. 94) – as in the first *Vindication* alliteration effectively conveys disdain. The attack on Gregory is less energetic because Wollstonecraft sees his concern with social 'decorum' as less damaging than Fordyce's libertinism disguised as morality.

The fourth section turns to women conduct writers, including Hester Thrale Piozzi, Madame de Staël, Madame de Genlis, Hester Chapone and Catharine Macaulay Graham, in ascending scale of approval. Full praise is reserved for Graham, 'the woman of the greatest abilities, undoubtedly, that this country has ever produced', and who combined male and female characteristics in her mind and writing:

Catharine Macaulay was an example of intellectual acquirements supposed to be incompatible with the weakness of her sex. In her style of writing, indeed, no sex appears, for it is like the sense it conveys, strong and clear.

I will not call hers a masculine understanding, because I admit not of such an arrogant assumption of reason; but I contend that it was a sound one, and that her judgment, the matured fruit of profound thinking, was a proof that a woman can acquire judgment, in the full extent of the word. Possessing more penetration than sagacity, more understanding than fancy, she writes with sober energy and argumentative closeness; yet sympathy and benevolence give an interest to her sentiments, and that vital heat to arguments, which forces the reader to weigh them.

This is an implied manifesto for *A Vindication* itself, though there is an implication that *A Vindication* contains the 'fancy' and 'sagacity' Macaulay lacks, and Wollstonecraft goes on to claim a relationship even beyond the grave: 'When I first thought of writing these strictures I anticipated Mrs. Macaulay's approbation, with a little of that sanguine ardour, which it has been the business of my life to depress; but soon heard with the sickly qualm of disappointed hope; and the still seriousness of regret – that she was no more!' (p. 106).

As a contrast, the fifth and last section considers Chesterfield's *Letters to His Son* (1774), a notorious expression of courtly ethics. Chesterfield makes a contrasting complement to Rousseau; he recommends the courtly social relations attacked by Rousseau, yet Rousseau restates Chesterfield's courtly trivialization of women. Wollstonecraft regards Chesterfield as an educational writer and treats his 'system' in terms of two interlocked economies the self: the relation of reason and the passions within an individual and the relation of the self to society, or 'the world' – that is, fashionable courtly society. She argues that experience of this 'world' in itself is not wisdom, but must be reflected upon by a balanced and rational mind in order to produce a truly moral being.

Chapter 6, 'The Effect Which an Early Association of Ideas Has Upon the Character', summarizes this model of self-construction in a brief, energetic essay combining a materialist epistemology with ideas of 'genius', innate 'temper' and Providential design. The gist is that gender is constructed culturally and socially by 'early association of ideas', and women are constructed for inferiority; the chapter closes celebrating the two emblems of professional middle-class subjectivity – Virtue and Reason – as professional self-discipline and professional order and method (pp. 120–1).

Wollstonecraft then turns by contrast to different forms of artificial, inauthentic personal identity. Chapter 7, 'Modesty. – Comprehensively Considered, and Not as a Sexual Virtue', deals with a common theme of conduct books; but Wollstonecraft redefines this 'feminine' trait by insisting on the subjective rather than merely social nature of modesty and its basis in what she celebrated at the end of the previous chapter: virtue and reason. Characteristically, she distinguishes 'modesty' from 'humility', describing the former as 'that purity of mind, which is the effect of chastity', 'by no means incompatible with a lofty consciousness of our own dignity' (p. 122). In effect 'modesty' is masculinized by making it sublime ('lofty'). She then rejects the view that knowledge of botany, including the sexual reproduction of plants, is incompatible with modesty, and gives her own experience as an example, insisting that, far from being a denial of the body, modesty leads to reverence for it (p. 126). 'Women as well as men ought to have the common appetites and passions of their nature', including sexual desire, and these are 'only brutal when unchecked by reason' (p. 130). 'Unchecked' here means 'uncontrolled' or 'undirected', not 'unsuppressed'. She concludes the chapter with another characteristic apostrophe, exhorting 'my sisters' to cultivate modesty as she has defined it.

Having dealt with modesty as inward identity, or 'virtue', she turns in Chapter 8 to outward identity and concludes that 'Morality [is] Undermined by Sexual Notions of the Importance of a Good Reputation'. She attacks the conduct books for defining reputation as merely social. This undermines both 'morality' and social relations, for she has observed that women involved in sexual intrigues are accepted in fashionable society as long as they keep up appearances, whereas the unfortunate woman caught in one slip is socially ostracized forever (p. 132). She rejects the Enlightenment argument that desire for reputation inspires great human achievements, and follows Richard Price in arguing that social standards are culturally and historically relative; therefore conduct should be guided by self-approbation in the light of heaven, not merely social renown (p. 135).

This argument develops into a characteristic lyrical passage on the pleasures and pains of self-reflection:

> Virtues, unobserved by man, drop their balmy fragrance at this cool hour, and the thirsty land, refreshed by the pure streams of comfort that suddenly gush out, is crowned with smiling verdure; this is the living green on which that eye may look with complacency that is too pure to behold iniquity!
> But my spirits flag; and I must silently indulge the reverie these reflections lead to, unable to describe the sentiments, that have calmed my soul, when watching the rising sun, a soft shower drizzling through the leaves of neighbouring trees, seemed to fall on my languid, yet tranquil spirits, to cool the heart that had been heated by the passions which reason laboured to tame.   (p. 136)

Textual continuity does break here, indicating a lapse into silent reverie, exhibiting the author's own plenitude of self and powers of reflection, and thereby validating the preceding argument that subjective identity is the only true basis of conduct and reputation.

The rest of Chapter 8 deals with 'reputation' in relation to the theme of the previous two chapters – the gendering of sexuality or the sexual double standard. Wollstonecraft quotes Macaulay Graham's view that loss of reputation for sexual chastity is much more serious for women than for men. She acknowledges that 'men are certainly more under the influence of their appetites than women', but explains this by social and cultural conditioning, arguing that the greater sexual licence allowed men depraves women by subjecting them to men's sexual appetite. Forced to arouse the male appetite in order to achieve and maintain social power, women weaken the body to make themselves attractive, leaving them unfit for the rigours of reproduction and reluctant to provide proper nourishment for their own babies by breast-feeding (p. 138). Thus 'the two sexes' must either corrupt or improve each other, and the consequences extend from private to public life.

This conclusion prepares for Chapter 9, 'Of the Pernicious Effects Which Arise from the Unnatural Distinctions Established in Society'. In both Vindications 'unnatural' social distinctions include class and gender, but the second Vindication foregrounds gender and shows more fully how the two 'distinctions' reinforce each other. Basing social status on hereditary wealth and titles obstructs the 'exercise' of 'reason' and 'virtue' or merit (pp. 140–1). But the growth of reason and virtue in women is obstructed not so much by inherited wealth and rank as by their dependence on men, which forces them to be 'cunning, mean, and selfish' in order to obtain a share of wealth and power (p. 141). Furthermore, 'women are more debased and cramped' by 'riches and hereditary honours' than men because men may 'unfold their faculties' by taking up a profession. A man may 'dare to think and act for himself', but a woman 'has difficulties peculiar to her sex to overcome', including 'propriety', slavery to her 'person' and the laws which 'make an absurd unit of a man and his wife' by the legal fiction of 'feme covert', in which the legal identity of a woman is supposed to be 'covered' by that of her husband (p. 145).

Wollstonecraft envisages women as 'citizens' on the home front, where their virtues may be as 'heroic' as those of men engaged in military service. If women are to be 'really virtuous and useful', however, they must have 'the protection of civil laws' and not be dependent on a 'husband's bounty', for no one can be 'virtuous' who is not 'free' (p. 146). It is true 'that women in the common walks of life are called to fulfil the duties of wives and mothers, by religion and reason', but the 'women of a superior cast' should be able to 'pursue more extensive plans of usefulness and independence' in certain professions. Indeed, 'women ought to have representatives, instead of being arbitrarily governed without having any direct share allowed them in the deliberations of government' (p. 147). Yet the electoral system is unjust to many groups, and women are as well represented as the 'numerous class of hard working mechanics' (that is, artisans and other skilled workers) 'whose very sweat supports the splendid stud of an heir apparent, or varnishes the chariot of some female favourite who looks down on shame' – a reference to the notorious extravagance and debauchery of the Prince of Wales. Thus the enfranchisement of women is linked to reform of the electorate and government as a whole.

Wollstonecraft then suggests professions for women of 'a superiour cast' – those fit to be equals and not just companions of professional men, and thus fit to participate in the state and political system directly. Many of these professions for women could include extensions of domestic roles: 'Women might certainly study the art of healing, and be physicians as well as nurses';

'decency' seems to allot midwifery to them as well, though this profession is being invaded by men. Women could 'study politics' and thereby 'settle their benevolence on the broadest basis', and they could take up 'business of various kinds', meaning not only commerce but management and administration. Thus women could avoid mercenary marriages, outright prostitution or becoming 'milliners and mantua-makers', whose wages were so low they were often forced into part-time prostitution. Being a governess is one opening for the well-educated woman, but Wollstonecraft condemns it as 'a fall in life', as she herself had reason to know. Above all, for the 'private virtue' of women to become 'a public benefit, they must have a civil existence in the state, married or single': 'Would men but generously snap our chains, and be content with rational fellowship instead of slavish obedience, they would find us more observant daughters, more affectionate sisters, more faithful wives, more reasonable mothers – in a word, better citizens' (p. 150).

Chapter 10, 'Parental Affection', and Chapter 11, 'Duty to Parents', are really two parts of one argument, take up some implications of the appeal to men at the end of Chapter 9, attack the family as constructed by court society, and call for the companionate, egalitarian family as a way to interiorize the political state in the individual and reproduce that state socially over time. Chapter 10 is a critique of the family constructed by court society, in which parental affection is a form of self-love, a desire to reproduce one's property and rank in the next generation. Such tyrannical 'affection' parallels and reproduces the tyranny of court government. Women are central to this cultural and political reproduction, enslaved so that they will prefer their children's interest to that of humanity at large. This brief chapter concludes by reaffirming the principles that would reform the family, and thus the whole of society – the proper physical, moral and intellectual education of women.

The next chapter considers the family from the other perspective – 'Duty to Parents'. The political language used throughout the chapter to describe family relations reinforces the connection of the moral economies of family and state. For example, the chapter opens with a traditional political analogy: 'The rights of kings are deduced in a direct line from the King of kings; and that of parents from our first parent' (p. 152). But Wollstonecraft argues that duty to parents should be based on the same principle as other social relations – respect sanctioned by reason – for on.y reciprocity between parents and children will guarantee the domestic affec- tions. If parental affection may be mere self-love, however, respect for parents may be self-interested regard for the parents' property and power. Selfish parents know this and enforce blind obedience on their children; but 'a slavish bondage to parents cramps every faculty of the mind' (p. 155). This is certainly so for girls and young women, who 'are more kept down by their parents' in order to defend a family, class or state against the aggrandizement of a rival or alien. The slavery of childhood leads to the 'slavery of marriage', but in order to elude 'arbitrary authority girls very early learn the lessons which they afterwards practise on their husbands', thus corrupting family life and society at large. Until 'esteem and love are blended together' and 'reason made the foundation' of dom- estic affection, 'morality will stumble at the threshold'. But this change cannot take place 'till society is very differently consti- tuted', that is, until there is a revolution (p. 157).

How this might be accomplished is outlined in Chapter 12, 'On National Education', the culmination of Wollstonecraft's opening critique of Talleyrand, thus bringing her argument full circle. Wollstonecraft plans a revolution through education, eradicating court culture and social emulation and transforming false distinc- tions of class and gender in her version of the professional middle- class cultural revolution. An introductory section dismisses both private or domestic education and public boarding schools: the former leaves the child too much with adults, resulting in prema- ture development and a habit of tyrannizing over servants; the latter are hotbeds of vice, where 'tyranny and abject slavery' are institutionalized (p. 159). She would reform this system but 'the fear of innovation, in this country, extends to every thing' – a reference to growing reaction in Britain against the French Revol- ution.

She attacks the teachers and administrators of public schools as disseminators of court culture and emulation, for the connection which the masters 'keep up with the nobility, introduces the same vanity and extravagance into their families'. Instead, public edu- cation should link the domestic affections to the state: 'Public education . . . should be directed to form citizens; but if you wish to make good citizens, you must first exercise the affections of a son and a brother' (p. 162). Because 'public affections, as well as public virtues, must ever grow out of the private character', the child's contact with home and family should not be broken by his or her being sent away to school. Accordingly, she proposes community day-schools. These should be 'national establishments' because the teachers must be independent of the parents or they will turn the schools into disseminators of the culture of the dominant élite. They will teach showy accomplishments to impress the parent-patrons, and overcrowd their schools for profit, thereby encouraging immodesty and 'vices' (masturbation and homosexuality) that 'render the body weak, whilst they effectually prevent the acquisition of any delicacy of mind' (p. 164).

Females acquire bad habits of their own when 'shut up together' in such schools; therefore 'to improve both sexes they ought . . . to be educated together' – an argument from Macaulay's *Letters on Education*. Furthermore, 'if nature destined woman, in particular, for the discharge of domestic duties', woman must be educated in what Wollstonecraft calls 'domestic taste' (p. 166). This *embourgeoisement* and domestication of 'taste' appropriates for women the qualities of 'mind' required by men in professional life, and parallels Wollstonecraft's earlier heroizing of women in the domestic sphere. Harking back to her opening attack on Talleyrand's marginalization of females within state education, she links 'domestic taste' to revolution by calling on France as an 'enlightened nation' to 'try what effect reason would have' in bringing women 'back to nature, and their duty', and by 'allowing them to share the advantages of education and government with man, see whether they will become better, as they grow wiser and become free'.

Wollstonecraft then details her own scheme of education (pp. 167–70). While boys and girls of all classes would be educated together from five to nine years of age, thereafter they would be streamed according to intellectual ability and vocational destination. Those intended for trades would be educated together in the morning and separated for the afternoon, when girls would be trained in 'plain-work, mantua-making, millinery, &c.'. Boys and girls 'of superiour abilities, or fortune' would go on to academic education. This system preserves both class and gender distinctions, while aiming for the *embourgeoisement* of children of all classes. The real objective of her political economy of national education, however, is to give women access to the professional culture – and some callings – available to men, otherwise women will reproduce court culture in their families and thus in society at

large (p. 174). Like many other professional middle-class revolutionaries, Wollstonecraft believes that the revolution in the state
should begin in the home, for if a man is a microcosm, 'every
family might also be called a state' (p. 177).

The book does not end with this Revolutionary feminist vision,
but returns to the obstacle to cultural revolution in the actual
condition of women, or rather of women's 'mind'. The last chapter
of *A Vindication* sketches 'Some Instances of the Folly Which the
Ignorance of Women Generates; with Concluding Reflections on
the Moral Improvement That a Revolution in Female Manners
Might Naturally Be Expected to Produce'. These follies stem from
'the weakness of mind and body, which men have endeavoured,
impelled by various motives, to perpetuate' in women (p. 178).
The first 'folly' is superstitious credulity, associated with the lottery mentality of the poor and other dependent social groups.
Then there is 'a romantic twist of the mind', or the false subjectivity of undisciplined desire, especially as represented by 'the
reveries of the stupid novelists' (p. 183). Because women are
excluded from public affairs and denied even a legal identity, they
'have their attention naturally drawn from the interest of the whole
community' to the plight of individuals in novels (pp. 183–4).
Fondness for dress is thought to be 'natural' to women, but
Wollstonecraft explains it by social psychology – 'want of cultivation of mind' – and historicizes and relativizes it. The next two
follies are often seen as female virtues. Women are supposed to
have superior 'humanity', or sympathy, rooted in their more
delicate and susceptible 'sensibility'. But this 'virtue' excludes
women from 'heroic' ones, such as 'generosity' and 'friendship',
which depend on 'reason'. Similarly, women's supposedly
'natural' aptitude as mothers is vitiated by their 'ignorance' (p.
189). In short, oppression deprives women of the professionalized
'mind' necessary for proper execution of their domestic duties, and
this situation will not be corrected 'till more equality be established
in society, till ranks are confounded and women freed' (p. 191). 'A
revolution in female manners' must be part of a wider social
revolution.

The last section of the chapter summarizes this central argument
of the book as a whole. Reason and virtue, signifiers for professional intellectual training and moral discipline, must be extended from 'man' to 'mankind' – from men to women – in order to
'render women truly useful members of society' while holding

their domestic place. Women and their domestic sphere must be professionalized. Only then will women 'acquire a rational affection for their country' and serve the state in the way appropriate for them – making the private sphere the basis for the public one. For 'public virtue is only an aggregate of private'. Using typography for emphasis, she claims 'that the most salutary effects tending to improve mankind might be expected from a REVOLUTION in female manners', but 'Virtue flies from a house divided against itself' (pp. 192–3). She concludes:

> Let woman share the rights and she will emulate the virtues of man; for she must grow more perfect when emancipated, or justify the authority that chains such a weak being to her duty. . . .
> Be just then, O ye men of understanding! (p. 194)

She closes with this exhortation, promising in a footnote to enlarge further in another volume 'on the advantages which might reasonably be expected to result from an improvement in female manners, towards the general reformation of society'.

This may seem a feeble conclusion, leaving the liberation of women to men, and admitting that women do not have it in their own power to emancipate themselves from the 'mind-forg'd manacles' of oppression. On the other hand, this conclusion is itself a rhetorical flourish, addressed to 'men of understanding', or the leaders of the bourgeois cultural revolution, warning them that the revolution they lead will fail if it continues to harbour court culture in the form of courtly woman, in the guise of domestic woman and culture. The address to men also informs women readers that their inferiority and oppression are not due to inherent weaknesses in their 'nature' but to culturally and socially constructed weaknesses imposed by and for men and a class-based culture.

Reaction to *A Vindication of the Rights of Woman* was mixed, and still is. It was burlesqued in the Platonist Thomas Taylor's *A Vindication of the Rights of Brutes* (1792), but on the whole it was well received by reviewers and readers alike and was translated into French and German.[10] Not surprisingly, reaction of reviewers tended to fall along the lines of the French Revolution debate. Those generally sympathetic to the Revolution praised it; those opposed to the

Revolution had reservations about it or ignored it; only the *Critical Review* attacked it. Most reviewers, who were of course men, took it to be a book on women's education and acknowledged its attempt to reconstruct the professional middle-class cultural revolution.

Many women readers were moved by the book, one way or another. Anna Seward, poet, Bluestocking and daughter of the English provincial Enlightenment, read the book soon after it came out and found it 'wonderful' yet perplexing, and was 'half-convinced' that its author was 'oftener right than wrong'. Anne MacVicar Grant, who disapproved of the book, nevertheless wrote from the Scottish Highlands in 1794 that the circulating-library copy 'is so run after here, that there is no keeping it long enough to read it leisurely'. In Blackburn, a woman named Rachel Prescott wrote some verses on reading *A Vindication* and later told Godwin, 'The opinions of a Wollstonecraft first induced me to think.' Even the aristocratic daughter of Lord Sheffield read the book with approval, finding in it 'many sensible and just observations'. Some readers also recognized that Wollstonecraft was engaged in a struggle within, not against, the bourgeois cultural revolution; Mary Berry, for example, found *A Vindication* to 'agree on all the great points of female education' with a writer of apparently very different politics such as Hannah More.[11]

Liberal intellectual young men of the time were often more enthusiastic about the book than women readers. John Henry Colls was inspired to write *A Poetical Epistle Addressed to Miss Wollstonecraft* (1793), praising her and *A Vindication*, and versifying its arguments in heroic couplets; yet he disagrees with her approval of the French Revolution. George Dyer, poet and leading Dissenting intellectual, praised Wollstonecraft along with a serried rank of Dissenting men and women, including Ann Jebb, Helen Maria Williams, A. L. Barbauld, Charlotte Smith and Mary Hays, in his ode 'On Liberty'. He imagines that Liberty has chosen 'to warm / With more than manly fire the female breast', urging Wollstonecraft 'to break the charm, / Where beauty lies in durance vile opprest'. Thomas Cooper the radical, who had been to Paris in 1792 and discussed women's rights with Théroigne de Méricourt, declared: 'I have seldom met with views more enlarged, more just, more truly patriotic; or with political reasonings more acute, or arguments more forcible, than in the conversation of Theroigne, and the Writings of Miss Wollstonecraft. Let the Defenders of male

Despotism answer, (if they can) "The Rights of Woman"'.[12] In part these responses were due to the comprehensiveness of Wollstonecraft's treatment of the 'woman question' in relation to class differences that had only been emphasized by the debate on the French Revolution and its import for Britain.

But in part the effect of A Vindication was also due to its form and style. It seems that some reviewers and many readers, especially those who approved of the book, recognized the revolutionary ambitions of Wollstonecraft's style and method, particularly her intention to infuse the work with the energy, 'nervousness' and personal tone of 'genius', as an exemplification of the book's arguments for women's equality of 'mind' with men. Indeed, these characteristics soon came to be attributed to Wollstonecraft's writing in a somewhat commonplace way. Other readers found, however, that these traits revealed her incapacity of 'mind' for what she had undertaken to prove. The *Critical Review* condemned the *Vindication*'s 'vague, inconclusive reasoning, strung together with little art, and no apparent plan', and described its style as 'flowing and flowery' but 'weak, diffuse, and confused' (vol. 5, January 1796, p. 397; May 1796, p. 141). In part this was taking Wollstonecraft at her word, for in the prefaces of her important works she herself claims a spontaneous, desultory, personal approach to the issues she addresses, even though this claim was partly a rhetorical ploy to authenticate her arguments. This negative view of the relation of her style and her 'mind' became the dominant one immediately after her death, when Godwin's *Memoir* revealed her transgressions in private life; then the style and method of *A Vindication* could be read with hindsight as discursive extravagance and transgression foreshadowing her emotional extravagance and sexual transgressions with Imlay and Godwin. This view was expressed by Thomas J. Mathias, a leading anti-feminist writer, in his satire *The Shade of Alexander Pope on the Banks of the Thames* (1799), where he describes Wollstonecraft as 'Fierce passion's slave, she veer'd with every gust, / Love, Rights, and Wrongs, Philosophy, and Lust'.

It is a view of *A Vindication* that has persisted down to the present, even among those sympathetic to the book, its arguments and its author. In her introduction to an 1891 edition of *A Vindication*, the suffragist Millicent Garrett Fawcett wrote: 'There is a want of order and system in it which may, perhaps, be attributed to the desultory education of the writer'. Eleanor Flexner, one of

Wollstonecraft's recent biographers, expresses a common modern view when she writes that Wollstonecraft 'is incapable either of the coherent organization of ideas or of avoiding repetition'. Another biographer, Claire Tomalin puts the same point in a more positive light when she writes that '*A Vindication* is a book without any logical structure: it is more in the nature of an extravaganza.' But what 'it lacks in method it makes up for in *élan*, and it is better to dip into than to read through at a sitting'. The critic Ellen Moers wrote that 'there are splendid passages' in *A Vindication*, but as a whole 'it is as boring as are all polemics which have been answered in the affirmative by history'; Wollstonecraft's 'best' passages – those relevant for today – 'will be found to be about love'.[13] Such views are still commonplace, but were particularly characteristic of the 1960s and 1970s, with the search for women intellectuals in the past who could be related to modern, university-trained, professional women intellectuals.

Feminist criticism in the 1980s shifted away from these already gendered criteria of order, coherence and artistry, and toward an interest in women and the politics of subjectivity, especially related to sexuality, and how these are written by women.[14] The arguments, style and structure of *A Vindication of the Rights of Woman* received a more sophisticated and sympathetic reading under this approach, but once again its apparent defects are traced to defects or contradictions in Wollstonecraft herself or the ideology that structured her consciousness. Mary Poovey, for example, finds that Wollstonecraft's contradictory attitude to middle-class values, especially the figure of the 'proper lady' in relation to women's sexuality and desire, was expressed stylistically in evasive 'use of euphemisms and circuitous phrasing': 'Whenever Wollstonecraft approaches a subject that arouses her own volatile emotions, her language becomes both obscure and abstract.' Furthermore, 'It is partly because Wollstonecraft so thoroughly distrusts her own sexuality that she rejects a female speaking voice' in *A Vindication*, and 'aspires not to a masculine voice but to a voice totally unconscious of sexuality'.[15]

It would not be surprising to find obscure, tangled, vague or inappropriate language in passages of an ambitious book, written in haste, in relation to an unprecedented social, cultural and political crisis of international dimensions. More importantly, transgressive writing, like irony, may fall between two incompatible standards of coherence and artistry, failing to meet either.

Anna Seward, one of the first readers of A Vindication, spoke for many readers of the time and since when she found that the book 'startled' her, and 'by turns, pleased and displeased'. Wollstonecraft shows every sign of recognizing that 'a revolution in female manners' required a revolution in women's discourse, but intending such a revolution is not the same thing as bringing it about. Not only may the revolutionary discursive project fail to elude the influence of the discursive order it seeks to overcome, but even its success may be all too easily 'misread' as failure to conform to the dominant order of discourse. Wollstonecraft's Revolutionary feminism was to be a reading and writing revolution in several ways; but such a revolution may simply substitute revolutionary writing for the real-life 'revolution in female manners' it proposes.

6

From Revolutionary Feminism to Revolutionary Paris

A Vindication of the Rights of Woman made Wollstonecraft a major figure in the French Revolution debate and the major voice of the feminist intervention in the bourgeois cultural revolution. It even brought an offer of marriage. She wrote to Everina in mock-formal style early in 1792, 'be it known unto you that my book &c &c has afforded me an opportunity of settling *very* advantageous in the matrimonial line, with a new acquaintance; but entre nous – a handsome house and a proper man did not tempt me' (*Letters*, p. 210). Meanwhile, 'a standing dish of family cares' continued to preoccupy her. She worried about finding 'situations' for her sisters, and eagerly passed on to them Ruth Barlow's assurance that they would be welcomed in the United States as English gentlewomen and have a good chance of finding husbands (*Letters*, p. 213). She pressed Charles to go to America with the Barlows and settle on a farm. But Barlow was part idealist and part opportunist. Though his political pamphlet, *Advice to the Privileged Orders*, was published by Johnson in February 1792, he was soon fishing for business opportunities with the government of France, and delayed his departure home. Wollstonecraft obtained work for Charles with Johnson in the autumn, and was told by Tom Paine that 'the habit of order' acquired 'by attending to business' would '"do him no harm in America"' (*Letters*, p. 215). Finally Charles left for the United States without the Barlows later in 1792. James was an officer in a merchant ship, and was off in the Atlantic by June 1792 for most of the year.

Her major preoccupation, however, was with Fuseli, and once *A Vindication of the Rights of Woman* was published her professional 'exertions seem to have been palsied'.[1] She wrote little but reviews for the *Analytical* 'and even these . . . would not have been written but for her daily necessities'.[2] Yet she believed that her 'attachment' for Fuseli was consistent with both her professional self-discipline and her politicized, professional middle-class morality. She told Fuseli that she 'was designed to rise superior to her earthly habitation' and that she 'always thought, with some degree of horror, of falling a sacrifice to a passion which may have a mixture of dross in it'.[3] When her obsession began to affect her health Fuseli reasoned with her, but she replied: 'If I thought my passion criminal, I would conquer it, or die in the attempt. For immodesty, in my eyes, is ugliness; my soul turns with disgust from pleasure tricked out in charms which shun the light of heaven' (p. 167). This is the same high, Revolutionary feminist morality informing *A Vindication of the Rights of Woman*.

She may have wondered if the Revolution itself would be more auspicious to her 'passion', for in June 1792 she, Johnson and Fuseli and his wife planned an excursion to Paris. They were to stay six weeks and combine pleasure with business. She told Everina: 'I shall be introduced to many people, my book has been translated and praised . . . and Fuseli, of course, is well known' (*Letters*, p. 213). The party reached Dover in late summer but turned back at news of political disturbances in Paris. Wollstonecraft became depressed and 'constantly vented complaints of being neglected'. According to Knowles, she at length grew 'desperate' and told Mrs Fuseli 'that she wished to become an inmate in her family': '"I find that I cannot live without the satisfaction of seeing and conversing with [Fuseli] daily"' (Knowles, p. 167). When Mrs Fuseli forbade her the house she had 'no resource' left 'but to fly from the object which she regarded: her determination was instantly fixed; she wrote a letter to Fuseli, in which she begged pardon "for having disturbed the quiet tenour of his life"', and left for Paris (p. 168). It was consistent to turn from a failed Revolutionary feminist relationship to the Revolution itself. Wollstonecraft thought her 'passion' for Fuseli different from the merely domestic and erotic relations of the Gabells, the Barlows and others she knew. The possibility – indeed, the necessity – of love of the 'mind' was called for in *A Vindication of the Rights of Woman*, and Fuseli seemed to offer such a relationship, a way of combining her private and professional identities in a revolutionary, vanguardist domesticity that would be the base of her public career.

One contemporary commentator on Wollstonecraft's involvement with Fuseli may have been William Blake. Though he was a marginal member of Johnson's circle and there is no evidence that he met Wollstonecraft, he knew Fuseli and his work, including perhaps Fuseli's private erotic art. Several critics have argued that Blake's first mature narrative poem, *Visions of the Daughters of Albion*, generalizes Wollstonecraft's failure with Fuseli into a denunciation of imaginative, erotic, social and political repression.[4] Certainly the name of the poem's female protagonist, Oothoon, seems to recall Wollstonecraft's sarcastic comment on Rousseau's picture of a young woman repeatedly writing the letter 'O', and Blake's poem refashions Wollstonecraft's attack on courtly amorousness as symptomatic of court culture. Echoes of Wollstonecraft's feminism and her relationship with Fuseli can also be found in Blake's 1793 notebook poems. Blake's political culture was that of the skilled urban artisans and not that of the professional intellectuals with whom Wollstonecraft associated, but their converging interest in a major theme of the cultural revolution indicates the possibilities for a revolutionary coalition of artisans and professionals in the early 1790s.

Though Wollstonecraft's attempt to establish a revolutionary domesticity with Fuseli seemed to 'palsy' her professional 'exertions' during 1792 and she only wrote reviews for the *Analytical*, this work was not much less in amount or vigour than what she had produced earlier. In 1792 'M.' reviewed books on natural history and education, Samuel Johnson, travel, history, the treatment of animals, prisons and the treatment of the poor, translations of the *Arabian Nights* and Lavater's *Physiognomy*, Elizabeth Benger's *The Female Geniad*, Thomas Holcroft's political novel *Anna St Ives*, Charlotte Smith's political novel *Desmond*, essays by the landscape architect William Gilpin, and Bible stories adapted for children. 'W.' reviewed a play by Hannah Cowley, a travel book and an attack on the sexual immorality of the time, *The Evils of Adultery and Prostitution*. Only after the abortive expedition to France, when Wollstonecraft became 'desperate' over Fuseli, did the reviews of 'M.' and 'W.' disappear.

The social side of Wollstonecraft's professional life continued to expand with her celebrity as an author, attracting the offer of marriage, increased respect in Johnson's 'Academy', new intellectual, artistic, political and literary friends such as the Barlows, Tom Paine, William Roscoe and the painter John Opie, and new acquaintances such as William Godwin and Mary Hays. In February 1792 she was even visited in Store Street by Talleyrand, who was in

London on an unofficial diplomatic mission. The story that she served Talleyrand wine in teacups seems to show her as a Bohemian intellectual, above 'feminine' niceties of housekeeping. More significant is that she received such a man herself, in her own rooms, as an author and public figure now above 'feminine' proprieties.

Talleyrand's visit may also have suggested new opportunities in Revolutionary France. Helen Maria Williams was making a controversial name for herself there as a 'female politician' with her series of *Letters* from France; Thomas Christie, Johnson's partner in the *Analytical*, explored political and business opportunities in France, and returned with a married Frenchwoman as his companion. Criticism of marriage as instituted for the courtly and landed classes made such relationships politically correct, and Wollstonecraft could believe revolutionary egalitarian love might be found in Revolutionary France. As she wrote to William Roscoe in November 1792, announcing her plan to abandon both England and her 'rational desire' for Fuseli: 'At Paris, indeed, I might take a husband for the time being, and get divorced when my truant heart longed again to nestle with its old friends' (p. 218).

Even her friendships at this time blended professional, political and personal interests. Mary Hays, for example, was a product of the English Nonconformist Enlightenment, developing her own version of feminism, and when *A Vindication of the Rights of Woman* was published she studied it carefully and approached its author as a literary adviser.[5] Wollstonecraft emphasized professionalism over gender, rebuking Hays for throwing herself on the public's mercy: 'the *honour* of publishing . . . is the cant of both trade and sex; for if really equality should ever take place in society the man who is employed and gives a just equivalent for the money he receives will not behave with the obsequiousness of a servant' (*Letters*, p. 219). She condemned pleading the limitations of female education: 'Disadvantages of education &c ought, in my opinion, never to be pleaded (with the public) in excuse for defects of any importance, because if the writer has not sufficient strength of mind to overcome the common difficulties which lie in his way, nature seems to command him, with a very audible voice, to leave the task of instructing others to those who can.' She rejected citing the approval of male mentors: 'Rest, on yourself – if your essays have merit they will stand alone, if not the *shouldering up* of D^r this

or that will not long keep them from falling to the ground' (p. 219).
One of the last professional tasks Wollstonecraft performed before
leaving for France was to read Hays's proofs.[6]

A more important friend was William Roscoe. Of modest social
origins, he educated himself in the English Nonconformist Enlightenment, went into law, took up the classics, arts and *belles-lettres*,
was an active poetaster, promoted literary and artistic societies,
and in the early 1780s became a friend of Fuseli through Johnson.
He associated with political and social reformers and in the late
1780s published attacks on the slave-trade and a celebration of the
Glorious Revolution of 1688. In 1789 he published an *Ode to the
People of France* and supported the Revolution during its early
phase. By October 1791 he knew Wollstonecraft well enough to
commission a portrait of her as the amazonian author of *A Vindication of the Rights of Men*, celebrated in his political ballad 'The Life,
Death, and Wonderful Atchievements of Edmund Burke':

> lo! an Amazon stept out,
>   One WOLSTONECRAFT her name,
> Resolv'd to stop his mad career,
>   Whatever chance became.[7]

Not only did her friendship with Roscoe validate her 'passion' for
Fuseli, it confirmed her ability to command the respect of professionally successful, broadly cultured and politically active men.

Roscoe also reinforced Fuseli's influence on her understanding
of the historical sociology of culture. He was a scholar of the Italian
Renaissance and connoisseur of Italian art, interests connected to
the social, cultural and political transformation of provincial
Britain. The rapid growth of provincial towns inspired the professional and commercial bourgeoisie to organize cultural activities
giving a focus to their social and political contacts, validating their
local importance with the cachet of high culture and dignifying
them in relation to both the 'county' landed classes and the metropolis. Roscoe, himself a 'new man', was a leader in the cultural
'renaissance' of Liverpool, and as a symbolic focus for this development he worked on an Enlightenment history of the life and
times of Lorenzo de' Medici, the political, commercial and cultural
leader of Florence in its golden age. Roscoe's models, such as
Voltaire's lives of Louis XIV and Charles XII and Robertson's life of
Charles V, are cultural histories of an age, using the past to

comment on the present, exposing the 'unreason' of monarchic governments and societies. Although not published until 1796, Roscoe's life of Lorenzo would expose the aristocratic factionalism and papist superstition directed against a man of the mercantile bourgeoisie trying to build a modern city-state in an age of revolutions, including the Protestant Reformation, the invention of printing, European exploration and the revival of vernacular literature in a standardized language. Wollstonecraft's next project, a social and cultural history of the early French Revolution, was informed by the same principles that inspired Roscoe's history of Lorenzo.

Wollstonecraft left London for Paris on 8 December 1792, intending to join circles of expatriate Britons and Americans, improve her French, look for suitable literary work and watch for openings for her sisters. Apparently she did not plan to stay for long.

She arrived in Paris during a comparative lull in the Revolutionary crisis after the overthrow of the monarchy, the September Massacres and the triumph of the citizen army at Valmy. But a new crisis was developing. The trial of the King had begun on 11 December and the capital was tense with political uncertainty. A month later, on 21 January 1793, he would be guillotined, leading to war with Britain and revolt in the Vendée. These crises in turn strengthened the Jacobins against the Girondins, with whom British pro-Revolutionists, including Wollstonecraft, had personal contacts and most in common politically. But when she wrote to Everina on 24 December she was struggling to master conversational French, planned to attend the King's trial and had seen Helen Maria Williams, who treated her 'very civilly': 'I shall visit her frequently, because I *rather* like her, and I meet french company at her house.' Yet she found Williams's manners 'affected', and moralized: 'Authorship is a heavy weight for female shoulders especially in the sunshine of prosperity' (*Letters*, p. 226). Wollstonecraft herself hoped to emulate Williams's literary, social and political career in Paris.

She still felt homesick, missed her study in Store Street and felt awkward and unnatural with French manners and speech. She realized that the political situation was deteriorating, and when 'a Gentleman' offered her a seat in his carriage back to England she had difficulty saying no. But she felt she was getting established professionally and told Ruth Barlow: 'I think it would be foolish to return when I have been at so much trouble to master a difficulty, when I am just turning the corner, and I am, besides, writing a plan of education for the Committee appointed to consider that subject' (p. 230). This would have been the committee on public instruction, at least one of whose members, Condorcet, advocated education for women.[8] If she was also falling in love with Gilbert Imlay she would have been expecting to merge her personal and professional lives at last. Her experience in the intellectual and political salons would confirm her desire to do so. Helen Maria Williams, for example, was involved with John Hurford Stone, who was already married. His wife Rachel was reported to have affairs of her own and Williams to have had other lovers, perhaps including Imlay.[9] In such circles, joining the domestic and amorous with the professional and political was considered politically advanced.

Such conduct was also found among the leaders of the Revolution, especially the circle of Marie Roland.[10] During 1791 and 1792 she presided over the most influential political salon in Paris, though seeming to keep in the background. Her husband was Minister of the Interior, she was known to advise him and she conducted political correspondence. But the Girondins broke with the Jacobins over war policy, and the Jacobins denounced the Rolands, attacking Madame Roland as a mere woman meddling in politics. Jacobin pressure forced Roland to resign his Ministry on 22 January 1793, just as Wollstonecraft was establishing contacts in Paris. Meanwhile, Madame Roland had fallen in love with the young politician Buzot. Raised on the ideals of stoic virtue celebrated in Plutarch and Rousseau, she confessed her love to her husband, but this demoralized him and divided the Girondin group. Thus by the time Wollstonecraft entered the Rolands' circle they were under a darkening political cloud. Madame Roland was the most important Revolutionary woman Wollstonecraft could have met and her fate left a lasting impression.

There is no evidence that Wollstonecraft met the Rolands, but she joined salons such as that of Fuseli's Swiss friends, Johann Carl Schweitzer and his wife Madeleine, and that of Thomas Christie and his new English wife. The most important expatriate salon, however, was that of Helen Maria Williams, attended by liberals, philosophers, writers, savants, politicians and intellectual-political tourists. In later life Williams described the political idealism and gender equality that prevailed in such circles:

> *On parlait peu des causeries ordinaires de la société. Les femmes paraissaient oublier le soin de plaire, et les hommes songeaient moins à les admirer. . . . Il y avait dans ce salon-là quelque chose de mieux que la galanterie. Une estime mutuelle, un intérêt commun pour les grandes questions du jour, étaient ce que paraissait le plus.*
> (We indulged little in common society chitchat. The women seemed to forget concern to please, and the men thought less about admiring them. . . . In that salon there was something better than gallantry. What appeared most were mutual esteem and a shared interest in the great issues of the day.)[11]

Such an ambience would have appealed strongly to the author of *A Vindication of the Rights of Woman*. But the declaration of war between France and Britain broke up these salons, depriving Wollstonecraft of their personal-political contacts and affecting her first professional undertaking in Paris, a book of letters on the Revolution like those published by Williams in 1790 and 1792.

Only one of the 'Series of Letters on the Present Character of the French Nation' was written, dated 'Paris, 15 February, 1793'. Though it is personal and sentimental and 'feminizes' politics, it is more detached, philosophical and reflective than Williams's *Letters*, and presented as Enlightenment sociology.[12] Wollstonecraft shows professional middle-class disdain for both the landed class and the commercial bourgeoisie: 'if the aristocracy of birth is levelled with the ground, only to make room for that of riches, I am afraid that the morals of the people will not be much improved by the change, or the government rendered less venal' (pp. 43–4). Richard Price made a similar point about the American Revolution.[13] Wollstonecraft also returns to one of her philosophical themes of the late 1780s – the problem of evil and misery under a benevolent deity – applied to the September Massacres and other apparently pointless episodes of Revolutionary violence. Such episodes were alienating many in Britain, but Wollstonecraft offers a commonplace apology for the Revolution: the frivolity of court culture and burden of aristocratic privilege produced an extreme reaction by 'the people'. This mechanical model implies that the pendulum swings of violence will gradually decrease. Yet hope for the future is counterbalanced by a fear that 'the turn of the tide has left the dregs of the old system to corrupt the new' (p. 50). The letter shows the vigorous style of the *Vindications* and a good grasp of the political situation, but the course of the Revolution deprived her of the intellectual and political contacts necessary to complete the project.

She may also have shelved it because of her growing involvement with Imlay, one of a group of Americans and Britons looking for opportunities from the overthrow of the *ancien régime*. He had experience of such a situation, having been in the American Revolutionary army and later a land speculator on the frontier. He knew the advantage of being an author in circles led by professional men and entrepreneurs, and showed his understanding of the state as patron of economic development in his *Topographical Description of the Western Territory of North America* (1792). When he met Wollstonecraft he was soon to publish a novel, *The Emigrants*, contrasting the decadence of the old world with the freedom of the new, and he was about to capitalize on his expertise about the American West. For the English radical Thomas Cooper was impressed with the *Topographical Description*; he introduced Imlay to the Girondin leader Brissot, and a scheme was devised for a French expedition to seize the Spanish territory of Louisiana. But the fall of the Girondins in April and May ended the plan.

It was at this time that Wollstonecraft became involved with Imlay. She met him at the Chisties' and his attentions began in February. At first, she disliked and avoided him, but soon changed her mind. By April their 'connection' was established and 'was carried on in a private manner for four months'.[14] By June Wollstonecraft had moved out of Paris to Neuilly because of increased tension in the capital over the deteriorating military situation. She was an enemy alien, subject to restrictions. He stayed in Paris, but since both saw their professional prospects suspended by the fall of the Girondins they planned to emigrate to the United States as soon as they could raise the money.

Throughout the summer of 1793 they met in a honeymoon atmosphere at Neuilly or the *barrière* that was part of the security system around the capital. The relationship transformed Wollstonecraft:

> Her sorrows, the depression of her spirits, were forgotten, and she assumed all the simplicity and the vivacity of a youthful

mind. She was like a serpent upon a rock, that casts its slough, and appears again with the brilliancy, the sleekness, and the elastic activity of its happiest age. She was playful, full of confidence, kindness and sympathy. Her eyes assumed new lustre, and her cheeks new colour and smoothness. Her voice became chearful; her temper overflowing with universal kindness; and that smile of bewitching tenderness from day to day illuminated her countenance, which all who knew her will so well recollect, and which won, both heart and soul, the affection of almost every one that beheld it. (*Memoirs*, p. 242)

She rejected marriage, less from feminist principle than concern for Imlay: according to law a husband was responsible for his wife's debts. But in August the National Convention decreed the imprisonment of Britons, and Imlay had Wollstonecraft registered as his wife at the American Embassy in order to protect her. Moreover, Wollstonecraft was pregnant and they both needed to be in Paris. He was acting for the Revolutionary government, circumventing the economic blockade; she was engaged on a new project. As early as June she had written to Eliza that she was 'writing a great book; and in better health and spirits than I have ever enjoyed since I came to France' (*Letters*, p. 231). Secure with Imlay, carrying his child and at work again as a writer, she seemed to have achieved her ambition of revolutionary domesticity. She 'was now arrived at the situation, which, for two or three pieceding years, her reason had pointed out to her as affording the most substantial prospect of happiness' (*Memoirs*, p. 241).

There was clearly a political dimension to such a relationship. The combination of domesticity, professionalism and egalitarian erotic love was of course part of the vanguardist culture of those French and Anglo-American circles to which Wollstonecraft and Imlay had access in Paris and in which they had met. Wollstonecraft's first anticipation of such a relationship was formed in the professional and political intensity of the years 1790 to 1792 with Fuseli. Wollstonecraft had in her youth and early adult years seen enough of what bourgeois cultural revolutionaries would consider decadent courtly eroticism, vulgar plebeian sexuality and banal petty bourgeois conjugality, and she had been repelled by all three. She had also become aware that, for both practical reasons and according to conventions of the day, development of her 'mind' and career were incompatible with either a private sexual life or conventional conjugality, and accordingly she had decided to forgo both. The erotic conjugality Wollstonecraft half-hoped for with Fuseli, saw in 'advanced' circles in paris and believed she had found with Imlay was meant to be a middle way between courtly and plebeian eroticism and conjugality, and thus to exemplify revolutionary vanguardist culture in general.

Certainly she gave herself fully and frankly to sexual love. After she and Imlay became lovers she was in conversation with a Frenchwoman who boasted of her lack of physical passion; Wollstonecraft replied: '*Tant pis pour vous, madame, c'est un défaut de la nature.*'[15] According to Godwin she was unrestrained in her love for Imlay (*Memoirs*, pp. 242–3). This made her dependent on him, but as soon as their relationship seemed firm she felt her professional confidence and ambition return, writing to him in summer 1793: 'you would smile to hear how many plans of employment I have in my head, now that I am confident my heart has found peace in your bosom' (*Letters*, p. 233). She had a clear philosophy of the physical self and its relation to 'mind' and she incorporated her new sexual experience, and then her experience of child-bearing, into this philosophy.[16] She saw her love for Imlay as physical feeling based on mental and moral perception of his 'tenderness and worth', as she called it, and she tried to describe and understand these feelings according to the materialist philosophy of Sensibility. While writing to Imlay in December 1794, for example, she was overcome by recollection of their intimacy:

> I have thy honest countenance before me – Pop – relaxed by tenderness; a little – little wounded by my whims; and thy eyes glistening with sympathy. – Thy lips then feel softer than soft – and I rest my cheek on thine, forgetting all the world. – I have not left the hue of love out of the picture – the rosy glow; and fancy has spread it over my own cheeks, I believe, for I feel them burning, whilst a delicious tear trembles in my eye, that would be all your own, if a grateful emotion directed to the Father of nature, who has made me thus alive to happiness, did not give more warmth to the sentiment it divides – I must pause a moment. (*Letters*, pp. 238–9)

Her erotic imagination is stirred by 'recollection', and immediately felt bodily in the blush and the tear – the body then silencing her writing of the body. Of course, the writing here is not a truly immediate expression of mind and body, but a re-presentation of them; nevertheless, her published writing uses the same figure of a mental experience expressed through the body, then impeding writing, in order to authenticate the writing.

In the same philosophical way she reflected on the sensations of pregnancy, writing to Imlay in January 1794 as the author of *A Vindication of the Rights of Woman*:

> Considering the care and anxiety a woman must have about a child before it comes into the world, it seems to me, by a *natural right*, to belong to her. When men get immersed in the world, they seem to lose all sensations, excepting those necessary to continue or produce life! – Are these the privileges of reason? Amongst the feathered race, whilst the hen keeps the young warm, her mate stays by to cheer her; but it is sufficient for man to condescend to get a child, in order to claim it. – A man is a tyrant! (*Letters*, p. 242)

Here is a new refinement on her sociology of gender difference, giving the moral superiority to women and leaving men, because of their 'immersion in the world', mere creatures of appetite – gustatory and erotic – rather than reason.

Not surprisingly for one so confident, and in spite of the dangers for a woman of 35, she had an easy childbirth on 14 May, recovered very quickly and by policy breast-fed her daughter, named Frances after her lost friend Fanny Blood. She was impatient of ladylike delicacy about childbearing and disdainful of the popular superstitions surrounding it. She relished the intensely physical quality of the experience, while taking a philosophical view of it. Six days after the birth she wrote to Ruth Barlow that she was 'so well, that were it not for the inundation of milk, which for the moment incommodes me, I could forget the pain I endured six days ago'. 'Yet', she added, 'nothing could be more natural or easy than my labour – still it is not smooth work – I dwell on these circumstances not only as I know it will give you pleasure; but to prove that this struggle of nature is rendered much more cruel by the ignorance and affectation of women.' 'Ignorance' refers to lower-class treatment of childbirth and 'affectation' to that of upper- and middle-class 'ladies'. She goes on to boast: 'My nurse has been twenty years in this employment, and she tells me, she never knew a woman [come through childbirth] so well – adding,

Frenchwoman like, that I ought to make children for the Republic, since I treat it so slightly' (p. 255). Wollstonecraft's sarcasm here may owe something to the Jacobin government's urging women to avoid politics and bear new republican citizens.[17] She took similar pride and delight in breast-feeding, the 'rational' course to follow, though she may also have smiled at the government's exhortation to women to provide *'le lait républicain'* for infant citizens rather than campaign for their own rights.

Wollstonecraft became tired of waiting for Imlay and followed him to Le Havre, only to find that he was often in Paris or London. These absences called forth her compensatory imagination. She could not bring herself to take his battered slippers away from her bedroom door (*Letters*, p. 239–40), and when she received a precious packet of books from London she saved them for him to read aloud while she mended her stockings. In his absence she turned to his side of the bed and clutched his pillow 'which you used to tell me I was churlish about' (p. 252). He drew glowing pictures in his letters of the domestic happiness they would enjoy one day – pictures to which she responded eagerly, in spite of the rather large family he thought they might have (pp. 246–7). Increasingly, she complained about his absorption in commerce, then reproved herself for being selfish while he toiled to assure their future of avant-garde domesticity.

Meanwhile she continued her writing. In February 1794 she wrote to Ruth Barlow from Le Havre that she was busy preparing 'a part of my M.S.' to send by courier to London; she empowered Joel Barlow to obtain her 'poor Books', left behind in Paris, and asked him to send the National Assembly's *Journal des débats et des décrets* so she could grasp the detail of the Revolutionary process. She assured the Barlows: 'I am now more seriously at *work* than I have ever been yet' (*Letters*, p. 250). In March she was anxious over the danger in communicating with Britain and wrote to Everina: 'I have just sent off great part of my M.S. which Miss Williams would fain have be [me] burn, following her example – and to tell you the truth – my life would not have been worth much, had it been *found'* (p. 250). These dangers are reflected in the way her book is written. But by the end of April Wollstonecraft reported to Ruth Barlow that 'the history is finished', though she designed further volumes, telling Everina in September that 'it is the commence[ment] of a considerable work' (pp. 253, 262).

It was published by Johnson in late summer 1794 as *An Historical and Moral View of the Origin and Progress of the French Revolution; and the Effect It Has Produced in Europe*, 'Volume the First', with Wollstonecraft's name on the title-page. In order to authenticate her Revolutionary feminist reading of the Revolution, Wollstonecraft had once again to combine discourses conventionally regarded as 'masculine' and 'feminine', in terms of the gendering of writing in her time, and especially in relation to the different English interpretations and eyewitness accounts of the Revolution already available. She aimed to be less immediate and personal than Helen Maria Williams's 'feminine' *Letters* from France, less dry and matter-of-fact than Dr John Moore's 'philosophical' account, and less polemically immediate than Burke's *Reflections* and her own reply to him. She aimed to be 'philosophical', in the sense of detached, historical and analytical, without being impersonal, like Enlightenment 'philosophical history', describing change in sociological and cultural rather than merely political terms. Such historiography conveyed Enlightenment critique of court culture in mid-century, but in the 1790s it was transformed by the French Revolution as history in the making.[18] Wollstonecraft's new experiment in writing was part of this transformation, applying 'philosophical history' to the present rather than the past.

Accordingly, her text again critically realigns differences of discourse, genre and style, and their relation to class and gender distinctions. It situates itself somewhere between the 'philosophical history' of Voltaire, David Hume and William Robertson and the immediate, Sentimental, epistolary, obviously feminine discourse invented by Helen Maria Williams to feminize politics and the Revolution. Historiography was seen as detached and 'philosophical', dealing with important and general issues; women were seen as specialists in the present, immediate and quotidian. Wollstonecraft's new work aims to combine these different 'views' by combining discourses and styles conventionally differentiated by gender. She does this in response to persistent, and in her view dangerous and destructive, gendering of the Revolution both in France and in the British debate on the Revolution.

For this reason, too, she restricts her treatment to the Revolution of 1789, but does so in a way that implies commentary on the Jacobin Revolution of 1793. She describes the Revolution of 1789 and its excesses in some detail, and forecasts a happy conclusion to the Revolution in spite of its excesses; but she says nothing of the

Jacobin Revolution of 1793, which was more violent and excessive than that of 1789. From this treatment reasonably well-informed readers would know or suspect that her book was written under this second, anti-feminine and anti-feminist Revolution, forcing her to a silence that nevertheless speaks in her book between the lines. Thus her argument posits, implicitly as well as explicitly, a 'good' if misguided Revolution of 1789 to 1792, a 'bad' Revolution of 1793 to the time of her writing, and a restoration of the 'good' Revolution in the future – a Revolution better, in fact, than that of 1789.

The Jacobin Revolution of 1793 was treated by Helen Maria Williams and others as a masculinization of the Revolution, breaking up families, destroying the domestic affections and wrongly excluding women from participation in the Revolution – something Wollstonecraft warned against in her second *Vindication*. Wollstonecraft knew of Burke's condemnation of women participants in the early Revolution and she would also have known that 'female politicians', women writers and Revolutionary feminism were being associated with political subversion by reactionary writers in Britain. In her own reply to Burke Wollstonecraft had rejected the effeminacy of pre-Revolutionary court culture and characterized Burke's attack on the Revolution as itself effeminate, while she herself aimed to exhibit in both *Vindications* the 'mind' of a woman qualified to write on public, political issues; in her second *Vindication* she went on to suggest that women should even participate in public, political life by exercising the vote. By combining 'men's' and 'women's' discourses in her new book, Wollstonecraft was implicitly reinforcing the book's plea for a reconciliation of 'bad' and 'good', 'masculine' and 'feminine' Revolutions, suggesting that Revolutionary feminism could save both the Revolution in France and the cultural revolution in Britain. Wollstonecraft's dialogical discourse models a solution beyond the apparent foundering of the Revolution in France and the consequent abandonment and repression of the revolutionary impulse in Britain in the mid-1790s. In order to see this solution, she suggests, a fresh and original 'view' of the Revolution is necessary.

The discursive innovativeness of her 'view' is indicated in her book's full title, *An Historical and Moral View of the Origin and Progress of the French Revolution; and the Effect It Has Produced in Europe*. The 'Historical' and the 'Moral' are designated as modes rather than grounds of discourse. Rather than the objectivity and authoritativeness presumed by a 'History', a 'View' suggests something personal, unique to an individual but inviting participation. Nor is the 'View' a classical, traditional, clearly established genre, but loose, open, obeying the particularities of its occasion rather than inherited institutional and cultural forces. A 'View' is like the 'Lines' or 'Stanzas' favoured in titles of Romantic poems. Yet 'Historical' and 'Moral' do suggest constraints of method and mode: 'historical' here means historicist, or the idea that society and culture are historically particular and determined, and 'moral' means having to do with standards of right and wrong and pertaining to *mores*, *mœurs* – in English, both morals and 'manners' or customs. A 'historical and moral' view takes a social culture as the product of history and judges it accordingly. Such a 'view' is 'philosophical' in the sense of analyzing and generalizing, but it is implicitly different from a legal, political or theological view. 'Origin and progress' is a catchphrase of Enlightenment analysis of institutions, ideas or movements, suggesting method, analysis, teleological assumptions – in short, critique rather than propaganda, celebration or apology. But Wollstonecraft deals less with the 'Effect' the French Revolution has 'produced' in Europe than with the Revolution's significance for Europe.

The book's prefatory 'Advertisement' again alerts the reader to the extemporaneous, mixed, open-ended character of the text, with its references to 'desultory disquisitions', 'descriptions' and 'theoretical investigations', which have 'grown' under the author's hand and will probably 'be extended to two or three more volumes'. A 'Preface' again outlines basic principles, central points and elements of method. As the Revolution is unprecedented in human history, comprehending it requires a 'mind' of a new kind, 'unsophisticated by old prejudices, and the inveterate habits of degeneracy', with 'an amelioration of temper, produced by the exercise of the most enlarged principles of humanity'. For the crimes and excesses 'which have clouded the vivid prospect that began to spread a ray of joy and gladness over the gloomy horizon of oppression' chill 'the sympathizing bosom, and palsy intellectual vigour'. To represent the contradictory nature of the Revolution requires a 'mind' properly balanced between 'sensibility' and 'reason' – conventionally seen as feminine and masculine traits. The author's qualifications of 'mind' are crucial because a 'just conclusion' as to the nature of the Revolution 'must ultimately sink the dignity of society into contempt, and its members into greater wretchedness;

or elevate it to a degree of grandeur not hitherto anticipated, but by the most enlightened statesmen and philosophers'.

Her 'conclusion' is the same as that reached by other apologists for the Revolution: it was produced by neither 'the abilities or intrigues of a few individuals' nor 'sudden and short-lived enthusiasm', but was 'the natural consequence of intellectual improvement, gradually proceeding to perfection in the advancement of communities, from a state of barbarism to that of polished society', now 'hastening the overthrow of the tremendous empire of superstition and hypocrisy, erected upon the ruins of gothic brutality and ignorance' (pp. vii–viii). But the excesses of the Revolution, its 'folly, selfishness, madness, treachery, and more fatal mock patriotism', were the legacy of the 'empire of superstition and hypocrisy', or court government and culture, 'erected upon the ruins of gothic brutality and ignorance', or the feudal system. This argument, that the defects of the Revolution are due to its retention of elements of court ideology and culture, is similar to Wollstonecraft's earlier argument in *A Vindication of the Rights of Woman* that the bourgeois cultural revolution is vitiated by its retention of elements of courtly gender ideology and culture. In order to validate this explanation of the Revolution here, and her optimistic 'View' of the Revolution's future, Wollstonecraft has to show that she has the 'mind' of the 'true' Revolutionary, 'unsophisticated by old prejudices, and the inveterate habits of degeneracy'. Her 'View' anticipates a state constituted by individual citizens, each an autonomous, independent, authentic self; her discourse must exemplify the citizen that this Revolutionary state should construct. Implicitly, however, the state is not yet made up of such individuals, otherwise the Revolution would have succeeded already; the 'true' Revolutionary citizen is as yet in a vanguard, one that includes the author.

The 'mind' of such a citizen should be feeling and rational, imaginative and analytical, transcendent, or above the historical scene it views, yet sympathizing in and with the actors in that scene. Accordingly, a *View* consists of a historical narrative rendered in a personal and often figurative style, interspersed with comments, analyses, arguments, apostrophes and personal reactions of various kinds. The tension between authorial 'voice' and personal method on one hand and overall structure on the other is presented more sharply in *A View* than in the *Vindications*, as the text is framed by opening remarks and a concluding chapter, and each of the five books closes with a reflective chapter. Wollstone-craft also gives 'voice' to the actors in Revolution, using quotations from figures such as the Revolutionary aristocrat and consti-tutional monarchist, Mirabeau. Less frequently she depicts an event from the perspective of the participants, as in her account of the attack on the Bastille. These devices imply that some Revolutionaries shared her own values, if not able to raise them-selves out of the immediacy of Revolutionary action to take her 'View' of it.

This documentary dialogism enables her to voice through others her own political values as radical critic of court government and culture, hereditary rank and property, yet a constitutional monar-chist, gradualist, supporter of capitalism and the rights of property and exponent of a merit system that would in effect ensure the social and political dominance of the professional middle class. By using such quotations she also represents the Revolution as an intense debate, an event inspired, conducted and interpreted through print – newspapers, magazines, pamphlets, legislative records, books. This is the approach of a professional writer and intellectual, who did not herself witness the events she describes. It is also the approach to be expected from a woman – indeed, forced on a woman – legally excluded from the public scene and from politics, especially after the seizure of power by the Jacobins, under whom this book was furtively written.

To indicate its element of histórical detachment, a *View* is the most obviously ordered and shapely of Wollstonecraft's texts. It comprises five books and eighteen chapters. Book I describes the Enlightenment background and the court system of the *ancien régime*. The Enlightenment made the people less willing to tolerate the excesses of the court and privileged orders, leading to the crisis of the late 1780s, expressed in a pamphlet war. Book II traces events from the people's statements of grievances and the opening of the States General in spring 1789, through the declaration of a National Assembly, the Tennis Court oath and the assault on the Bastille. Book III deals with the joyful and patriotic atmosphere of July and early August, and the abandonment by the aristocracy of their feudal privileges. Book IV focuses on the Declaration of the Rights of Man and Citizen of August 1789 and the debate over the King's power. Finally, Book V describes the march of the women of Paris on Versailles in October and the background and aftermath of that event. In spite of this clear over-arching structure, however, the personal response to the event narrated is more prominent in the reading experience. For example, there are relatively few footnotes and, again, most are personal remarks rather than citations of facts or sources. Similarly, the chapter headings connect comment with exposition. Yet the characteristics of Enlightenment 'philosophic history' are strong in a *View*. If 'philosophical history' informs the textual structure of a *View*, the 'voice' of the viewer informs its texture.

For example, the first chapter's heading resembles those opening many 'philosophical histories'. It starts by laying down basic principles: 'INTRODUCTION. PROGRESS OF SOCIETY. END OF GOVERNMENT'. Then it goes on to events: 'RISE OF POLITICAL DISCUSSION AMONGST THE FRENCH. REVOLUTION IN AMERICA.' It then considers social, cultural, institutional and political factors: 'VIRTUE ATTEMPTED TO BE BUILT ON FALSE PRINCIPLES. THE CROISADES, AND THE AGE OF CHIVALRY. ADMINISTRATION OF RICHELIEU, AND OF CARDINAL MAZARIN. THEATRICAL ENTERTAINMENTS, AND DRAMATIC POETS OF THE FRENCH, – MOLIERE, – CORNEILLE, – RACINE. LOUIS XIV. THE REGENCY. LOUIS XV'. The progression from generalities to particularities is characteristic of 'philosophical history'.

So too is the co-ordination of political factors with cultural ones. 'Theatrical entertainments' may seem tangential here, but a *View* argues that court government is theatrical because it has to dazzle those it rules; thus the whole of French society became theatrical, more concerned with display and appearance than with 'reality'. Moreover, drama was considered the great cultural achievement of the age of Louis XIV – so pervasive, Wollstonecraft argues, that even Louis XIV's wars were theatrical exhibitions. Furthermore, this cultural legacy has continued down to the present, just like the legacy of despotism. Finally, the theme is appropriate because Burke had accused the Revolution of being merely theatrical. Later in the book Wollstonecraft agrees, but argues that the theatricality of the French carried over from the *ancien régime* to the Revolution. In 'philosophical history' the outward cultural products of a society are symptomatic of its inner moral character. In her analysis of the theatricality of French society and culture, as elsewhere in a *View*, Wollstonecraft shows that she had mastered the characteristic critical method of 'philosophical history' and could apply it to the history of the present.

She does so in order to argue that the plot of history concludes with her own version of the professional middle-class cultural revolution. Like other 'philosophical historians', she attributes the superiority of modern civilization to inventions that furthered travel, trade and empire, as well as 'the fortunate invention of printing'. Printing and trade brought mankind more together, and 'the friction of arts and commerce have given to society the transcendently pleasing polish of urbanity'. Unfortunately, 'the remains of superstition, and the unnatural distinction of privileged classes, which had their origin in barbarous folly, still fettered the opinions of man, and fettered his native dignity'. But English writers such as John Locke broke these fetters, leading directly to Paine's *Rights of Man*, 'which, in spite of the fatal errours of ignorance, and the perverse obstinacy of selfishness, is now converting sublime theories into practical truths' (pp. 3–4).

This plot of history also privileges writing and print as agents of 'progress'. She goes on to contrast English and French political writing and argues that opinions circulated faster in France than in Britain because there was greater social conformity in France: 'The idle caprices of an effeminate court had long given the tone to the awe-struck populace, who, stupidly admiring what they did not understand, lived on a *vive le roi*, whilst his blood-sucking minions drained every vein, that should have warmed their honest hearts' (p. 12). This is a common middle-class view of the way court culture achieves ideological domination of the lower orders by influencing their 'passions', which should be educated by 'reason' – the 'mind' of the professional bourgeoisie. Wollstonecraft emplots the relationship of passion and reason in history, from passion's dominion in the past to the future dominion of reason; she transcendentalizes this relationship as the divinely ordained golden rule of 'do unto others'. Here she digresses into one of her enthusiastic and visionary flights, imagining the glorious future of reason – 'the image of God implanted in our nature' – as it spreads ideas of liberty.

She then considers the related Enlightenment debate on whether 'civilization' has brought more harm or good to mankind. She disagrees with Rousseau and others that departure from primitive 'simplicity' causes decline; rather, it is the court system that causes degeneration (pp. 19–20). The apparently superior energy of the ancient heroic age is due to mere flashes of passion and imagination, not systematic reason: 'Ignorant people, when they appear to reflect, exercise their imagination more than their understanding . . . and thus grow romantic, like the croisaders; or like women' (p. 21). The bold comparison of crusaders and women is characteristic of both *A Vindication of the Rights of Woman* and Enlightenment social criticism, which saw 'chivalry' as the false front of modern court society and mounted a steady attack on it, treating the Crusades as characteristic of chivalry's excess, folly, and hypocrisy.

She goes on in Book I to describe the rise of the court system in France and attributes the miseries of Europe not to an imperfect state of civilization but to the court economy. The patronage system of acquiring wealth and honours requires the courtier to practise both deceit and tyranny, to dupe patrons and keep down competitors. This system pervades all levels of society: 'Kings have been the dupes of ministers, of mistresses, and secretaries, not to notice sly valets and cunning waiting-maids . . . till in the circle of corruption no one can point out the first mover' (pp. 46–7). She then shows how the court economy inevitably produced the economy of Revolutionary excess up to October 1789; this explanation also applies to the event she could not describe – the Jacobin Revolution of 1793–4. This is the central point of her 'View' of the 'Origin and Progress of the French Revolution' and implicitly accounts for 'The Effects It Has Produced in Europe'.

This explanation justifies her optimism 'that the people are essentially good, and that knowledge is rapidly advancing to that degree of perfectibility, when the proud distinctions of sophisticating fools will be eclipsed by the mild rays of philosophy, and man be considered as man – acting with the dignity of an intelligent being'. 'Knowledge' and 'the mild rays of philosophy' stand for the professional cultural revolution; 'the proud distinctions' are those of a court-dominated class system; 'man' is used as a general noun. As she does throughout, she figures the cultural revolution as a natural process (dawning day), according to human nature ('the people are essentially good'), rather than as the programme of a particular class or its vanguard. She concludes Book I by declaring: 'it is perhaps, difficult to bring ourselves to believe, that out of this chaotic mass a fairer government is rising than has ever shed the sweets of social life on the world. – But things must have time to find their level' (pp. 72–3). Again, she explains the Revolution as a 'natural' process ('things . . . find their level'), but she cannot deny Revolutionary violence, so she introduces a tone of sensibility and hesitant hopefulness at the end.

In the following Books she deals more particularly with events of May to October 1789. Book II begins with a vigorous review of the people's grievances addressed to the States General. She uses a favourite device – the distinction of terms – to account for these grievances by the relation of rich and poor, when 'the rich necessarily became robbers, and the poor thieves. Talking of honour, honesty was overlooked' (p. 77). The distinction between 'robbers' and 'thieves' attributes lower-class crime to necessity and makes rich and poor morally equal. Her distinction between 'honour' and 'honesty' employs a favourite theme: the contrast of outward, social appearance and inner, moral reality; the aristocratic code of 'honour' is mere appearance contrasted to the moral virtue of 'honesty'. She uses social psychology to attribute the improvidence of the common people to the feudal structure of the *ancien régime*. Because 'neither the life nor property of the citizens was secured by equal laws, both were often wantonly sported with by those who could do it with impunity'. Such 'despotism' inspired 'continual fear' and uncertainty, producing 'abject manners' which were then used to justify continued despotism. This also accounts for the lottery mentality of the common people in France: 'people are very apt to sport away their time, when they cannot look forward, with some degree of certainty, to the consolidation of a plan of future ease' (pp. 138–9).

Thus the French were caught up in a process of revolutionary transformation that they could not understand because the ideological hegemony of the old order persisted even after that order had been swept away. This explanation underpins the terse, racy, yet analytical narrative of the assault on the Bastille in July 1789 (Book II, ch. 3), one of the events widely thought to reveal the Revolution's 'true' character and thus pointing to its outcome. Wollstonecraft now eschews the detachment of historical hindsight and gives journalistic immediacy and a feeling of spontaneity to her narrative by blending together reports of eyewitnesses and participants. This method is appropriate here because she argues that such events and the Revolution as a whole were spontaneous expressions of political fervour by the people and not, as some in Britain claimed, results of a secret conspiracy. By writing with apparent immediacy herself, she gives the impression of a true revolutionary sensibility responding to the authentically Revolutionary event she describes. As in the other Books, the last chapter of Book II is reflective, offering a survey of the diffusion of knowledge that laid the groundwork for the kind of popular outburst exemplified by the attack on the Bastille.

Book III continues the narrative of political events, describing the confusion and indecision among both court and reformers after the popular Revolutionary destruction of the Bastille. Again, the explanation is to be found in the ideological and cultural legacy of court government (p. 252). Again, too, the explanation could be extended to more recent events of 1793 and 1794. Appropriately, the central chapter of a *View* (Book III, ch. 2) describes the Declaration of the Rights of Man and Citizen in August 1789 – to Wollstonecraft, Paine and others, the representative event of the Revolution. Wollstonecraft does not idealize these events, but portrays them as a contest in extremes of public display. The last chapter of the Book again explains the economy of such 'display' as the legacy of the *ancien régime*: 'It was by debasing artifices, under the old government, that men obtained favour and consequence; and whilst such men, men who were educated and ossified by the ancient *regimen*, act on the political stage of France, mankind will be continually distressed and amused by their tragic and comic exhibitions' (p. 299). The theatrical metaphor reinforces the point, cashing in on her exposition of the theatre of court politics in Book I, while the phrase 'tragic and comic' also suggests the Revolution's contradictory extremes.

The chapter ends by tracing social relations and conflicts from primitive societies down to the 'polished slavery' of the *ancien régime*. Yet, she insists, there were some among the French who 'really learned the true art of living' – to give 'that degree of elegance to domestic intercourse, which, prohibiting gross familiarity, alone can render permanent the family affections, whence all the social virtues spring' (p. 309). This ideal conjugality will be the basis of society and the state in the future, post-Revolutionary age, therefore it is itself revolutionary. Furthermore, female sexuality now has a place in this revolutionary force, as it replaces both the repressed sexuality of mere bourgeois 'propriety' and the subservient sexuality of courtly 'gallantry', coquetry and the 'mistress system'. Wollstonecraft argued in *A Vindication* that sexual passion had to die out of a marriage for true conjugality to grow, because she saw such passion as subordinating women in the courtly politics of sexuality; she now argues that egalitarian sexuality is necessary to 'true' conjugality, which must be the basis of a truly revolutionary society and state. In fact, she argues, the greater acceptance of female sexuality in France makes domesticity and thus political culture more advanced than they are in England (p. 311).

At this point the book's argument gains particular force from its author being identified on the title-page. A book on history and politics by a woman would be dismissed by many readers, as she had seen with reviews of her first *Vindication*, whereas an analysis of the Revolution in terms of sexual politics would gain authority from such an author. As many readers would know, Wollstonecraft had already written on the politics of courtly sexuality in *A Vindication of the Rights of Woman*. She could also be supposed to have authority on the political, intellectual and sexual vanguard that she claims makes French political culture more advanced, more potentially revolutionary, than elsewhere. The same authority applies to her picture of gentrified middle-class domesticity, where it is 'pursuing employments not absolutely necessary to support life, that the finest polish is given to the mind, and those personal graces, which are instantly felt, but cannot be described'. Such aestheticized domesticity – what she called 'domestic taste' in the second *Vindication* – would be most available to the professional bourgeoisie, but especially to writers, intellectuals and artists, of which the author of a *View* is self-evidently one.

Book IV discusses the events and debates that founded the Revolutionary state in August 1789 yet left it vitiated by errors inherited from the old order. For example, the failure to protect property, the guarantor of citizens' loyalty to the state (p. 317), was caused by vices of court culture such as fondness for 'eloquence', and impulsiveness. Yet Wollstonecraft sees signs of progress in two areas, government and dress: 'In the progressive influence of knowledge on manners, both dress and governments appear to be acquiring simplicity; it may therefore be inferred, that, as the people attain dignity of character, their amusements will flow from a more rational source than the pageantry of kings, or the view of the fopperies exhibited at courts' (p. 351). Under court governments fashion in dress is merely social, based on emulation within a hierarchical society dominated by the court and its culture of ceremony, display and conspicuous consumption. Under constitutional government fashion will be 'rational', not based on inequalities of wealth and power. Moreover, women were thought to be more interested in 'dress' than 'government'; Wollstonecraft

shows that dress is not only political in itself and a way of expressing political sentiments but may reveal as much about the state of
the nation and its future as government does.

For ideology and culture are the focus of her analysis and she
deals only briefly with constitutional, legislative and financial
issues. Nevertheless, she argues that in neglecting political economy, 'the most important, and most difficult of all human improvements' (p. 397), France 'probably lost most of the advantages,
which her finances might have gained by the revolution'. Instead,
the impatient Revolutionaries relied on 'the full blown bladders of
public credit, which may be destroyed by the prick of a pin'
(p. 395), proving once again 'the necessity of a gradual reform': 'All
sudden revolutions have been as suddenly overturned, and things
thrown back below their former state' – another obvious if oblique
reference to events of 1793 and 1794. As usual, she closes the Book
with general reflections, portraying the Revolution as fundamen-
tally an intellectual and cultural event, because 'the improvements
in the science of politics have been still more slow in their advancement than those of philosophy and morals' (p. 396). But because
the Revolution was 'progressive' and 'in the minds of men' she
finds reason to hope (p. 398).

The fifth and last Book describes events of autumn 1789 that
arose from the summer's errors and excesses and that show how a
poorly founded revolution degenerates into extreme acts, such as
the Paris mob's attack on Versailles in October 1789. This event
inspired Burke's best known rhetorical flight in *Reflections*, where
he laments that 'ten thousand swords' did not leap from their
scabbards to avenge the mob's insult to the Queen. This event is
also the centrepiece of Wollstonecraft's Book v (ch. 2) and, surprisingly, her view of it resembles Burke's. By 1794 she and others
recognized that, though Burke's reasoning may have been wrong,
he was right to see the events of October as forerunners of worse to
come. But she explains these events differently from Burke, and so
explains the later excesses too. This is her dual mission: to reclaim
revolutionary optimism for those in Britain, like herself and those
in Johnson's 'Academy', who had sympathized with the Revolution of 1789 to 1792, and to turn back the tide of British anti-
Revolutionary reaction that had alarmed her since 1792. Thus this
section is the culmination of her Revolutionary feminist reading of
the Revolution.

Her focus is the role of women in the attack on Versailles. She invokes a conspiracy theory, that men exploited the grievances of Parisian women in order to achieve their own political ends:

> From the enjoyment of more freedom than the women of other parts of the world, those of France have acquired more indepen- dence of spirit than any others; it has, therefore, been the scheme of designing men very often since the revolution, to lurk behind them as a kind of safeguard, working them up to some desperate act, and then terming it a folly, because merely the rage of women, who were supposed to be actuated only by the emotions of the moment.   (pp. 425–6)

This explanation is aimed as much at the Jacobin suppression of women's political clubs in 1793 as at the women who marched on Versailles in October 1789.

Like most professional middle-class revolutionaries, Wollstone- craft had a limited understanding of what E. P. Thompson calls 'the moral economy' of the common people – communal values that could mobilize many individuals into spontaneous, orderly, purposeful protest – according to George Rudé, a 'crowd' rather than a 'mob'.[19] Wollstonecraft distinguishes between the 'mob' of 5 October and the 'honest multitude, who took the Bastille', but, like Burke and many others of her class, she tends to see crowds as mobs. As Joan Landes points out: 'Wollstonecraft dismisses the march on Versailles in an almost Burkean fashion.'[20] Her account of the attack on Versailles resembles Burke's and even echoes its language and rhythm:

> The laws had been trampled on by a gang of banditti the most desperate – The altar of humanity had been profaned – The dignity of freedom had been tarnished – The sanctuary of re- pose, the asylum of care and fatigue, the chaste temple of a woman, I consider the queen only as one, the apartment where she consigns her senses to the bosom of sleep, folded in it's arms forgetful of the world, was violated with murderous fury – (p. 457)

Burke provides more detail, adds erotic titillation, prolongs his indignation and pushes it further than Wollstonecraft does. But where Burke sees only Revolutionary crime and madness Woll- stonecraft sees another consequence of sudden and extreme change 'from the most fettering tyranny to an unbridled liberty'. Nevertheless, the last chapter of the book seeks consolation and hope even in the violence of October 1789 and, tacitly, the Jacobin violence of 1793 and 1794, explaining again how the social and cultural habits acquired under the *ancien régime* were carried into the Revolution, causing fluctuation between extremes that will eventually be modified into rational government by 'progress of knowledge' and the spread of revolutionary domesticity.

But she also adduces a new explanation of the Revolution, based on the theory of the French '*économistes*' that 'the roots of human social existence lie in the material conditions of life which provide for survival and physical well-being'.[21] These writers, also known as 'physiocrats', had promoted a programme of agrarian capitalism hostile to the centralized economic control characteristic of the *ancien régime*. Not surprisingly, this programme influenced the first wave of Revolutionaries, including Mirabeau, a writer Wollstone-craft cites often in a *View*, and their ideas would have been frequent topics of discussion among the business-minded denizens of the Christies' Paris salon and those acquainted with Imlay. The '*économistes*' were also connected with Adam Smith, whose *Theory of Moral Sentiments* was an important source for Wollstone-craft's Sentimental social theories.

Wollstonecraft uses the theory of the '*économistes*' specifically to suggest the common interest of professional and capitalist bour-geoisie, while maintaining justice for the labouring classes. She also relates the free market economy promoted by the '*économistes*' to her own argument, expressed in her first *Vindication*, for a free market in 'mind' – merit or what she here calls 'talents': 'The economists . . . showed that the prosperity of a state depends on the freedom of industry; that talents should be permitted to find their level; that the unshackling of commerce is the only secret to render it flourishing, and answer more effectually the ends for which it is politically necessary' (p. 499). By contrast, the economy of court government corrupts the upper and middle ranks, includ-ing professions and commerce:

> Extravagance forces the peer to prostitute his talents and influ-ence for a place, to repair his broken fortune; and the country gentleman becomes venal in the senate, to enable himself to live on a par with him, or reimburse himself for the expences of electioneering, into which he was led by sheer vanity. The

professions, on the same account, become equally unprincipled. The one, whose characteristic ought to be integrity, descends to chicanery; whilst another trifles with the health, of which it knows all the importance. The merchant likewise enters into speculations so closely bordering on fraudulency, that common straight forward minds can scarcely distinguish the devious art of selling any thing for a price far beyond that necessary to ensure a just profit, from sheer dishonesty, aggravated by hard-heartedness, when it is to take advantage of the necessities of the indigent. (pp. 517–18)

The court system also criminalizes the lower ranks: 'The deprivation of natural, equal, civil and political rights, reduced the most cunning of the lower orders to practise fraud, and the rest to habits of stealing, audacious robberies, and murders' (p. 520). This description could apply as well to Britain as to France.

She concludes that the ranks corrupted by court government have a common interest in overthrowing this system, though in doing so they would only be supporting a natural process:

Thus had France grown up, and sickened on the corruption of a state diseased. But, as in medicine there is a species of complaint in the bowels which works it's own cure, and, leaving the body healthy, gives an invigorated tone to the system, so there is in politics: and whilst the agitation of it's regeneration continues, the excrementitious humours exuding from the contaminated body will excite a general dislike and contempt for the nation; and it is only the philosophical eye, which looks into the nature and weighs the consequences of human actions, that will be able to discern the cause, which has produced so many dreadful effects. (p. 522)

The figures of disease and medicine are taken from Burke, but used here to argue for Revolutionary optimism, while accounting for the 'general dislike and contempt' of the Revolution as it has unfolded so far.

Appropriately, this passage ends a *View*, returning to the 'philosophical eye' claimed by the author at the outset. Yet the 'eye' now transcends even the plane of 'philosophical history'. The 'philosophical eye which looks into the nature and weighs the consequences of human actions' parallels God the searcher of hearts and weigher of deeds. This is a purposeful parallel. Wollstonecraft often recurred to a question that vexed eighteenth-century thought: how a benevolent God could allow evil, or the human misery seen everywhere in the present and past. Revolutionary violence was seen as an extreme case of such evil and misery, and Wollstonecraft takes up that issue in suggesting that 'the philosophical eye . . . will be able to discern the cause, which has produced so many dreadful effects'. But unlike anti-Revolutionists she does not invoke divine retribution for Revolutionary violence, and unlike disillusioned pro-Revolutionists she does not abandon explanation of the Revolution's 'origin and progress' to the deity or a later age. A *View* is a secular, properly 'philosophical' view of the Revolution; yet it is also a 'moral' view, affirming a divine purpose for human life and history. In its attempt so to combine a secular and yet providential view it is implicitly the view of a 'female philosopher'. A *View* is a Revolutionary feminist reading of what was widely seen as the most important event in human history. As such, the book was designed to explain apparent paradoxes in the course of the Revolution and, more important, to suggest how such feminism could contribute to resolving the future of both the Revolution in France and the cultural revolution in Britain.

Critics generally recognized this design and Wollstonecraft's intention to write as a 'female philosopher', for better or for worse. The *Analytical Review*, not surprisingly, found it was for the better: Wollstonecraft had conducted 'a diligent and accurate examination of the facts' with a 'sound judgment', 'enlightened understanding' and 'a liberal spirit', 'warmed by the steady flame of universal philanthropy' – qualifications 'which in a woman may appear to male vanity highly astonishing'. The *Analytical* saw a *View* as a 'production of genius' combining distinctive and conventionally gendered traits: 'energy of diction' and 'richness of imagery' on one hand and on the other 'a degree of impartiality scarcely at present to be expected' and 'truly philosophical', 'notwithstanding the odium that has of late fallen upon philosophy' (December 1794, p. 337).

Other reviews were mixed. The *Monthly Review* also thought the work combined 'masculine' and 'feminine' qualities, but was more ambivalent about this. It found that Wollstonecraft wrote 'not like an annalist, but like a philosopher', and though the 'vigour' of her 'imagination' was shown 'throughout the work in the metaphorical cast of her language', it sometimes became 'too figurative to be perfectly clear' (April 1795, pp. 393–4). This failing was often attributed to women writers. The *New Annual Register*, which was written by leading men (and the occasional woman) of the Scottish and English Nonconformist Enlightenments, agreed with this view. It thought that 'history and discussion', subjects many readers would see as men's intellectual domain, were treated by Wollstonecraft 'with a calm and philosophic eye' and merited 'the attention of politicians of every party, and statesmen of every country'. Even the style 'is peculiarly energetic and impressive'. But once again Wollstonecraft's gender and gendered culture were revealed in 'some obscurities occasioned by the too frequent recurrence of metaphorical and figurative language' (vol. for 1794, p. 222).

Reviews hostile to Wollstonecraft's pro-Revolutionary point of view made the same criticisms but treated them as more serious defects. These reviews suggested that in tackling history and politics Wollstonecraft inevitably showed her and her sex's intellectual and literary limitations. The *Critical Review* advised Wollstonecraft to stick to either simple narrative or philosophical reflections, and not try to combine both. The reviewer warned those readers 'who are acquainted with the strong mind of Mrs Wollstonecraft' that they could again 'expect to meet with many just remarks and forcible observations' as well as 'want of grace and amenity' and a 'tendency to the turgid in her expressions'. At the same time, he advised Wollstonecraft to be more feminine, to 'add a little grace and delicacy' to the 'vigour' of her style and avoid such unladylike expressions as the comparison of the Revolution to a complaint of the bowels.

The *British Critic* went much further, claiming that the good part of the book – its information – was plagiarized from the *New Annual Register*. This charge cannot in fact be substantiated. The reviewer then found that Wollstonecraft's 'reflections' on this material showed lack of the intellectual method that would be expected of a man:

Mrs. W. . . . seems to have considered each part of the history separately; her attention, very frequently, not being extended to what precedes or follows her immediate subject; so as to modify the conclusion she draws from it, by the collateral lights which such a process might afford. Hence her conceptions are not digested into the diversified, but concordant parts, of a whole;

nor resemble, in any degree, the operations of an extensive and firm judgement.

Finally, the reviewer also found that Wollstonecraft's style showed its author's gender by its rhetorical excesses, misuse of language and ignorance of discursive decorum: 'The prevalent fault of it is, that it is more florid than the tone of the subject allows; mixing too much that of the novelist with that of the historian; the dignity of whose matter very ill accords with tinsel and tawdriness' (July 1795, pp. 34–5).

Whatever their political bias or judgement, all these reviews hit the mark. For it was precisely the gendering of discourse, culture and politics that Wollstonecraft was challenging – first in *A Vindication of the Rights of Woman* in the revolutionary state, and now in her account of how a revolutionary state had gone wrong by allowing the wrongly gendered culture and politics of the *ancien régime* to persist into the new order, splitting the Revolution into an effeminate early phase and its ferociously masculine Jacobin successor. Helen Maria Williams had already presented such an analysis in her *Letters* from France, and predicted (or hoped for) a restoration of the feminized Revolution of the Girondins in the circle of Marie Roland. Williams's Sentimental style aimed to exemplify such a feminized revolutionary consciousness. Wollstonecraft first intended to follow Williams with her projected 'Series of Letters on the Present Character of the French Nation'. But her *View* argues and exemplifies stylistically a more thoroughly feminist way through the destructive gendering of political and cultural revolution. Wollstonecraft would be disappointed but not surprised that the reviewers could not see that. But by the time the reviews appeared she would be more concerned by the breakdown of her vanguardist revolutionary conjugality with Imlay than by the failure of her vanguardist revolutionary writing.

7

'A Solitary Wanderer'

By the time *An Historical and Moral View of the . . . French Revolution* was published Wollstonecraft's relationship with Imlay was disintegrating. She thought she had found with him a revolutionary domesticity and sexuality based on 'mind' and supporting her public identity and professional career. She could not believe that her revolution was over and continued to pursue the ideal and Imlay. Even her next book was a by-product of that pursuit.

She joined Imlay at Le Havre in February 1794 but when he went to London she returned to Paris. At the same time, the war prevented regular communication with her sisters, brothers and friends in England. She followed political events, rejoiced in Robespierre's downfall in July 1794 and adopted one of his leading opponents, Tallien, as her Revolutionary hero (*Letters*, p. 260). In September she took Fanny to a Revolutionary fête and planned to buy her a sash in honour of Rousseau – 'and why not? – for I have always been half in love with him' (*Letters*, p. 263). She met Rouget de l'Isle, author of the Revolutionary anthem, the 'Marseillaise', and found herself ready to be 'half in love' with him, too (p. 268). She welcomed relaxation of restrictions on the press, telling Imlay: 'they write now with great freedom and truth, and this liberty of the press will overthrow the Jacobins' (p. 264). The hopeful predictions of *An Historical and Moral View* seemed to be coming true, though her confidence was mixed with fear: 'The liberty of the press will produce a great effect here . . . and the Jacobins are conquered. – Yet I almost fear the last flap of the tail of the beast' (p. 267).

But her main interest now was in saving her revolutionary domesticity. She saw herself representing domesticity and the life of the imagination as Imlay became more immersed in 'business'. In September she wrote:

Believe me, sage sir, you have not sufficient respect for the imagination – I could prove to you in a trice that it is the mother of sentiment, the great distinction of our nature, the only

purifier of the passions. . . . The impulse of the senses, passions,
if you will, and the conclusions of reason, draw men together; but
the imagination is the true fire, stolen from heaven, to animate
this cold creature of clay, producing all those fine sympathies
that lead to rapture, rendering men social by expanding their
hearts, instead of leaving them leisure to calculate how many
comforts society affords.

If you call these observations romantic, a phrase in this place
which would be tantamount to nonsensical, I shall be apt to
retort, that you are embruted by trade and the vulgar enjoyments of life. . . .   (p. 263)

Throughout the vicissitudes of the following year she philos-
ophized in this way, as she had done in her struggle for independence in the late 1780s.

Her chief domestic pleasure now was Fanny; but this pleasure
only heightened her pain at Imlay's absence. In September 1794
she wrote:

I have been playing and laughing with the little girl so long, that
I cannot take up my pen to address you without emotion.
Pressing her to my bosom, she looked so like you (*entre nous*,
your best looks, for I do not admire your commercial face) every
nerve seemed to vibrate to the touch, and I began to think that
there was something in the assertion of man and wife being one
– for you seemed to pervade my whole frame. . . .   (p. 264)

Her capacity for intense physical experience of mental and moral
affections, which she saw as the basis of her love for Imlay, now
became a source of more acute suffering and she felt herself
'almost a slave to the child'. Her domestic paradise had become a
place of torture and bondage.

She complained that he was being drawn into further 'schemes
and projects', and urged a professional rather than speculative
approach to earning a livelihood; a career should stimulate the
'mind' and domestic affections, not stultify them. In December she
learned of his sexual infidelity, and wrote with philosophical
indignation:

The common run of men have such an ignoble way of thinking,
that, if they debauch their hearts, and prostitute their persons,

following perhaps a gust of inebriation, they suppose the wife, slave rather, whom they maintain, has no right to complain, and ought to receive the sultan, whenever he deigns to return, with open arms, though his have been polluted by half an hundred promiscuous amours during his absence.

I consider fidelity and constancy as two distinct things; yet the former is necessary, to give life to the other – and such a degree of respect do I think due to myself, that, if only probity, which is a good thing in its place, brings you back, never return! – for, if a wandering of the heart, or even a caprice of the imagination detains you – there is an end of all my hopes of happiness – I could not forgive it, if I would.

I have gotten into a melancholy mood, you perceive. You know my opinion of men in general; you know that I think them systematic tyrants, and that it is the rarest thing in the world, to meet with a man with sufficient delicacy of feeling to govern desire. When I am thus sad, I lament that my little darling, fondly as I doat on her, is a girl.   (p. 273)

The author of A Vindication of the Rights of Woman is seen in the distinction between 'fidelity' and 'constancy', in the Enlightenment topos of oriental despotism (the 'sultan'), and in the Sentimental economy of habits, feeling and self-discipline. Her Revolutionary feminism returns home in concern for her daughter and her intention to resume her career, making herself and Fanny independent of Imlay.

In the early months of 1795, weakened by illness and anxiety, she recurs to the morbidness characteristic of the mid-1780s. The dissolution of her domestic idyll seemed to deny the power of her mind to shape her career as a self-determined progress in life, and she imagined various ways out, including death, solitude, madness and Imlay's eventual remorse. She even tried placing her own suffering in relation to that caused by the Revolution, a strategy that would inform her next book:

This has been such a period of barbarity and misery, I ought not to complain of having my share. I wish one moment that I had never heard of the cruelties that have been practised here, and the next envy the mothers who have been killed with their children. Surely I had suffered enough in life, not to be cursed with a fondness, that burns up the vital stream I am imparting.

You will think me mad: I would I were so, that I could forget my misery. . . . (p. 279)

'Fondness' here means excessive affection, for Imlay; 'the vital stream' is her mother's milk which she feels drying up from distress, but which also symbolizes her ability to pass on life as she has made it for herself. Imlay's betrayal has brought into conflict domestic relations that should be united. Imagining herself a victim of the Jacobin Revolution heroizes her suffering, raising it above the merely personal; she also invokes the common characterization of the Jacobin Revolution as tyrannically and oppressively masculine, destroying families and domestic affections for (merely) public goals.

When Imlay summoned her to England, she turned her resentment against her own nation, exclaiming: 'am I only to return to a country, that has not merely lost all charms for me, but for which I feel a repugnance that almost amounts to horror, only to be left there a prey to it!' (p. 280). Once in London, she resorted to a politicized professionalism, or 'plans of usefulness'. She wrote to her sisters with schemes to help them and her father, but when she learned for certain that Imlay had taken another mistress she attempted suicide. Afterwards she met him and agreed to recruit herself by vigorous – even dangerous – activity. She would go to Scandinavia as Imlay's business agent; she would also resume professional work by keeping an account of her trip, to be published by Johnson.

In his business of breaking the blockade against France Imlay had sent a large quantity of silver and gold to Scandinavia, presumably to pay for goods sought by the French government. But his agent had absconded with the treasure and Imlay was trying to recover it, partly by lawsuit and partly by mediation.[1] He gave Wollstonecraft power of attorney, as his 'best friend and wife', to go and mediate a settlement. She was to sail from Hull in Yorkshire with Fanny and her French maid Marguerite. Delayed by unfavourable winds, she wrote expostulating letters to Imlay. 'Why do you not attach those tender emotions round the idea of home', she asked. 'This alone is affection – every thing else is only humanity, electrified by sympathy' (p. 289). Behind the remark is a common observation of the French Revolution debate – that Revolutionaries worshipped 'humanity' but disregarded the domestic affections. A couple of days later she reflected on his confession that he lived for the 'zest of life' in the moment:

> The common run of men, I know, with strong health and gross appetites, must have variety to banish *ennui*, because the imagination never lends its magic wand, to convert appetite into love, cemented by according reason. – Ah! my friend, you know not the ineffable delight, the exquisite pleasure, which arises from a unison of affection and desire, when the whole soul and senses are abandoned to a lively imagination, that renders every emotion delicate and rapturous.

These emotions are 'the distinctive characteristic of genius, the foundation of taste, and of that exquisite relish for the beauties of nature, of which the common herd of eaters and drinkers and *child-begeters*, certainly have no idea' (p. 291).

While at Hull she was taken to Beverley, and reflected on the distance between herself and most of those who still lived there: 'when I found that many of the inhabitants had lived in the same houses ever since I left it, I could not help wondering how they could thus have vegetated, whilst I was running over a world of sorrow, snatching at pleasure, and throwing off prejudices'. Yet she was shocked at 'what strides aristocracy and fanaticism have made, since I resided in this country' (*Letters*, p. 294). The reaction against the French Revolution, its British supporters and any kind of reform had overtaken her. Betrayal of what she had tried to make of her life seemed complete.

The voyage across the North Sea was rough, the welcome she received was gratifying but fatiguing and her feelings continued to fluctuate. She wrote more letters to Imlay and longed for their meeting on the Continent at the end of the summer. When she could not hope she recurred to familiar anodynes: self-sacrifice, hope for early death, retreat into herself, physical activity and exercise, what she called 'dissipation' or socializing, professional self-dedication and living for her child, or fantasies of Imlay's remorse. To her surprise she found the glorious summer weather and rural recreations improved her health and appearance (*Letters*, p. 302). This in turn stimulated philosophical reflection on her own sexuality and its relation to her feminism: 'To act up to my principles, I have laid the strictest restraint on my very thoughts'; 'I have reined in my imagination' and avoided 'every sensation' that might arouse sexual desire. She realized, however, that 'Love, in some minds, is an affair of sentiment, arising from the same delicacy of perception (or taste) as renders them alive to the beauties of nature, poetry, &c'; therefore sexual love need not mean subordination. In fact, she realizes now that 'Love is a want of my heart' and 'to deaden is not to calm the mind – Aiming at tranquillity, I have almost destroyed all the energy of my soul' (*Letters*, p. 302). Her passion for Imlay was no self-betrayal, to be erased by apathy, as she had tried to erase more generalized desire in the mid-1780s. Books and her own writing also helped reconstruct her self. She had brought books with her, probably including Shakespeare's plays, for in her letters she heroizes herself as a male tragic hero, Lear (pp. 297, 305) or Hamlet (p. 300). More sentimentally, she thought of herself as Laurence Sterne's pathetic Maria in *A Sentimental Journey* (*Letters*, p. 305). But by the middle of July she had 'recovered herself' enough to begin her new book (p. 306). By the end of July she was feeling new pride in self-dedication to Fanny and her profession, and told Imlay: 'When we meet again, you shall be convinced that I have more resolution than you give me credit for' (p. 307). By August her own self-discipline, self-analysis and professional commitment had virtually restored her to herself.

By September, however, it was clear that Imlay was not going to meet her on the Continent and he hinted at the reason – he had taken a new mistress. This possibility upset her new, fragile equilibrium. In response she adopted her earlier heroic posture, setting herself above his 'caprices'. She planned to confront him, and with Johnson's help earn enough to settle with Fanny in France (*Letters*, pp. 313–14). Back in London in early October, she found that he had indeed 'formed some new attachment'. She wrote a suicide note, asking him to pay off her servants and have Fanny sent to Paris to be cared for (pp. 316–17). On 10 October she went to Battersea Bridge, but there were people around and she hired a boat to Putney Bridge, where she walked up and down in the rain to soak her clothes and ensure that she would sink, and then she jumped into the river. She was underwater long enough to lose consciousness, but she had been observed and was pulled out, revived and taken to the Christies' home. She continued writing to Imlay through November and into December, appealing to what she believed was his better nature, adopting a posture of dignified independence, refusing his offers of monetary help, reprimanding him for showing little concern for her and stoically resolving to face shame as an unmarried and abandoned mother. Only in the spring of 1796 could she acknowledge that the 'affair' was at last over, and take up her career again. The view taken by many then and since was that in spite of her pretensions to be a woman of 'mind' above the weaknesses of her sex she had acted like a 'mere' woman. But her 'attachment' for Imlay, like that for Fuseli, was part of her Revolutionary feminism and vanguardism. At first Imlay seemed the ideal revolutionary man she had called for in *A Vindication of the Rights of Woman* – uncontaminated by court culture, fit for the revolutionary domesticity that was to bring about a revolutionary society. Unfortunately, he turned out to be tainted with the courtly erotic culture that she had criticized in *A Vindication* as the source of women's oppression and thereby the source of social and political corruption. Imlay also became 'embruted' by 'business' and 'commerce' – the false outcome of revolutionary process warned against by Richard Price in his critique of the American Revolution and in Wollstonecraft's account of the French Revolution. The course of her relationship with Imlay simply confirmed with bitter personal experience the arguments of her Revolutionary feminism.

Letters Written During a Short Residence in Sweden, Norway, and Denmark brought these arguments and experience together in one text. It was published by Johnson in January 1796 and purports to be a travel book.

The eighteenth century was a golden age of travel writing.[2] In the middle decades of the century distinct kinds emerged, including scientific travels, aesthetic or picturesque travels, Enlightenment 'philosophical' travels and 'sentimental' travels; Wollstonecraft reviewed books in all these categories for the *Analytical*. Stylistically and discursively, travels were considered a branch of the *belles-lettres*, situated between the formal and learned and the personal and familiar. Travels also affected other kinds of writing, especially the novel. Novels increasingly contained factual travel descriptions and travels often adopted a partly fictitious narrative form. The classic travel novel, which Wollstonecraft knew and referred to in her *Letters* from Scandinavia, was Laurence Sterne's *A Sentimental Journey through France and Italy*. Ann Radcliffe's novels, which Wollstonecraft also knew, contain descriptions imitated from travel books. Travel description permeated such forms as the fictional narrative poem, often authenticated by footnotes.

This 'novelization' of travel writing was part of literary Sensibility, seen in foregrounded first-person narration, emphasis on the individuality of characters rather than outward description, description through the sensibility of the narrator and emphasis on common quotidian life rather than large political and social institutions. Various styles, modes or discourses may be combined in one text, making it dialogical; personal forms such as the letter or diary are used rather than the objective, 'philosophical' survey; and the structure is desultory rather than analytic. The novelization of travel writing opened it to other discourses in order to relativize, upset or even overturn distinctions and hierarchies found in earlier, aristocratic or scholarly travel writing. Since these hierarchies were perceived to be controlled by dominant upper-class culture, novelizing them was a subversive and revolutionary move, part of the *embourgeoisement* of travel writing and writing in general.

Letters from Scandinavia combines 'philosophical' and 'sentimental' travel writing in the same kind of cultural critique found in the two *Vindications* and *An Historical and Moral View of the . . . French Revolution*. Writing again as a woman (her name was on the title-page), in another genre and subject rarely ventured on by women, Wollstonecraft avoids the scientific, learned or 'philosophical' approaches that might be expected of men travellers. Yet she also avoids the merely personal, desultory, 'sentimental' approach of women travel writers such as Lady Anne Miller, Elizabeth Craven and Hester Piozzi (whose *Journey* Wollstonecraft had reviewed in the *Analytical*). Wollstonecraft's aim, again, is to write as that paradoxical, implicitly revolutionary and avant-garde being, the 'female philosopher', for reasons similar to those behind her adoption of this style in her *View* of the French Revolution: to give a textual representation of the exemplary 'mind' of a true revolutionary. Accordingly, *Letters* includes lyrical description, apostrophe, self-reflection, political disquisition, deictic expressions, anecdotes, autobiographical allusions, literary quotations, maxims and typographical devices of expressivity. As with Wollstonecraft's other works, modern readers have difficulty finding coherence in such a form. But as Mitzi Myers argues, 'far from being digressive or disorganized', *Letters* is a purposeful 'literary experiment, thematically unified and formally organized through a very personal version of associationism'.[3] As in her previous three works, Wollstonecraft uses style to exhibit a 'mind' both 'rational' and 'feeling', the 'mind' of a woman lacking a professional man's education yet capable of 'philosophizing'. *Letters* extends Revolutionary feminism to another discourse not considered the cultural property of women, further revolutionizing the professional middle-class revolution's institution of writing.

The prefatory 'Advertisement' affirms this programme, rejecting both the 'vanity' of the Grand Tourist or savant and the 'sensibility' of the picturesque or sentimental traveller. Wollstonecraft admits that in writing 'these desultory letters' she 'could not avoid being continually the first person', and that though the letters were written for publication, 'in proportion as I arranged my thoughts, my letter, I found, became stiff and affected: I, therefore, determined to let my remarks and reflections flow unrestrained, as I perceived that I could not give a just description of what I saw, but by relating the effect different objects had produced on my mind and feelings, whilst the impression was still fresh'. This is not an admission of 'sentimental' travelling but a claim to authenticity and philosophical purpose, rooted in her intellectual and affective individuality, her 'mind and feelings'. The text is 'about' the traveller rather than the travels, but textualizing of the self is not an end in itself.

For as Mary Poovey points out, Wollstonecraft emphasizes the relationship 'between herself as a particular subject and humanity in general'.[4] The self in the text validates the critique of a pre-revolutionary, provincial society corrupted by the same courtly culture represented as the root of social misery in the *Vindications* and *An Historical and Moral View of the . . . French Revolution*. But Wollstonecraft now emphasizes the debasing effect of commerce as well. This is hardly surprising, since she rarely left the coasts of Scandinavia, most of the people she met were involved in trade, and she herself was on a commercial mission arising from a dispute between business partners. In fact, she omits any direct reference to this mission; to do so would undermine the authority of her apparent detachment from the society she views, and lessen the 'philosophical' character of her observations. For *Letters* continues the closing theme of *An Historical and Moral View*, showing the economic base of the social and cultural superstructure in Scandinavia. Hitherto she had focused on upper-class dominance and lower-class subordination; she now turns to the professional middle-class's other rival for power, the commercial bourgeoisie. For Wollstonecraft, as for Richard Price, a society and state dominated by commerce are little better than those dominated by court government. But as in her three previous books, she sets social and economic determinism against progress from increased knowledge and understanding. This hope relies on the intellectual culture of the professional middle class themselves.

Her critique again encompasses both class and gender difference. For example, she illustrates the evils of court government by the fate of Queen Caroline Matilda, a wronged woman yet a rational mother and a public-spirited stateswoman. She was married to the mentally defective young King of Denmark, but fell under the spell of an ambitious professional man and courtier, Struensee, and became his mistress. They aroused court factions by premature attempts at reform, Struensee was overthrown and Caroline died in exile in 1775 at the age of 24. Caroline Matilda resembles predecessors such as Mary Queen of Scots, Christina of Sweden and even Marie Antoinette. But for Wollstonecraft her fate exemplifies the present condition of Denmark, as she exclaims: 'Poor Matilda! thou hast haunted me ever since my arrival; and the view I have had of the manners of the country, exciting my sympathy, has increased my respect for thy memory!'[5]

This 'view' shows that court government vitiates the rest of society, even in Denmark and Norway (then ruled by Denmark), as seen in the Norwegian estate of Herregaarden. This is the property of the count of Laurvig who, like many 'progressive' landed magnates in Britain, combines an agrarian estate economy with capitalist investment in resources such as iron and timber. Yet his effect on the local economy has been negative because he applied his financial power and court 'influence' to secure a local monopoly in the timber trade. This kind of economic practice, associated with court mercantilism and restriction on trade, was contrary to the doctrines of the '*économistes*' Wollstonecraft refers to at the end of her *View* of the French Revolution. Furthermore, the presence of the previous count of Laurvig introduced the courtly evil of social emulation into the nearby town, producing 'a degree of profligacy of manners which has been ruinous to the inhabitants in every respect' (p. 125).

Elsewhere in Norway class relations are dominated by the commercial class, but they do not yet have 'a sufficient monied interest to induce them to reinforce the upper class, at the expence of the yeomanry' (p. 149). For Wollstonecraft, the 'yeomanry' combine the best qualities of the common people and those of the middle classes, and are to be the foundation of civic liberty. But the rise of the commercial class will be as bad for the yeomanry as domination by the landed class. 'England and America owe their liberty to commerce', she writes, 'which created a new species of power to undermine the feudal system', just as in France during the Revolution of 1793. 'But', she warns, 'let them beware of the consequence; the tyranny of wealth is still more galling and debasing than that of rank' (p. 150). She hopes for a different outcome, invoking an Enlightenment model of the progress of civilization: a commercial society such as Norway is on the threshold of true civilization and may cross it thanks to the French Revolution (p. 103). This analysis implies that the narrator is at the stage the Norwegians may soon reach – a mature culture in possession of 'the arts and sciences', 'the grand virtues of the heart' and 'the enlarged humanity' that depend 'on the understanding'. Implicitly, too, the narrator must already possess whatever the French Revolution may effect, and be one of the revolutionary vanguard.

Wollstonecraft's critique of commercial society, as Richard Holmes notes, reaches a climax toward the end of her travels, at Hamburg.[6] The outports of Sweden and Norway are near the countryside, but Hamburg is a major European free port – a state dominated by the commercial bourgeoisie. Like other free towns, it is 'governed in a manner which bears hard on the poor, whilst narrowing the minds of the rich', and commercial competition, rather than invigorating the mind, demeans it (p. 190). Hamburg prospered from the Revolutionary wars, but 'the insolent vulgarity which a sudden influx of wealth usually produces in common minds' contrasts with the 'sentiments of honour and delicacy' and 'greatness of soul' of the French émigrés who sought refuge there (p. 191). Her preference for aristocratic émigrés over 'vulgar accumulators' seems reactionary but represents current professional middle-class opinion, turning away from an anti-court coalition with the commercial bourgeoisie toward gentrification through coalition with the landed classes.

She goes on to argue that both Hamburg and Revolutionary France have been depraved by the domination of commerce, which is worse than Revolutionary violence: 'The sword has been merciful, compared with the depredations made on human life by contractors, and by the swarm of locusts who have battened on the pestilence they spread abroad' (p. 195). She applies Enlightenment sociology of culture to explain the indifference of 'men of commerce' to Revolutionary ideals:

> An ostentatious display of wealth without elegance, and a greedy enjoyment of pleasure without sentiment, embrutes them till they term all virtue, of an heroic cast, romantic attempts at something above our nature; and anxiety about the welfare of others, a search after misery, in which we have no concern. But you will say that I am growing bitter, perhaps, personal. Ah! shall I whisper to you – that you – yourself, are strangely altered, since you have entered deeply into commerce. . . . (p. 191)

The reference to 'all virtue, of an heroic cast' being dismissed as 'romantic' echoes one of her letters to Imlay, while referring to a common way of dismissing Revolutionary optimism. The personal twist at the end of the passage may be a direct reference to Imlay; but it also signals the narrator's superiority to the debased culture she has just described, while authenticating that criticism by reference to her own experience and feelings. The personal and the public are inextricable.

The same sociological analysis explains domestic relations in the commercial bourgeoisie, for the 'mind' produced by commerce enforces both domestic and state tyranny. 'The men of business are domestic tyrants, coldly immersed in their own affairs'; as a result, the women 'are simply notable house-wives; without accomplishments, or any of the charms that adorn more advanced social life' (p. 165). This in turn makes them bad parents, spoiling their children and reproducing the same culture in the next generation, as she argued in her educational writings.

She accounts for gender relations in the lower ranks by the same economy. Thus 'the total want of chastity in the lower class of women' in Scandinavia is the product of social culture: 'The country girls of Ireland and Wales equally feel the first impulse of nature, which, restrained in England by fear or delicacy, proves that society is there in a more advanced state.' For when 'the mind is cultivated, and taste gains ground, the passions become stronger, and rest on something more stable than the casual sympathies of the moment' (p. 83). The fact that she makes such a claim implies that she herself knows the 'passions' strengthened by 'taste' into authentic female sexuality. She also attributes the different sexual conduct in city and country to cultural causes: 'The manners of Stockholm are refined, I hear, by the introduction of gallantry; but in the country, romping [boisterous frolic] and coarse freedoms, with coarser allusions, keep the spirits awake.' Her social psychology here is limited, ignoring the possibility that the 'promiscuous amours' of the lower classes may be a way to select a marriage partner by pre-marital pregnancy, when a subsistence economy makes children important assets.[7] Furthermore, her attitude to lower-class women shares the moralistic tone of middle-class social reformers such as Sarah Trimmer and Hannah More. Yet her sociological approach avoids much of the essentialism and the biologism in late eighteenth-century discussions of women's 'nature'.

As in *A Vindication of the Rights of Woman*, corrupt gender relations are attributed to court culture emulated by other classes, linking class and gender exploitation:

> I have every where been struck by one characteristic difference in the conduct of the two sexes; women, in general, are seduced by their superiors, and men jilted by their inferiors; rank and manners awe the one, and cunning and wantonness subjugate the other; ambition creeping into the woman's passion, and tyranny giving force to the man's; for most men treat their mistresses as kings do their favourites: *ergo* is not man then the tyrant of the creation? (p. 171)

Wollstonecraft then gives a doubly personal resonance to her point: 'Still harping on the same subject, you will exclaim – How can I avoid it, when most of the struggles of an eventful life have been occasioned by the oppressed state of my sex: we reason deeply, when we forcibly feel.' Experience is both the genesis and the validation of the text's Revolutionary feminism. This plot of developing revolutionary consciousness would be carried over into her next work, a Revolutionary feminist novel.

Wollstonecraft uses the personal in two major ways in *Letters*. Many readers would know her as the author of *A Vindication of the Rights of Woman*, thus strengthening her analysis of gender relations here. Her private identity as woman and mother is also manifested in the text. For example, she uses her child, who is not named and thus becomes representative of all daughters, to particularize her feminist motivation. On parting from her she writes:

You know that as a female I am particularly attached to her – I feel more than a mother's fondness and anxiety, when I reflect on the dependent and oppressed state of her sex. I dread lest she should be forced to sacrifice her heart to her principles, or principles to her heart. With trembling hand I shall cultivate sensibility, and cherish delicacy of sentiment, lest, whilst I lend fresh blushes to the rose, I sharpen the thorns that will wound the breast I would fain guard – I dread to unfold her mind, lest it should render her unfit for the world she is to inhabit – Hapless woman! what a fate is thine! (p. 97)

If the world is not fit for a daughter of 'sensibility' and 'mind', it cannot be fit for the mother able to 'cultivate' these in her daughter. If a daughter with 'sensibility' and 'mind' is likely to be wounded on the 'thorns', the mother must have been so wounded already. The passage claims the author's authority for treating gender difference and oppression as she does.

Letters does not treat the professional middle class itself in detail because they are not prominent in a pre-revolutionary society dominated by the commercial bourgeoisie on one hand and an absentee landed class on the other. As in France during the last years of the *ancien régime*, the professionals in Scandinavia are inevitably 'moulded' by their 'situation'. For example, lawyers take on the character of Scandinavian commercial society: 'The profession of the law renders a set of men still shrewder and more selfish than the rest; and it is these men, whose wits have been sharpened by knavery, who here undermine morality, confounding right and wrong' (p. 124). It was notorious that lawyers led the French Revolution, and Wollstonecraft may be alluding to this fact when she advocates replacing them with citizen mediators, for lawyers 'have, for a long time . . . set the people by the ears, and lived by the spoil they caught up in the scramble' (p. 124).

The proper leaders of society, she suggests, are professional intellectuals, who will be the revolutionary vanguard of Scandinavia because they are already sympathetic to the French Revolution. She reports meeting 'an intelligent literary man' whom she takes as representative of an international revolutionary class, for he 'was anxious to gather information from me, relative to the past and present situation of France'. Discussion of the Revolution is in fact 'confined to the few', professionals such as 'the clergy and physician, with a small portion of people who have a literary turn and leisure'. Thus Wollstonecraft is 'now more than ever convinced, that it is an intercourse with men of science and artists, which not only diffuses taste, but gives that freedom to the understanding, without which I have seldom met with much benevolence of character, on a large scale' (p. 141). By 'benevolence . . . on a large scale' she means the 'philanthropy' of Revolutionary slogans. 'Taste', 'freedom' of understanding and 'benevolence . . . on a large scale' are qualifications of the revolutionary élite because they indicate independence from both the courtly and commercial classes. The passage also indicates that the narrator herself has those qualifications.

Her treatment of the lower classes, however, shows the mixture of sympathy and condescension found in her earlier works and in other professional middle-class revolutionaries of the time. Though regarded as backward, the northern regions of Europe, like the northern regions of Britain, were then thought to be the home of simple rustic people whose way of life was not only authentic but the fount of the 'national' culture. The mixture of sympathy and condescension is presented in the first letter (p. 66). Later, in Sweden, she compares the lower classes favourably to the middle classes:

> I must own to you, that the lower class of people here amuse and interest me much more than the middling, with their apish good breeding and prejudices. The sympathy and frankness of heart conspicuous in the peasantry produces even a simple graceful-ness of deportment, which has frequently struck me as very picturesque. . . . (pp. 83–4)

This too is condescending, but the important point is that the lower classes, unlike the bourgeoisie, are as yet free from the social emulation ('apish good breeding and prejudices') that spreads court culture through the 'middling' class.

There are evils and inequalities in this northern Eden, such as the traditional curse of the lower classes, 'dram-drinking'. But Wollstonecraft understands the economic, social and even climatic and dietary causes of this 'vice' (p. 76). Later she broadens this analysis, defending the lower classes against the charge of being 'stupid', or insensitive, and attacking Enlightenment travel writers who are too quick to dismiss the 'primitive' peoples they en-counter: 'A people have been characterized as stupid by nature;

what a paradox! because they [the social critics] did not consider that slaves, having no object to stimulate industry, have not their faculties sharpened by the only thing that can exercise them, self-interest' (pp. 92–3). The argument from economic base to social and cultural superstructure is used here to plead for understanding of lower-class culture. She criticizes the use of religion for social control in England (p. 120) and shows an understanding of the 'moral economy' of the common people in 'rioting' when they feel there is an artificial shortage of provisions brought about by the greed of the grain merchants (p. 143). She finds the poor in various countries to be in much the same plight, and she criticizes charity as a form of social politics masking exploitation (p. 187), in the 1790s serving the charitable as what Roy Porter calls 'a prophylactic against, or an antidote to, mutinous grassroots stirrings'.[8]

Not surprisingly, then, she sees the better lower-class folk as a potential source of revolutionary social transformation. Having reached the point furthest north in her journey, she wishes to go further, 'not only because the country . . . is most romantic', but because what she has heard of the inhabitants 'carried me back to the fables of the golden age: independence and virtue; affluence without vice; cultivation of mind, without depravity of heart; with "ever smiling liberty", the nymph of the mountain' (pp. 148–9). Critiques of decadent court society, in cultural movements of primitivism and mediaevalism, idealized northern and mountain peoples, such as Highland Scots and the alpine Swiss, as lower-class folk imbued with middle-class values and culture.[9] Wollstonecraft transfers that political fantasy to Norway and claims it consoles her for both disillusionment with the common people elsewhere and her personal 'disappointments', again linking her destiny with that of the revolutionary age.

This link also offers hope, as she envisages a special role for herself in a revolutionary dialectic of common people and professional élite, or rather in the political use of the idea of the 'common people' in order to carry out a revolution against the 'privileged orders'.[10] The Revolutionary excess of the French has been blamed on their 'depravity', yet where, she asks, 'has more virtuous enthusiasm been displayed than during the two last years, by the common people of France and in their armies?'. She acknowledges the Revolutionary 'horrors' and 'vices', but concludes that they 'are the concomitants of ignorance' (p. 172). Therefore those best situated to draw out the 'virtuous enthusiasm' of the 'common people' and suppress their 'gross vices' would be the professional intellectual élite she describes in the text, and to which she herself obviously belongs. This analysis of class relations in *Letters* was not an academic exercise but addressed to the British crisis of class relations in the mid-1790s. Yet she herself is prepared with alternatives if this revolutionary coalition of people and professionals should not come about. Before the Revolutionary decade, the Sentimental culture of subjectivity, domesticity, transcendent nature and emotional religion was a response by professional middle-class revolutionaries to the apparently overwhelming dominance of the upper classes. After the Revolutionary violence of 1792 and the Jacobin *coup d'état* many cultural revolutionaries returned to these alternatives, reformulating them not as alternatives to revolutionary action but alternative, cultural forms of such action. *Letters* presents all these alternatives.

Subjectivity is foregrounded by the narrator's 'secret sorrow', which appears in the first paragraph of the first letter, hindering her ability to give her 'observations' (p. 7), and in later passages of lyrical, expressive intensity. Its source is love, conventional figure for the absolute self, beyond the merely social. For example, after a descriptive passage that prefigures the method of Wordsworth's 'Tintern Abbey', Wollstonecraft, or the narrative figure who stands for her in the text, goes on to a characteristic passage of Sentimental self-revelation, marked by broken sentences and dashes:

– I must love and admire with warmth, or I sink into sadness. Tokens of love which I have received have rapt me in elysium – purifying the heart they enchanted. – My bosom still glows. – Do not saucily ask, repeating Sterne's question, 'Maria, is it still so warm?' Sufficiently, O my God! has it been chilled by sorrow and unkindness – still nature will prevail – and if I blush at recollecting past enjoyment, it is the rosy hue of pleasure heightened by modesty; for the blush of modesty and shame are as distinct as the emotions by which they are produced.   (p. 111)

This seems sentimental, but it is more complex and original than it looks. She revives the hackneyed image of the 'glowing bosom' by insisting delicately on both the blushing appearance and the physical warmth of a 'glowing' bosom in the half-joking reference to Sterne, a joke made in any case as if by her correspondent. The similarity of 'Mary' (Wollstonecraft) and 'Maria' reinforces the reference. In Sterne's *Sentimental Journey* Yorick meets Maria, a young woman half-crazed by disappointed love. Affected by her story, he soaks his handkerchief with tears, and when she offers to wash it in a nearby stream he asks where she will dry it. She replies, in her bosom, and he asks: 'And is your heart still so warm, Maria?' The near-absurdity of this episode helped make Sterne's travel novel notorious, but the episode dramatizes an important philosophical point – the relation of mind and body, including erotic desire and sexual pleasure. Wollstonecraft's use of the episode indicates that her 'glowing' bosom and the 'blush at recollecting past enjoyment' refer to both her own sexual desire and the blushing afterglow of sexual pleasure. But lest this suggestion dominate the passage and vulgarize it in the eyes of her readers, she makes it conditional with an 'if' and quickly sweeps on to a philosophical reflection about the difference between modesty and shame.

The narrator's taste for the domestic affections is another aspect of her rich subjectivity. In the first letter, for example, she turns from her 'secret sorrow' and social disappointment: 'Some recollections, attached to the idea of home, mingled with reflections respecting the state of society I had been contemplating that evening', while 'emotions that trembled on the brink of extacy and agony gave a poignancy to my sensations, which made me feel more alive than usual' (p. 69). Domestic disappointment afflicts her, but domestic affections are an anodyne for the melancholy bitterness aroused by contemplating the wider social scene. Later she links her domestic disappointments to the state of society:

> How illusive, perhaps the most so, are the plans of happiness founded on virtue and principle; what inlets of misery do they not open in a half civilized society? The satisfaction arising from conscious rectitude, will not calm an injured heart, when tenderness is ever finding excuses; and self-applause is a cold solitary feeling, that cannot supply the place of disappointed affection. . . . (pp. 135–6)

The consciousness of belonging to the revolutionary vanguard ('virtue and principle', 'conscious rectitude') may not compensate for disappointment of the domestic affections, including sexual desire, in an unrevolutionized ('half civilized') society.

She can turn to nature, however, for in the natural sublime she finds validation of her revolutionary self and hope that general misery and the failure of her own domestic relations will be repaired by revolutionary transformation of society. In the first letter, for example, she contemplates nature:

> I gazed around with rapture, and felt more of that spontaneous pleasure which gives credibility to our expectation of happiness, than I had for a long, long time before. I forgot the horrors I had witnessed in France, which had cast a gloom over all nature, and suffering the enthusiasm of my character, too often, gracious God! damped by the tears of disappointed affection, to be lighted up afresh, care took wing while simple fellow feeling expanded my heart.   (pp. 67–8)

Nature overcomes social disillusionment and 'disappointed [domestic] affection' to produce general social sympathy experienced as plenitude of self.[11] Indeed, the self constructed by sublime nature must sicken at the imperfection of society, and thus becomes a potential revolutionary (p. 99). For Wollstonecraft, as for Wordsworth during the mid-1790s, love of nature leads to human love, both individual and general; but society disappoints while nature does not.

Nature also constructs the revolutionary by inspiring paradisal visions. When the narrator is lulled asleep by nature's beauties, for example:

> Light slumbers produced dreams, where Paradise was before me. My little cherub was again hiding her face in my bosom. . . . New-born hopes seemed, like the rainbow, to appear in the clouds of sorrow, faint, yet sufficient to amuse away despair. (p. 127)

The vision is given a 'philosophical', physiological basis, in the way 'light slumbers' produce dreams, while the association of Paradise with the rainbow evokes the archetypal cycle of human history, from the Fall and Expulsion from Paradise to the Flood and rainbow of promise. But the archetype is particularized in both the fate of the narrator and her daughter ('my cherub') and the cycle of the Revolution.

Nature is assigned a role both 'philosophical' and religious in construction of the individual, for Wollstonecraft goes beyond the familiar argument that nature is, with Scripture, God's book. She takes a materialist line: 'the beauties of nature' are pleasures of the senses, and 'If we wish to render mankind moral from principle, we must . . . give a greater scope to the enjoyments of the senses, by blending taste with them' (p. 147). Thus nature is part of a divine plan that includes human progress. Since she has already suggested that 'progress' means something like the ideal programme of the French Revolution, nature is hereby incorporated into her divinely sanctioned revolutionary project. Elsewhere, however, she makes sublime nature an alternative to such projects. Her visit to a waterfall, prime site of sublime nature for Sentimental and Romantic tourists, is described with intermingled immediacy and reflectiveness that again prefigure Wordsworth (pp. 152–3). But the passage shows Wollstonecraft divided between three different images of 'nature': as refuge from a society inevitably hostile to sensibility; as the standard for constructing a state that will in turn construct mankind according to 'nature'; and as the transcendental sublime in a culture pretending to turn away from social experiments such as the French Revolution, but in fact using 'nature' as a trope in the rhetoric of cultural revolution.

The economy comprising nature, self, text and society is central to both the argument and the rhetoric of *Letters*. Like other transcendental signifieds such as God or 'History', 'Nature' addresses the individual across the merely temporal and relative domain of the social, thereby transcendentalizing the individual. Like later Romantic writers, Wollstonecraft suggests that if nature successfully addresses enough individuals in this way then society itself will be naturalized and its relativities cured. Thus nature can revolutionize both the individual and society. The author able to represent this process in herself is self-evidently naturalized and revolutionized already. She re-presents nature in a secondary address – writing, which is now another transcendental signifier. Henceforth revolution will take place through writing and reading.

'To naturalize' means 'to bring into conformity with nature; to free from conventionality', and convention is the domain of the social and cultural. But this is the secondary sense of 'naturalize'. The primary sense is 'to put on a level with what is native', and even 'to invest an alien with the privileges of a native-born subject'. The narrator of *Letters* puts herself on a level with what is native in Scandinavia, while remaining alien and, by implication, superior. Her superiority is seen to depend on her naturalization in the secondary sense, her 'conformity with nature', her freedom from 'conventionality' and thus from the custom and culture that narrow the vision and obstruct the self-understanding of the natives. The narrator's relationship with what is native is parallel to that of the 'enlightened', progressive, revolutionary intellectual with his or her own society and culture. *Letters* exemplifies the revolutionary 'mind' as one that is naturalized.

It does so with formal devices she had used before, for different rhetorical occasions, but generally seen at the time as natural, spontaneous and authentic – a personal range of allusion and reference, footnotes that are personal comments, lyrical and expressive passages, autobiographical references, frequent apostrophes, sentimental description, informal epistolary form and self-conscious digression with such phrases as 'But I have rambled away again . . .'. Most important is the desultory movement of the prose – always Wollstonecraft's stylistic forte – from one phrase, sentence, paragraph, passage and letter to the next, turning from brisk narrative, to sentimental description, to apostrophe, to self-reflection, to firm statement (often as a maxim), to quotation and so on. The text supposedly represents the movement of the author's mind immediately, although a re-presentation that is immediate – that is, unmediated – is a paradox. This is a version of the style of 'genius' that Wollstonecraft had already practised in different ways for various ends.

She characterizes the 'mind' of her narrator from the outset as rational and 'sensible', practical and susceptible, relishing the 'picturesque' and the sublime yet determined in action, especially for a woman (as the contrast with her servant Marguerite in the first letter shows), able to 'read' both the landscape and the people and to account for the ways of the latter in terms of Enlightenment social psychology. It is a mind responsive to its circumambient natural and social worlds, yet able to analyse its own responses and responsiveness – the mind of a 'female philosopher'. But at times the 'woman' is more to the fore; at times it is more the 'philosopher'. This purposive tension represents the difficulty of being both a woman and a philosopher in a pre-revolutionary society.

The dialogue of woman and philosopher is played out through a text that is open yet represents an individual 'mind' or 'genius'. All of Wollstonecraft's texts, but especially those of the 1790s, are open in this way, as part of their textual politics, undermining established generic, discursive and formal practices, though at the risk of seeming merely ignorant of them (as many contemporary reviewers and later critics thought). *Letters* departs from this politics of open form in one significant respect, however. It closes as its three predecessors do, with the affirmation of revolutionary optimism, but in a way that indicates ambivalence and perhaps the disintegration of the 'female philosopher' – the prefiguratively revolutionary, personally validated union of 'head' and 'heart', reason and sensibility, philosophy and feeling, 'masculine' and 'feminine' discourse.

Ominously, the last letter, from Altona near Hamburg, begins by announcing a diversion. The narrator will not go on through Germany to Switzerland as intended – not just because the Revolution itself, or its armies, block her way, but because her will, her revolutionary desire, has failed: 'I do not feel inclined to ramble any farther this year; nay, I am weary of changing the scene, and quitting people and places the moment they begin to interest me. – This also is vanity!' (p. 197). 'Vanity' here has the root meaning Wollstonecraft often gives it: not only self-conceit but futility and emptiness. The plenitude of self, the display of which lends rhetorical authority to the politics of *Letters*, is apparently running out, for personal as well as political reasons. This last letter is not even completed; it breaks off and is resumed from Dover and England, which are a complete contrast to the heroic sublimities and paradisal simplicity found in Scandinavia. She writes, 'at the sight of Dover cliffs, I wondered how any body could term them grand; they appear so insignificant to me, after those I had seen in Sweden and Norway'. She closes the letter:

> Adieu! My spirit of observation seems to be fled – and I have been wandering round this dirty place, literally speaking, to kill time; though the thoughts, I would fain fly from, lie too close to my heart to be easily shook off, or even beguiled, by any employment, except that of preparing for my journey to London. – God bless you!
>
> MARY ——

The journey and all it represents are abandoned, apparently because her secret sorrow, alluded to in the first paragraph of the first letter and struggled with from time to time throughout the text, is now overwhelming. Mitzi Myers argues that Wollstonecraft's travels 'constitute a metaphoric as well as an actual journey' – 'an evolution toward maturation . . . uniting masculine concerns', such as politics and progress, 'with female needs', such as love and domesticity.[12] But from the last letter it might seem that the journey leads to disintegration, and the prefiguratively revolutionary female philosopher turns out to be more a woman – or a mere woman – after all.

This impression seems to be confirmed by the book's 'Appendix', the last part of *Letters*. (In fact, the Appendix is not the end of *Letters* either: there are 'Author's Supplementary Notes' giving facts and figures on Norway's size, shape, population, trade, economy, armed forces and taxes.) The Appendix is like the postscript of a letter – conventionally supposed to convey the real message. If so, this Appendix is paradoxical, both an apology and an affirmation. It begins with the narrator's confession that 'private business and cares' prevented her from gathering all the information she should have. She deplores this 'insensibility to present objects' because 'a person of any thought' wishes to compare the past with the present state of manners, and would conclude as she has that the 'knowledge and happiness' of the lands she visited are 'increasing', 'and the gigantic evils of despotism and anarchy have in a great measure vanished before the meliorating manners of Europe' (p. 198). A true revolution is emerging between the alternatives of 'depotism', or monarchic court government, and premature revolution, or 'anarchy', but this revolution 'must be the growth of each particular soil, and the gradual fruit of the ripening understanding of the nation' – that is, it must be native and natural. Nature the transcendental signified, rather than the revolutionary actions of men and women, will bring about the paradisal vision glimpsed in the early Revolution and in Scandinavia.

Nevertheless, the Appendix, though apologetic, ends as a revolutionary affirmation rooted in the personal experience and thus the authority of the narrator. The apparent conclusion of the text, the last letter, seems to be a false conclusion; but it is recontextualized, not cancelled, by the Appendix. If the text ended with the last letter the reader could conclude that the prefiguratively revolutionary female philosopher had disintegrated, retaken by the very social divisions – particularly divisions of gender – that *Letters* criticizes as part of the old order. But in spite of the Appendix's apology, it reaffirms, however hesitantly, the 'female philosopher's' confidence – or hope – that the divided social order that seemed to have retaken her in the last letter is after all passing away, and will leave her and humanity free at last.

Letters was well received by reviewers, who praised its personal yet philosophical and even 'political' outlook, though some found it over-written, with the usual 'feminine' stylistic defects of extravagance, disorder and incorrectness. Most other readers also found the book moving yet philosophical, though it did not, as Wollstonecraft probably hoped it would, reinspire Imlay with love for her as a 'female philosopher', superior to the mere courtly amorousness of his other women. Yet its exhibition of her 'mind' as that of a woman and philosopher, in the revolutionary vanguard, does seem to have inspired that feeling in other men, themselves in the vanguard of the cultural revolution. These included Thomas Holcroft and William Godwin, leaders of the 'English Jacobins', as well as young radicals and Romantics.

Referring to *Letters*, Robert Southey looked back on Wollstonecraft after her death as 'her / Who among women left no equal mind / When from this world she pass'd'.[13] Some had their image of her as the Amazonian vindicator of the rights of woman suddenly transformed, such as a writer ('L. M.') in the New York *Monthly Magazine*:

> I saw her there the child of nature and the sport of feeling: yet, like a lovely infant smiling through its tears, changing alternately from anguish to delight; for in the midst of gloom her exquisite genius darted ever and anew, like sunshine on her mind, through the crevices of the clouds which hung upon it. I saw her there reasoning and philosophizing with all the powers and the skill of a rational being, yet secretly preyed upon by circumstances which her reflections on the vicissitudes of life might have taught her to expect, and her firmness of mind should have prepared her to encounter. (vol. 1, August 1799, pp. 330–1)

Yet in such responses is already seen the impression of Wollstonecraft too much the woman for her own good and the good of her 'philosophy'.

Indeed, the editors of the *Monthly Mirror* were moved by the book to enquire into Wollstonecraft's private life, because 'public opinion is sometimes guided, and often confirmed by the private conduct of the most eminent literary characters' (vol. 1, January

1796, p. 132). Not surprisingly, the *Monthly Mirror*'s review of *Letters* was one of the few to be mainly unfavourable. After Wollstonecraft's death and the revelations of Godwin's *Memoirs* about her private life, *Letters* from Scandinavia could be read more conclusively as an exhibition of the 'mind' and 'private conduct' that vitiated her feminism. The Professor of Moral Philosophy at Edinburgh University could even turn the *Letters* into a moralistic narrative poem illustrating the dangers of a woman, even one with 'a mind of no common order', indulging in passion.[14] *Letters* was in fact the beginning of the breakdown of Wollstonecraft's attempt to fashion her career into the public figure of 'female philosopher' validating and anticipating the triumph of her Revolutionary feminism, though the breakdown was due to Revolutionary circumstances beyond her control.

8

Love, Marriage and the Wrongs of Woman

In the winter of 1795–6 Wollstonecraft faced social ostracism as a single woman with a child. She faced the possibility of public vilification, as reaction against the French Revolution was being orchestrated into an attack on radical wings of the professional cultural revolution in Britain, including advocates of the rights of women. She also faced the immediate task of recommencing her career. In January 1796 she wrote to the Irish revolutionary Archibald Hamilton Rowan, then in the United States: 'I live, but for my child – for I am weary of myself.' But she had resumed her professional career: 'now I am writing for independence' (*Letters*, p. 328). In a postscript she noted that the political reaction in England might make things more difficult for her – 'The state of public affairs here are not in a posture to assuage private sorrow.'

Joseph Johnson tried to help out by encouraging a marriage proposal from someone who may have become infatuated with the textual figure of Wollstonecraft in *Letters* from Scandinavia. The man in question might have been Thomas Holcroft, self-educated playwright and novelist, self-styled 'philosopher' and a leader of the intellectual wing of the 'English Jacobins'. An unsigned letter of early January 1796 to Wollstonecraft offers a vision of avant-garde revolutionary conjugality that would have been characteristic of him and corresponds to the plea for such conjugality in *Letters*. But the writer doubts his ability to make her happy, especially since her heart is 'irrevocably given to another'. These doubts then give way to erotic yet philosophical fancies; he wishes to fall on her 'bosom and there dissolve in bliss such as I have never known', and urges her to 'try if this Lover's Millenium may not yet be ours'.[1] In these suggestions Wollstonecraft would see courtly libertinism masquerading as revolutionary vanguardism of a kind she had seen already in Paris and experienced to her cost with Imlay. Not surprisingly she rejected the offer with indignation (*Letters*, p. 327).

It was not Holcroft, but his friend William Godwin who turned out to be Wollstonecraft's new partner in revolutionary domesticity. Godwin was a product of the English Nonconformist Enlightenment, but in the early 1790s he worked out a system of philosophical anarchism with Holcroft, which he published in 1793 as *An Enquiry Concerning Political Justice*.[2] It caused a sensation, especially among younger professional middle-class cultural revolutionaries. Though a contribution to the French Revolution debate, it was a full-scale philosophical treatise, combining materialist epistemology, sociology and political philosophy from the English, Scottish and French Enlightenments, and arguing that material and social circumstances form the character of an individual and a society by process of 'necessity'. This determinism seems to leave no room for the will, but Godwin insists that humanity is not only improvable but 'perfectible' by 'the spread of truth' through print and free rational discussion. 'Political justice' would be achieved by applying reason to every act according to principles of justice and utility. In a passage from *Political Justice* that became infamous, Godwin argued that if he could rescue either the philosopher Fénelon or some personal relation from a fire, he ought to rescue Fénelon because the philosopher would be of more benefit to humanity. Like religion, property and other social institutions, the domestic affections are 'prejudices' that impede 'political justice'.

Wollstonecraft would not agree, but *Political Justice*, like her writings, was part of the critique of court culture in the 1790s, and Godwin, like Wollstonecraft, refounds social relations on individual being constituted as professional intellectual practices, labelled 'reason', and bourgeois ethical values, labelled 'benevolence' or 'virtue'. When Godwin and Wollstonecraft met at Mary Hays's for tea in January 1796 he was already modifying *Political Justice*. The social and political crisis of Britain in late 1793 and early 1794 persuaded him that demand for 'rights' and 'justice' could implicate oppressed and oppressor in the same chain of error and guilt. He toned down the second edition of *Political Justice* (1796), making it less political and more philosophical, and softened controversial passages such as his condemnation of marriage.

Hays later claimed that she was matchmaking when she invited Godwin to tea with Wollstonecraft and Holcroft.[3] The meeting was friendly though not intimate; Godwin felt 'sympathy in her anguish, added . . . to the respect I had always entertained for her talents'.[4] In fact he was interested in several other women at the time, but in

late January and early February he read the recently published
Letters from Scandinavia. He found it lacked the 'occasional harshness and ruggedness' of *A Vindication of the Rights of Woman* and,
like other politically 'advanced' men, found it deeply moving.
Later he wrote: 'If ever there was a book calculated to make a man
in love with its author, this appears to me to be the book' (*Memoirs*,
p. 249). Meanwhile Wollstonecraft was finally breaking away from
Imlay. She went to visit her friend Mrs Cotton in Berkshire for
most of March, and letters from Imlay finally convinced her all was
over. When she accidentally met him again in April the encounter
passed 'without producing in her any oppressive emotion' (*Memoirs*,
p. 254).

She called on Godwin herself on 14 April, 'a deviation from
etiquette' that impressed him; 'but', he wrote, 'she had through
life trampled on those rules which are built on the assumption of
the imbecility of her sex; and had trusted to the clearness of her
spirit for the direction of her conduct, and to the integrity of her
views for the vindication of her character'. Their egalitarian 'intimacy' grew gradually:

> The partiality we conceived for each other, was in that mode,
> which I have always regarded as the purest and most refined
> style of love. It grew with equal advances in the mind of each. It
> would have been impossible for the most minute observer to
> have said who was before, and who was after. One sex did not
> take the priority which long-established custom has awarded it,
> nor the other overstep that delicacy which is so severely im-
> posed. I am not conscious that either party can assume to have
> been the agent or the patient, the toil-spreader or the prey, in the
> affair. (*Memoirs*, p. 257)

Even so, in May Wollstonecraft was still feeling betrayed and
thinking of leaving England, perhaps for Switzerland or Italy
(*Letters*, p. 330). But on 1 July she sent Godwin a flirtatious yet
philosophical letter with the last volume of Rousseau's *La nouvelle
Héloïse*, a novel that would figure in the plot of the feminist novel
she herself was beginning to write.

Godwin left for his annual visit to family and friends in East
Anglia, but the separation brought him and Wollstonecraft closer,
and when they met again they felt 'a more decisive preference for
each other'. As Godwin wrote: 'It was friendship melting into love'

(*Memoirs*, p. 258). Three weeks later on 16 August there was a mutual confession of love, and perhaps an attempt at love-making. Godwin was inexperienced and either suffered temporary impotence or shocked Wollstonecraft with his impetuousness, leaving her confused and remorseful. Casting him as the 'philosopher' and herself as the Rousseauist victim of sensibility, she wrote: 'Consider what has passed as a fever of your imagination; one of the slight mortal shakes to which you are liable – and I – will become again a *Solitary Walker*' (*Letters*, p. 337). Godwin replied: 'I was not aware that the fervour of my imagination was exhausting itself', urged her not to become a 'solitary walker' or let her 'feelings of nature' tyrannize over her, and hoped that in time he would be 'completely happy' – a conventional euphemism for achieving sexual union.[5] They became lovers on 21 August, but kept the affair secret and continued to work apart and see their friends separately. Godwin also became attached to little Fanny, who called him 'Man'.

Though Wollstonecraft still passed as 'Mrs Imlay' she was free to marry Godwin, but he later explained philosophically that 'nothing can be so ridiculous upon the face of it, or so contrary to the genuine march of sentiment, as to require the overflowing of the soul to wait upon a ceremony' (*Memoirs*, p. 258).[6] Both had published criticism of marriage as an institution subjecting women, their children and their property to patriarchal control. Not marrying was for them a gesture of political vanguardism, though Wollstonecraft was also in debt and marrying Godwin would have made him liable. But she now had to be more concerned about pregnancy than in the heady days of Revolutionary love in the summer of 1793. Godwin responded as a philosopher and feminist, taking responsibility by exercising self-control and calculating when love-making would be safe for her.[7]

It was a struggle to keep up their intimacy while maintaining secrecy, avoiding pregnancy, continuing their writing and coping with the distractions of everyday life. In September Fanny was ill with chicken-pox; in October Wollstonecraft had Mrs Cotton to stay; in November both Godwin and Wollstonecraft were ill. In addition, Wollstonecraft found her lover's philosophical earnestness sometimes overbearing, sometimes charming; Godwin found her enthusiasm, sensitivity and spontaneity sometimes exasperating, but usually engaging and often instructive. She teased him about being too much the philosopher, and when their rhythm

method of contraception made love-making risky, she reminded
him that their visit must consist of *'rien que philosophie'* (*Letters*,
p. 355). But she also conceded that her work might be improved by
more careful study, greater attention to standard English and more
conscious artistry.

Set against this was their mutual desire. She was more forthright
about this than he was. In September she wrote playfully:

> Now by these presents let me assure you that you are not only in
> my heart, but my veins, this morning. I turn from you half
> abashed – yet you haunt me, and some look, word or touch
> thrills through my whole frame. . . .
> When the heart and reason accord there is no flying from
> voluptuous sensations, I find, do what a woman can – Can a
> philosopher do more? (pp. 349–50)

Her sexual pleasure with Godwin equalled that with Imlay, but
differed in Godwin's being indeed a 'philosopher'. When she read
his essays (later published as *The Enquirer*) in October they made
her love and desire him more:

> I should have liked to have dined with you to day, after finishing
> your essay – that my eyes, and lips, I do not exactly mean my
> voice, might have told you that they [the essays] had raised you
> in my *esteem*. What a cold word! I would say love, if you will
> promise not to dispute about its propriety, when I want to
> express an increasing affection, founded on a more intimate
> acquaintance with your heart and understanding.

The thought of the author being her lover gives her 'voluptuous'
sensations, which she goes on to define philosophically:

> I would describe one of those moments, when the senses are
> exactly tuned by the rising tenderness of the heart, and accord-
> ing reason entices you to live in the present moment, regardless
> of the past or future – It is not rapture. – It is a sublime
> tranquillity. I have felt it in your arms – (pp. 356–7)

Shortly afterward she became pregnant.[8] This might expose her
to social ostracism, and childbirth was perilous for any woman –
more so for one 37 years old. But she resolved to take the burden

herself, writing to Godwin on 31 December: 'I can abide by the consequence of my own conduct, and do not wish to envolve any one in my difficulties' (p. 372).

She was depressed and sick, and even found the requirements of women's dress to be oppressive. When it snowed on 12 January she doubted she could keep her appointment with Godwin: 'But you have no petticoats to dangle in the snow. Poor Women how they are beset with plagues – within – and without' (p. 374). She blamed Godwin's 'philosophy' for making him over-confident in his system of birth control at her expense, and wrote: 'Women are certainly great fools; but nature made them so' (p. 377). In February she recovered health and spirits, though still worried about money. On 22 March she wrote to Everina: 'My pecuniary distress I know arises from myself – or rather from my not having had the power of employing my mind and fancy, when my soul was on the rack' (p. 384). Yet she preferred 'the solitude of my fire side' to the company of merely fashionable females at Everina's new employer's, Josiah Wedgwood.

On 29 March Godwin and Wollstonecraft were married quietly in St Pancras church. Godwin admitted that they did so on practical, even political grounds: 'She was unwilling, and perhaps with reason, to incur that exclusion from the society of many valuable and excellent individuals, which custom awards in cases of this sort'; besides, 'after the experiment of seven months' of intimacy 'there was certainly less hazard to either' of them 'in the subjecting ourselves to those consequences which the laws of England annex to the relations of husband and wife' (*Memoirs*, pp. 259–60). On 6 April they moved into common lodgings, and he explained matters to his friends and hers. He had some difficulty reconciling marriage with his past principles, especially to disciples and financial supporters such as Tom Wedgwood. Their marriage also revealed that she had not been married to Imlay, and several friends, including Elizabeth Inchbald and Sarah Siddons, dropped her, a rejection that Godwin tied to the persistence of courtly values in society. Nevertheless, marriage benefited her immediately, for as Godwin put it, 'She was a worshipper of domestic life' (*Memoirs*, p. 262). There were petty difficulties: in April she complained to him about 'the state of the sink' and his laxness in seeing to repairs and dealing with tradespeople. But they arranged their lives in accordance with their principles as cultural revolutionaries, so each had a distinct if overlapping professional life, circle of friends, interests, pursuits and even working space (Godwin rented a study down the street from their lodgings). Above all, they kept up their respective 'literary pursuits'.

Wollstonecraft had been working on 'a series of books for the instruction of children' at the time of her suicide attempt in October 1795. One of these was completed as 'The first book of a series which I intended to have written for my unfortunate girl', and Godwin published it with Wollstonecraft's *Posthumous Works* in 1798. It resembles Anna Laetitia Barbauld's *Lessons for Children* (1778–88), a series of moral tales for children of two to four years old. Wollstonecraft's 'Lessons' are designed to come before the first of Barbauld's books; they take a child through a structured acquisition of language, from a series of nouns (Lesson I); verbs, times of the day, qualities and numbers (II); simple subject–verb–object sentences describing domestic life (III); more complex statements, often implying a dialogue with the child and representing domestic relationships (IV and V); connected explanations of situations and relationships, often implying or stating a moral (VI to X); and moralistic accounts and explanations of social relationships and responsibilities based on bourgeois domesticity and social leadership (XI to XIII). There is a final lesson, which assures the child that she knows 'how to think', as illustrated by some domestic incidents.[9] Though a slight work, 'Lessons' shows Wollstonecraft's idea of how the self and social relations are constructed in and through the structure of language.

Wollstonecraft resumed her 'literary pursuits' when she abandoned hope of reconciliation with Imlay. She wrote 'the sketch of a comedy' – probably what would have been called then a 'sentimental comedy' or serious play with a happy ending. According to Godwin, the play turned 'upon the incidents of her own story', and it was finished enough to be offered to the managers of Drury Lane and Covent Garden theatres (*Memoirs*, p. 255). From this account of the work it would seem to have been a version of the story that was soon turned into her feminist novel. She planned 'a series of seven *Letters on the Management of Infants*', the surviving fragment of which addresses the high rate of infant mortality – as high as one in three – through educating women to abandon traditional customs.[10] In Rousseauist vein she calls for a return to 'simplicity', invokes the professional authority of 'physicians', and appeals to the middle classes: 'My advice will probably be found most useful to mothers in the middle class; and it is from them that the lower imperceptibly gains improvement.' The middle classes are open to reason, whereas the lower classes can only learn by 'imitation'. A table of contents for the projected book shows it was to cover 'management of the mother during pregnancy', childbirth and the first two years of the child's life.

In April 1797 she published an essay 'On Poetry, and Our Relish for the Beauties of Nature' in the *Monthly Magazine*.[11] This periodical was closely associated with the English Nonconformist Enlightenment and had published essays on the novel and politics of culture by Mary Hays and others whom Wollstonecraft knew. Godwin was writing essays of a similar kind, eventually published in 1798 as *The Enquirer*, popularizing the arguments of *Political Justice* as Hume had popularized his *Treatise of Human Nature* in essays. Wollstonecraft's essay shows her moving in a similar direction, to disseminate her ideas on the politics of culture to a wider readership and add another dimension to her literary career and her professional income. Situated now in a loose network of politically and intellectually avant-garde writers and artists, she may have been planning to move her Revolutionary feminism into wide-ranging cultural criticism. Her essay on poetry is partly a restatement of her theory of primitivism and progress, recently set forth piecemeal in *Letters* from Scandinavia, and partly a response to continuing discussions with Godwin and others on the relation of reason and imagination, 'philosophy' and 'genius'.

The essay restates commonplaces of the bourgeois critique of court culture, coincides with certain ideas of the young Romantic poets and anticipates the preface to *Lyrical Ballads*. Wollstonecraft attacks the contemporary enthusiasm for nature as mere cultural emulation rather than authentic personal and subjective response. She then argues that 'the poetry written in the infancy of society, is most natural' because it is 'the transcript of immediate sensations', and unmediated by 'civilization'. Similarly, the best modern poets are untainted by emulation, relying instead on 'genius' – 'only another word for exquisite sensibility'. This enables the poet to respond directly to 'nature' and build up stores 'within', so that his poetry 'gives us only an image of his mind, when he was actually alone, conversing with himself'. By contrast, 'gross minds are only to be moved by forcible representations': 'It is not within that they seek amusement; their eyes are seldom turned on themselves. . . .' This is 'why the beauties of nature are not forcibly felt, when civilization, or rather luxury, has made considerable advances'. The essay warns that 'sensibility' is an ambiguous gift, as liable to make a 'libertine' as a 'genius', but concludes that contentment, if not happiness, is to be found in the domestic affections if they are based on 'sensibility' and not 'civilization, or rather luxury'.

Wollstonecraft was also compiling a collection of maxims on a variety of subjects, later published by Godwin as 'Hints, Chiefly designed to have been incorporated in the Second Part of the *Vindication of the Rights of Woman*'.[12] But they seem to have been written over some years and not all deal with the condition of women. Taken together they suggest the broad cultural critique that was the basis for all her books, and they are the kind of maxims Wollstonecraft used to anchor descriptive, discursive, expressive or argumentative passages in her writing. Furthermore, such aphorisms were considered appropriate to subjects unsuited for systematic treatment, and were also considered a characteristic device of the 'genius'. 'Hints' is the kind of collection kept by many intellectuals, artists and writers of the time, including Fuseli, as Wollstonecraft would have known, and could as easily have been published separately as 'incorporated' into a sequel to *A Vindication of the Rights of Woman*. She may also have been building up a collection of observations to be used in essays such as the one on modern poetry in the *Monthly Magazine*.

But according to Godwin, 'the principal work, in which she was engaged for more than twelve months before her decease, was a novel, entitled, *The Wrongs of Woman*'. Even her work for the *Analytical*, which paid her household bills, was directed to this major project. She managed the fiction section of the *Analytical* and increased the length and quality of reviews, getting friends such as Hays and Godwin to review novels. She herself reviewed almost nothing but fiction, in order to help herself to become a better novelist. The ideological and cultural role of the novel was a major theme in her feminism, and the title of her new work indicates its relationship to *A Vindication of the Rights of Woman*. On the other hand, the relation between the *Vindication* and the English novel had been noted in a review of *Robert and Adela; or, The Rights of Women Best Maintained by the Sentiments of Nature* in the September 1795 *Analytical Review*. The reviewer claimed that *A Vindication* was not popular with novelists because, 'Were the doctrines of that work to become prevalent, and the female mind universally braced up to the tone of vigour which they are adapted to produce, where would be found women with nerves sufficiently relaxed to write, or to read, soft sentimental tales?' (p. 285). *Maria; or, The Wrongs of Woman* was designed to fulfil this potential by converting this despised, merely 'feminine' genre into another vehicle for Revolutionary feminism.

Wollstonecraft reviewed for the *Analytical* from March 1796 to May 1797 and covered major novelists of the time, including Mary Robinson, Elizabeth Inchbald, Frances Burney, Robert Bage, M. G. Lewis, Dr John Moore, Ann Radcliffe and Charlotte Smith, the first two of whom were known to her personally. She also read and commented privately on novels she gave others to review. Her own reviews show her gradually sharpening her critical language while applying her own idea of what a good novel should be. It should evince its author's 'mind', depict the 'passions' with psychological realism, have realistic characters and situations and a tight plot, and be carefully written according to its particular rhetorical objective. She insists on high artistic standards because of the ideological, cultural and political power of the novel. A review that may be hers notes: 'It was said by Rousseau, that to a refined and sensible people instruction can be offered only in the form of a novel, and it is certain, that in the present age – "Sermons are less read than tales"' (September 1796, p. 315).

She also raises points relevant to her own novel. For example, 'M. I.' (Mary Imlay) praises Mary Robinson's *Angelina* for showing a heroine who is 'an assemblage of almost every excellence which can adorn the female mind, beaming mildly through clouds of affliction and melancholy' and for revealing the character of the author, breathing 'a spirit of independence, and a dignified superiority to whatever is unessential to the true respectability and genuine excellence of human beings' (March 1796). 'M.'s' review of Elizabeth Inchbald's *Nature and Art* (May 1796) concludes with extracts illustrating the novel's treatment of class and gender oppression in a court-dominated society. 'M.' praises Bage's *Hermsprong; or, Man As He Is Not* for the character of the lively feminist, Miss Fluart (December 1796). This is hardly surprising, since *Hermsprong* refers to *A Vindication of the Rights of Woman* and advances feminist arguments at several points. When Wollstonecraft assigned Jane West's *A Gossip's Story* to Mary Hays, she sent her opinion that 'The great merit of this work is . . . the display of the small causes which destroy matrimonial felicity & peace' – a theme of her own novel (*Letters*, p. 375). Hays's review is itself a manifesto for the group of novelists around Wollstonecraft and Godwin, calling for takeover of the novel by 'superiour writers' in the cause of the cultural revolution – 'reform, whether moral or political'.

The urgency of producing a Revolutionary feminist novel was increasing. War and the political and social crisis of the mid-1790s were being used to justify greater control of dissenting social groups, including women.[13] For example, the *Analytical's* review of Thomas Gisborne's *An Enquiry into the Duties of the Female Sex* notes that it 'ventures to dispute the high claim, which has lately been asserted, of perfect equality in point of intellect between the sexes' (February 1797, p. 121) – a reference to Wollstonecraft's *Vindication of the Rights of Woman*. But Wollstonecraft's reviews express disappointment in the work of contemporary women novelists, even those with a feminist bent. As 'M.' observes, with possibly the last words Wollstonecraft published in the *Analytical Review*, 'the writing of a good book is no easy task' (May 1797, p. 523). She must have felt that if someone were to publish a good feminist novel it would have to be herself. She did not live to do so, but the fragments she left show how she intended to convert the mere novel to her Revolutionary feminist revision of the professional middle-class cultural revolution.

In her earlier, educational and feminist work she, like other social critics, attacked the novel for reproducing women's cultural and social inferiority by depicting and disseminating court culture and emulation. She had tried to reclaim the Sentimental novel in *Mary: A Fiction*, and she would now make the novel serve Revolutionary feminism by finding a form answerable to both her revolutionary purpose and an unrevolutionized readership. The English Jacobin novelists, led by Godwin and Holcroft, thought the novel could carry 'truth' to a wide readership, with a persuasive force that 'philosophy' could not equal, and they were already experimenting with the novel form to make it serve their version of the bourgeois cultural revolution.[14] Other novelists, representing different factions within the cultural revolution, countered with political novels of their own, some of which Wollstonecraft had also reviewed in the *Analytical*.[15] *Maria; or, The Wrongs of Woman* aims to be 'philosophical' yet represent the 'mind' of women, thus eliminating the gap between men and women within both the revolutionary vanguard of 'English Jacobin' novelists and in society at large. In order to do so Wollstonecraft adapts the English Jacobin novel to Revolutionary feminism.

In an 'Author's Preface' assembled by Godwin from her notes, she repeats her argument that oppression of any kind produces inferiority which is then used to justify further oppression.[16] She calls on a vanguard – 'a few, who will dare to advance before the improvement of the age' – to recognize that her 'sketches' are 'not the abortion of a distempered fancy, or the strong delineations of a wounded heart'. This call refers to the way transgressive work by women writers was dismissed as madness or merely individual discontent. She goes on to emphasize psychological realism rather than 'manners' to avoid heightening character and incident and thus weakening the general implications of the novel, for 'the history ought rather to be considered, as of woman, than of an individual'. On the other hand, she claims to embody theme and argument in character and plot, and thus to avoid the common error of detaching the novel's 'philosophy' from the formal elements.

In part of a letter to George Dyson included in the 'Author's Preface' she discusses her themes in more detail, declaring that she 'cannot suppose any situation more distressing, than for a woman of sensibility, with an improving mind, to be bound' for life to such a man as her heroine's husband, 'obliged to renounce all the humanizing affections, and to avoid cultivating her taste, lest her perception of grace and refinement of sentiment, should sharpen to agony the pangs of disappointment'. This refers to the conduct-book injunction that a woman unhappily married should bear the situation. She intends 'to show the wrongs of different classes of women, equally oppressive, though, from the difference of education, necessarily various', but she emphasizes 'wrongs' of the 'mind' – those most likely to be experienced by women in the middle ranks. Other so-called 'great misfortunes' favoured by novelists, such as abduction, rape and forced marriage, 'may more forcibly impress the mind of common readers' of novels, 'but it is the delineation of finer sensations, which, in my opinion, constitutes the merit of our best novels'.

Wollstonecraft's novel is shaped accordingly, foregrounding a central subject consciousness. The surviving fragment is dominated by the thoughts and feelings of a gentlewoman, Maria Venables. Most of this fragment consists of her 'memoirs' (chs 7 to

14), and in the remainder the third-person narrator represents Maria's thoughts through the technique of 'free indirect discourse'. Thus the plot also depends on representation of the central subject, showing how 'things as they are' form 'mind' in early life and condition its development later. The form of the memoir shows the damaging relationship of society and self as a continuing process, one inherited from the past and reproduced into the future, unless there is a revolution in the self. For Maria this is a revolution in feminist consciousness, as the novel's full title indicates. The focus on individual subjectivity is reinforced by evidently autobiographical material. The title-page of *Maria* would have carried the name of its author, already known for *A Vindication of the Rights of Woman*. There are passages in the novel that would suggest autobiographical reference, such as Maria's account of the sublimities of childbearing, the pleasures of breast-feeding or the vicissitudes of sexual desire.

These intimations of autobiography are not merely designed to represent the author through a discreet veil of fiction; nor are they traces of writing as author's self-therapy, left for the edification of the reader. S. D. Harasym is right to reprimand readers who 'conceive of the author's or character's self as an essence', and the text as merely 'the intersection of self and literature'.[17] Such apparently autobiographical signs in the text are a rhetorical device, authenticating the fiction for the reader, in terms of the order of discourse at that time, and giving the impression that personal experience has been shaped into a fictional structure, thus generalizing it. Furthermore, as in other English Jacobin novels, the implications of the individual life are broadened by the inclusion of several parallel life-stories. Readers at the time would recognize from the very title of Wollstonecraft's novel that it claimed membership of a recognized sub-genre – the 'philosophical' or political novel – in which 'autobiographical' material was to be expected. Such novels were seen as political in the sense that *philosophes* and 'philosophers' were seen as political in the 1790s: the former were widely believed to have brought about the French Revolution and the latter were believed to be working for a revolution in Britain.[18] But such 'philosophers' were also widely supposed to have personal cause or motives for their general social critique. Whether or not readers agreed with this critique, they would expect 'philosophical' novels to generalize, or 'philosophize' the personal experience of the alienated and disaffected into social critique, for unlike general and abstract discourse such as philosophy, the novel was understood to be amenable to such use.

It was widely thought, however, that this 'philosophical' tendency clashed with the mimetic and artistic aims of the novel. For example, in 'philosophical' novels dialogue often expounds social criticism, straining conventional 'realism'. Like other English Jacobin novelists, Wollstonecraft compensates in part with convincingly characteristic speech for each character, such as the 'common' speech of Maria's landlady (pp. 177–8). Like other English Jacobin novelists, she tries to construct dialogue so that 'philosophical' points arise out of the novel's central conflict, as in the climactic trial scene (ch. 17). She also uses dialogue to assign theorizing power to certain characters, constructing a hierarchy of 'mind' among them. In this way Wollstonecraft shows how Godwinian 'necessitarianism' can break out of the deterministic impasse. In *Maria* the heroine develops a feminist social critique from her own experience; she then uses this critique in dialogue, to empower herself and intervene in 'things as they are'. She out-argues her dissipated husband, helps other women see the general character of their individual oppression, and philosophizes with her lover Darnford. In the trial scene she generalizes from her own experience to a public statement of feminism. Even her 'memoirs', though written, are a form of activist dialogue, theorizing her personal experience for her lover, her daughter and her female dependant. Such dialogue shows that women may be intellectual and social critics in their sphere. But Maria is the only such female character, suggesting that feminism is as yet for the revolutionary vanguard.

The significance of Maria's situation is filled out by the English Jacobin novelists' device of using names to reinforce the political implications. Maria's name could allude to other historical prisoners of sex, such as Mary Queen of Scots and Marie Roland, victims of their own sensibility and Revolutionary anti-feminism; Maria could also stand for her author. The name of Maria's helper and companion, Jemima, ironically echoes that of Job's daughter, who was supposed to share her father's inheritance (Job 42: 13–15). Henry Darnford's last name is a variation on Darnley, the lover of Mary Queen of Scots and the cause of her downfall. The name of Maria's husband, George Venables, embodies topical allusions. He is obsessed with commerce and tries to sell his wife, though himself a womanizer. His last name plays on 'able to sell' (ven[d]-

able) and 'able in venery' (or the pursuit of pleasure, as womaniz-
ing). Such word-play was common in novels of the time, especially
English Jacobin novels. Venables also has the Christian name of
the notorious royal womanizer, George, Prince of Wales, whose
marriage broke up in 1796. The Prince restricted his wife's conduct
and access to their daughter, heir apparent to the throne. His wife
played the role of the wronged wife and mother, gaining sympathy from political reformers and the general public.[19] Conserva-
tives feared the royal marriage breakup was furthering the cause of
these 'English Jacobins'. Maria's domestic situation is an exaggerated and common-life version of that occupying public attention at
the time Wollstonecraft was writing her novel. The names are not
intended as a key to the novel, but to deepen and authenticate its
implications.

This device is reinforced by pointed and apt literary quotations,
historical allusions and factual references. For example, Wollstonecraft's familiarity with Shakespeare and heroic drama received
feminist inspiration from seeing her new friend, Sarah Siddons, in
leading roles. Siddons was the greatest tragic actor of her time,
especially in the role of heroic wronged woman in which she was
thought to reach heights of 'sublimity' hitherto unattained by a
woman. *Maria* refers directly to Siddons (p. 144) and to several
roles played by her, including Calista, the seduced and abandoned
heroine of Rowe's *The Fair Penitent*, the wronged Queen Katherine
in Shakespeare's *Henry VIII* and Roxana in Lee's *The Rival Queens*.

Less obvious is Wollstonecraft's feminist adaptation of the story
of Mrs Fitzpatrick in Book XI of Fielding's *Tom Jones* – a novel highly
regarded by English Jacobin novelists for its artistry, critique of
court culture and vision of the landed classes renovated by bourgeois morality. Mrs Fitzpatrick's and Maria's stories are inset
narratives and each is a warning to another woman. Each woman
is taken in by an unscrupulous man because of her limited education and knowledge of the world, each finds marriage resembles
Hogarth's 'Marriage à la Mode', each finds her husband to be
intellectually her inferior, each is deceived by him, nevertheless
becomes pregnant by him, is then cajoled into giving him money,
is confined by him when she refuses, escapes and finds another
man as a 'protector'. Each uses philosophical language, a broad
social critique of courtly gallantry, and even feminist arguments to
account for her plight. But whereas Mrs Fitzpatrick turns out to be
a hypocrite, using bad treatment by her husband to mask her own

courtly amours and feminist protest to justify her own gallantries, Maria becomes a feminist heroine and martyr.

The English Jacobin novelists studied their predecessors and contemporaries with the practical aim of improving the rhetorical effectiveness of their own work. There are hints in *Maria* that Wollstonecraft studied Defoe's *Roxana* and *Moll Flanders* for their 'realistic' representation of women in high and low life. (Godwin had studied Defoe's other works for his own novel of 1794, *Things As They Are; or, The Adventures of Caleb Williams*.) The English Jacobin novelists also tried to improve their fiction by including obviously factual material, especially on social and economic conditions and on legal issues. Wollstonecraft may have used sources such as *The Newgate Calendar* and Bladon's *Trials for Adultery* (again, these were known to Godwin), and *Maria* includes much factual material appropriate for a continuation of *A Vindication of the Rights of Woman*: on the legal situation of women; their property and marriage rights; divorce and child custody; employment opportunities; wages and working conditions; prostitution and policing; charitable institutions; control of the poor through parish relief and workhouses; crime and punishment; treatment of the insane; patronage in politics and the professions; conditions of military service; and so on. In fact, to achieve accuracy in her novel's madhouse scenes Wollstonecraft visited Bedlam Hospital in February 1797 with Godwin and Johnson.[20]

Influenced – perhaps even awed – by Godwin and the other English Jacobin novelists, but 'impressed . . . with the consciousness of her talents', Wollstonecraft realized 'how arduous a task it is to produce a truly excellent novel; and she roused her faculties to grapple with it' (*Memoirs*, p. 264). She consulted Godwin, who insisted that she base her unrivalled 'power of expressing feeling' on a clear plot, energetic incidents and progressive psychological realism.[21] She turned her back on her first novel, telling Everina in March 1797: 'As for my Mary, I consider it as a crude production, and do not very willingly put it in the way of people whose good opinion, as a writer, I wish for' (*Letters*, p. 385). As Godwin put it, her 'other works were produced with a rapidity, that did not give her powers time fully to expand', but *Maria* 'was written slowly and with mature considerations'. She tried 'several forms, which she successively rejected', and 'wrote many parts of the work again and again'. After 'she had finished what she intended for the first part, she felt herself more urgently stimulated to revise and improve what she had written, than to proceed' (*Memoirs*, p. 264). Though only a fragment was completed, it shows how carefully constructed and pervasively political she intended the novel to be.

It opens *in medias res* – an increasingly favoured device at this time, perhaps borrowed from the theatre – with Maria imprisoned in a madhouse, her infant daughter apparently abducted. Much of the first chapter describes her feelings of despair and anguish. But she interests her warder, Jemima, who brings some books and materials for writing. At first Maria writes only 'some rhapsodies descriptive of the state of her mind', but gradually she connects these into a narrative that 'might perhaps instruct her daughter', should she ever receive it, 'and shield her from the misery, the tyranny, her mother knew not how to avoid' (p. 82). Merely expressive acts of self-consolation are converted into a political self-vindication and manual of instruction, a Revolutionary feminist conduct book. Jemima brings more books, belonging to a 'gentleman' (Henry Darnford) also confined in the house. Maria is interested by the books' marginal notes, including 'various observations on the present state of society and government, with a comparative view of the politics of Europe and America'. The books also include Rousseau's *La nouvelle Héloïse*, and after a rapturous reading of it, Maria imagines the stranger to be an ideal lover. Writing initiates desire, for better or worse.

With Jemima's help, Maria begins a correspondence with Darnford that leads to love. When they meet, he recounts his life story (which resembles that of Mary Robinson's former lover, Banastre Tarleton, as some readers would recognize – the affair was a topic in the newspapers over many years, including 1796).[22] The son of 'people of fashion', Darnford was bred 'a thoughtless, extravagant young man'. He wasted his patrimony, fought against the American Revolution and homesteaded on the frontier. But disgusted by the new republic's commercialism he returned to England, where he was abducted by a relative who wanted his property and immured in the same madhouse as Maria. Confinement for such reasons was a known scandal at the time.[23] But prison turns out to be a site of liberation – of 'mind' if not body. Maria is captivated by Darnford's tale, and narrative unleashes love. This love then arouses Jemima's sympathy and unleashes her narrative, for she 'was so softened by the air of confidence which breathed around her, that she voluntarily began an account of herself' (p. 101).

Jemima was born a bastard, rejected by her father, abused by her stepmother, raped by her employer, almost killed by a self-induced abortion and forced by poverty into prostitution. She became the kept mistress of a sentimental libertine from whom she acquired genteel culture, but she was thrown out of the house at his death and driven to manual labour as a washerwoman. Illness forced her to a charity hospital, originally designed for the poor but now 'conducted for the accommodation of the medical men and their pupils, who came to make experiments on the poor, for the benefit of the rich' (p. 117). Unable to work, she 'began to consider the rich and poor as natural enemies, and became a thief from principle', ending up in the house of correction and the work-house, institutions for suppressing and oppressing the poor (p. 118). Eventually one of the workhouse overseers set up a private madhouse and hired her as a warder. Maria sympathizes with Jemima and generalizes from her tale: 'Thinking of Jemima's peculiar fate and her own, she was led to consider the oppressed state of women, and to lament that she had given birth to a daughter' (p. 120). To reciprocate, Jemima tries to trace Maria's child, but learns she has died. Maria is now grateful for Darnford's love and lets him read 'the memoirs which had been written for her daughter' (p. 123). These express the hope that 'From my narrative, my dear girl, you may gather the instruction' necessary to avoid a similar fate (p. 124).

Maternal domestic affections give rhetorical force to this social critique, and personal narrative illustrates the general condition of women. Writing the 'memoirs' also relieves the pain of imprison-ment; thus their very existence is evidence of what Maria claims they illustrate – 'the misery, which the constitution of society seems to have entailed on all her kind'. Finally, the 'memoirs' are an act of social rebellion against 'the constitution of society', for in writing them Maria has to 'break through all restraint' in order to authenticate their picture of oppression with details too indelicate for a lady's – or even a woman's – pen. This discursive situation had precedents. Lady Sarah Pennington adopted the same posture for *An Unfortunate Mother's Advice to Her Absent Daughters* (1761). The English Jacobin novelists also used personal apology for social protest. Even more pertinent was Marie Roland's confessional political memoir, addressed to her daughter but titled *Appel à l'impartiel postérité* and published in 1795.[24] Maria's 'memoirs', like Roland's, are expressly designed to intervene in 'things as they are' and, though addressed to one individual, are meant for society at large.

In Godwinian fashion, Maria's memoirs trace the circumstances 'which, during my childhood, occurred to fashion my mind' (p. 126). These circumstances are the interrelated differences of class and gender that constitute women's oppression. Maria was the daughter of a weak mother and despotic father, but neglected by them for her older brother. She was favoured by an uncle who brought her books, 'for which I had a passion', but these led her to 'form an ideal picture of life' (p. 128), making her susceptible to a courtly hypocrite, George Venables. The second son of a merchant, he 'had acquired habits of libertinism', but she saw him as a novel hero. His courtly skills deceived Maria and her uncle, whose property Venables would gain by marrying her. Maria's life to this point is meant to typify the education – or miseducation – of women as mere vessels of feeling unrestrained by reason and 'reality', and therefore susceptible to seduction by the courtly social other and to being used as a means of transferring property from one man to another.

This realization seizes Maria again in the midst of her narrative, and she stops writing, exclaiming, 'Why was I not born a man, or why was I born at all?' (p. 139). When she resumes her pen, it is 'to fly from thought' (p. 143). The moment of recognizing patriarchal oppression arises from the narrative and momentarily arrests its progress, thereby seeming to authenticate it; but the narrative may also be a refuge from consciousness of oppression and a substitute for self-emancipatory action. It is true that Maria is imprisoned, unable to do much for herself, but able to write her self for the emancipation of another. Nevertheless, the turn from writing revolutionary consciousness to taking revolutionary action is not clearly made in the novel. This does not signal the failure of the novel's feminism, though it does mark the revolution as, again, a writing revolution. Maria's experience of oppression authenticates her feminism in her writing; it is left to her readers to turn the lesson of the text into appropriate action in 'real life'.

Maria herself made the classic mistake of the oppressed woman in patriarchal society: she married to escape a family divided by gender and corrupted by false class values, but found marriage a prison. At first the relative freedom of having her own home enabled her mind to improve, while George's absorption in business schemes and secret vice narrowed his mind. Maria quotes

Calista from Nicholas Rowe's well-known 'she-tragedy', *The Fair Penitent*: 'Hearts like ours were pair'd . . . not match'd' (p. 144). Observing that her husband's deterioration produced in him a contempt for women, Maria states one of the principles of social psychology that generalize her narrative: 'Men who are inferior to their fellow men, are always most anxious to establish their superiority over women' (p. 147). She protests the injustice of the conduct-book advice that wives put up with slovenliness in their husbands but continue to make themselves attractive, and she gives a satiric picture of her marriage that parallels Hogarth's 'Marriage à la Mode'.

At this point nature inspired her, helping her progress to feminist consciousness. In her 'native village' she was refreshed by the sublime pleasures of memory and the picturesque, and revisiting her mother's grave she moved from the natural sublime to 'devotional feelings' that affirmed her autonomy and plenitude of self at the very time that she was being socially degraded and exploited (pp. 151–2). This recollection returns to her, again interrupting her narrative: 'I pause – feeling forcibly all the emotions I am describing' (p. 152). The plenitude of self that validates the confessional narrative is manifested by a breakdown of narrative caused by 'overflow' of that self.

Appropriately, she then asserts that female sexual desire is equal in nature and worth to men's desire, evidence of full subjectivity and a strong, active and virtuous mind, and the moral basis of conjugal relations. As Jane Spencer says, 'The novel boldly vindicates its heroine's recognition of her sexuality.'[25] As Maria puts it, 'Truth is the only basis of virtue; and we cannot, without depraving our minds, endeavour to please a lover or husband, but in proportion as he pleases us' – that is, pleases both morally and physically. Thus Maria reclaims female sexuality from instrument of the trivialization and oppression of women in court society to manifestation of women's equality of 'mind'. Sexual transgression should not be the symptom of women's inferiority of 'mind' but a proclamation of women's subjective equality with men. These remarks are dramatized by Maria's vigorous description of her husband's physical repulsiveness, and then by her shame in having to admit that she was pregnant by him.

Yet this mistake made possible the joy she experienced as the mother of her to whom the memoirs are addressed. This joy is represented as a uniquely female experience of the sublime, the recollection of which again interrupts her narrative.[26] It is as if the oppression of women, represented here by Maria's sexual submission to her husband, which the law requires of her, can yet produce a uniquely female experience of liberation in bondage. Similarly, Maria's oppression and imprisonment seem to produce feminist consciousness as a form of liberation in bondage. This liberation of the 'mind' seems to be the only kind available to Maria. For by a cruel irony she discovered her pregnancy just as she realized that 'Marriage had bastilled me for life' (pp. 154–5). 'To bastille', meaning to imprison, was a verb in English before the French Revolution, but here it recalls the Revolutionary symbol of domestic and political tyranny: the Bastille and other prisons were widely believed to house victims of the infamous *lettres de cachet*, decrees of arbitrary imprisonment used by upper-class parents to prevent 'improper' marriages, or love-matches, by their children. Yet neither Maria's feminist realization of oppression nor the Revolutionary destruction of the Bastille has produced real freedom. Appropriately, Maria's realization that she is 'bastilled for life' also leads to reflections on the inequality of the marriage laws (pp. 155–6), and these in turn look back to Wollstonecraft's own statement of Revolutionary feminism, for consideration of these laws was to have been included in a sequel to *A Vindication of the Rights of Woman*.

These reflections are followed by Maria's description of her financial exploitation by Venables and his attempt to sell her to one of his creditors in payment for a debt. Maria's recollection of the episode produces another bitter outburst, on the legal privileges of husbands even in France, and again links Maria's plight to Revolutionary failure (p. 159). The passage, which could also have gone into a sequel to *A Vindication of the Rights of Woman*, has dramatic validity by being placed before her declaration of independence from her husband, leading to feelings of sublime freedom even while literally imprisoned in her own home:

> How had I panted for liberty – liberty, that I would have purchased at any price, but that of my own esteem!. . . . I was all soul, and (wild as it may appear) felt as if I could have dissolved in the soft balmy gale that kissed my cheek. . . . A seraphic satisfaction animated, without agitating my spirits; and my imagination collected, in visions sublimely terrible, or soothingly beautiful, an immense variety of the endless images, which

nature affords, and fancy combines, of the grand and fair. (p. 163)

Transcendent self-recognition is associated with nature in terms of the sublime and the beautiful, the two highest forms of aesthetic experience in eighteenth-century theory, and conventionally gendered as masculine and feminine respectively. Such transcendence again confirms Maria's authenticity and plenitude of self, and her superiority, subjective if not social and legal, to her husband and to institutionalized patriarchy. Many readers would also recognize in this passage strong echoes of the autobiographical-political writings of Rousseau, adopted father of the Revolution and masterwriter of the poetics and politics of subjective transcendence as a prelude to social and cultural revolution.

Maria's account of her escape and subsequent persecution by her husband looks like a cliché of the late eighteenth-century women's novel, a variation on numerous tales of abduction, forced marriage and Gothic entrapment. But Godwin showed how to give a political resonance to such 'adventures of flight and pursuit' in his *Things As They Are; or, The Adventures of Caleb Williams*, which Wollstonecraft was reading while she worked on her own novel. Further resonance would be gained from widely reported true stories of Revolutionary persecution. Wollstonecraft uses such adventures to further dramatize her heroine's superiority of self, here called 'reason' and 'duty', over society, state and social convention.

While in flight Maria encountered again the way patriarchy, or the social and legal power of men, forces women to become each other's enemies. For she sought a lodging with a woman whom she had helped in business, but who was controlled by her husband, or 'master': 'no slave in the West Indies had one more despotic; but fortunately she was of the true Russian breed of wives', proverbial for submissiveness. These references broaden the significance of women's oppression to other races and cultures, and to other regimes of tyranny; at the same time they suggest that such oppression is somehow 'not British'. The husband of Maria's landlady forced his wife to evict Maria, who continued to be 'hunted out like a felon', only able to express her feelings with a refrain from *Judas Maccabeus*, Handel's oratorio about the heroic resistance of the Jews to Roman oppression (p. 174) – the reference gives another historical and cultural resonance to Maria's plight.

Self-narrative again furthered self-emancipation and reciprocity, however, for Maria gained her landlady's assistance by relating her wrongs, and the woman then related her own experience of legally sanctioned oppression (pp. 177–8). Maria planned to go to Italy where she could escape 'in the contemplation of the heart-enlarging virtues of antiquity, from the turmoil of cares that had depressed all the daring purposes of my soul' (p. 179). But no sooner did she deliver a daughter than she learned that her uncle had died, leaving his fortune to the child in order to keep it from Venables. Maria then devised a plan to protect her daughter from '"the killing frost"' to which she was 'destined to be exposed' as a woman. The quotation is again apt, from Shakespeare's *Henry VIII*, in which Sarah Siddons recently played the role of the wronged Queen Katherine. The narrative precipitates another reflection, as Maria exclaims, 'born a woman – and born to suffer . . . I feel more acutely the various ills my sex are fated to bear – I feel that the evils they are subject to endure, degrade them so far below their op-pressors, as almost to justify their tyranny; leading at the same time superficial reasoners to term that weakness the cause, which is only the consequence of short-sighted despotism' (p. 181). This is the main argument of *A Vindication of the Rights of Woman*, but it also characterizes the speaker and sets up the final episode of Maria's narrative: Venables used Maria's maidservant to abduct the child and have Maria thrown into the madhouse – a last example of how patriarchy uses women against each other.

This concludes Maria's inset narrative; the rest of the text is fragmentary. Maria's story evokes love in Darnford and almost immediately, as if their revolutionary egalitarian love were literally liberating, the manager of the madhouse decamps and Maria and Darnford are free (pp. 189–90). She visits the grave of her daughter and, wishing to live with Darnford, negotiates a settlement with Venables. Jemima insists on being their housekeeper, accepting only 'the customary stipend': once out of prison the community of sympathy between Darnford, Maria and Jemima must conform to conventional class distinctions. Venables sues Darnford for 'seduc-tion and adultery', but Maria is left to conduct the defence. She is dropped by her women acquaintances, even those who are them-selves secret adulteresses. Maria feels she should marry Darnford: 'Marriage, as at present constituted, she considered as leading to immorality – yet, as the odium of society impedes usefulness, she wished to avow her affection to Darnford, by becoming his wife according to established rules; not to be confounded with women who act from very different motives, though her conduct would be just the same without the ceremony as with it, and her expectations from him not less firm' (pp. 193–4). Behind this reflection lies an intense debate among 'English Jacobins' on the relation of principle to expediency in the changing political climate of the mid-1790s.

There is also political significance in the next episode, Maria's defence of Darnford against Venables's suit for adultery and seduction. This is the last complete chapter and was probably meant as the novel's climactic episode. Trials occur in many texts of the Revolutionary decade, given additional significance by French Revolutionary tribunals and British treason trials of the mid-1790s. The trial is a complex figure in the Revolutionary decade, representing conflict of opinions within the political classes, individual judicial reason in a period of intense polemical struggle and professional middle-class culture itself, for judicial process and argument were methods used in many professions besides law. Thus the trial scene also dramatizes ideological conflict within the revolutionary professional middle class in terms familiar to that class, thereby seeming to give that class exclusive power to resolve the conflict. Trial scenes in literature of this time often represent professional virtues tried by the old order and condemned, revealing the gap between law, an institution still commanded by the landed classes in their own interest, and justice, an ideology of personal merit. Finally, English Jacobin writers, like Enlightenment philosophers, often represent challenge to the old order as 'curiosity', a 'passion' that serves 'progress' by challenging irrational 'custom' and 'prejudice'. But 'curiosity' may also represent the investigative and critical method of the professionals, as a revolutionary vanguard. Curiosity is the ruling passion of Godwin's fictional hero and archetypal social rebel, Caleb Williams, and curiosity also impels Maria to understand her internalization of social difference, as self-division, by developing a broad feminist social critique.

In *Maria* Wollstonecraft adapts the figure of the trial to Revolutionary feminism, so that both the structure and content of the scene tell. The trial is in three parts. First, Venables's counsel exculpates his client's conduct and condemns Maria's, appealing to social convention rather than the law. His legalistic précis of the case contrasts with the expressive vigour of Maria's previous autobiographical account of the marriage and thus seems a distortion of the story the reader already knows. The reader would share Maria's 'strong sense of injustice' at the lawyer's account and feel that his discourse exemplifies the law's formalization of (mistaken) social convention at the expense of individual motive and merit. For Maria insists 'on the privilege of her nature', claiming that her subjective absolute – love for Darnford – transcends social convention and the law: 'The sarcasms of society, and the condemnation of a mistaken world, were nothing to her, compared with acting contrary to those feelings which were the foundation of her principles' (p. 195).

Since she cannot plead in person, 'she wrote a paper, which she expressly desired might be read in court' – this is the second part of the trial. Silenced in public by legal procedure that again formalizes social convention and even Paul's injunction in the New Testament, she can only 'speak' in writing. Her paper asserts that she married before the age of reason, that her husband violated the marriage contract but that under 'proper restrictions' she reveres marriage, for it is 'the institution which fraternizes the world', even though the laws make wives 'dependent on the caprice of the tyrant, whom choice or necessity has appointed to reign over them' (p. 195). The political resonance in 'tyrant' and 'reign over' would invite readers to associate the 'wrongs of woman' with the social wrongs in society under court government and culture. Asserting Richard Price's moral rationalism again, Maria argues that a wife 'must be allowed to consult her conscience, and regulate her conduct, in some degree, by her own sense of right', even if disapproved by the state: 'I wish my country to approve of my conduct; but, if laws exist, made by the strong to oppress the weak, I appeal to my own sense of justice, and declare that I will not live with the individual, who has violated every moral obligation which binds man to man' (p. 197). The phrase 'man to man' may seem odd here, but Wollstonecraft usually employs 'man' as a general noun encompassing both sexes; here 'man to man' suggests that the relation of woman to man is only a particular case of the general principles of 'right' and 'justice' that should apply to all relationships and be embodied in the laws.

Maria then appeals 'to the justice and humanity of the jury – a body of men, whose private judgment must be allowed to modify laws, that must be unjust, because definite rules can never apply to indefinite circumstances'. This is not just a feminine plea against the generalizing, categorizing tendency of men's 'philosophy' and professional discourse, but a restatement of a basic principle in Godwin's *Political Justice* – a kind of radical individualism, or 'philosophical anarchy', against any collective or state pre-emption of individual freedom of judgement. In fact, however, juries did recognize particular circumstances and refuse (as they still do) to bring in guilty verdicts even when the law had obviously been broken; and during the mid-1790s the ability of juries to place justice above the unjust laws was much discussed. Maria's appeal to the jury is against laws serving a particular class, but this appeal cannot extend to gender. Her description of the jury as a 'body of *men*' also changes her use of the general pronoun, reminding the reader that women could not be jurors – indeed, could not participate in the legal process as judge or lawyer, either. Her appeal is not addressed to a jury of *her* peers but to men, who may hold the same anti-feminist prejudices embodied in the laws. Not surprisingly, she then closes her written vindication by claiming a transcendentally validated standard of conduct, declaring that she is 'free' from her husband 'in the sight of heaven', 'and no power on earth shall force me to renounce my resolution' (p. 198). The style of the declaration supports its claim. It eschews the expressive, lyrical and personal for the brisk, clear, detached but firm style of one confident that 'right' and 'reason' are on her side. It also exhibits Maria's capacity to reason from personal experience, and thereby make her own choices in life.

Maria's claim is immediately denied, however, in the third part of the trial – the judge's summation to the jury, denouncing 'the fallacy of letting women plead their feelings, as an excuse for the violation of the marriage-vow', and opposing 'the new-fangled notions' enroaching on 'the good old rules of conduct'. Like Burke, the judge pretends to speak for all Englishmen and connects the public and domestic spheres in the light of the French Revolution, asserting that 'we' do not want 'French principles in public or private life' (pp. 198–9). He dismisses the evidence against Venables, concedes that Maria has grounds for a legal separation, but reaffirms the principle of English common law that a woman's legal personality is always 'covered' by that of some man, who should control her property as well as her freedom of action. Such restrictions 'might bear a little hard on a few, very few individuals', he concludes, but it is 'for the good of the whole'. But the novel's various inset narratives have suggested that the oppression of women in marriage is in fact widespread. The chapter and the completed portion of the novel leave the jury's decision in the air. Godwin published Wollstonecraft's notes for continuations and conclusions, which show that the close of the novel was not clearly determined when Wollstonecraft stopped work. Two continuations indicate that Darnford's return from Paris is delayed, causing Maria anxiety. There are four other continuations and conclusions. In one Maria obtains a legal separation but her property is tied up in the Court of Chancery, notoriously slow and expensive, and she 'goes into the country', presumably to be restored by nature again. In the second continuation Maria becomes pregnant again but is deserted by Darnford. The third outline continues from the first, as Maria returns to London, becomes pregnant, and makes a discovery that causes her to miscarry. The fourth outline is the most decisive and pessimistic: Maria is 'Divorced by her husband – Her lover unfaithful – Pregnancy – Miscarriage – Suicide'.

The sketch of a conclusion headed 'The End' comprises six paragraphs and takes a different, more hopeful course. Maria attempts suicide by overdose of laudanum in order 'to forget herself' and 'to escape from thought'. In an expressive passage she has broken impressions of important events in her recent life as she sinks into unconsciousness, but at the last moment Jemima enters with a little child – Maria's lost daughter. When Maria recovers, Jemima describes the plot between Venables and Maria's older brother to sequester the child in order to get her property – a conspiracy of patriarchy to dispossess women. When the girl utters the word 'Mamma' Maria decides 'The conflict is over! – I will live for my child!' (p. 203). These last words of the novel, as assembled and edited by Godwin, suggest how, even in an unrevolutionized society, Maria was to escape the contradictions of gender that made her wish to die, to destroy the autonomous being that she had constructed from her own experience but that society does not allow women to have.

Wollstonecraft's best hope for Maria was to leave her as an independent woman free of any man, and as a publicly professed feminist prepared to disseminate her feminism onward to the next generation, represented by her daughter, and downward to the class beneath her, represented by Jemima. Whereas domestic woman is subjugated within 'her' class so that she will reproduce its culture without altering or intervening in it, Maria presides over a social unit also based on the domestic affections but reproducing the professional middle-class cultural revolution as revised by Revolutionary feminism.

At the end of Wollstonecraft's text Godwin added a paragraph of his own, restating the main points of the 'Author's Preface', especially the rhetorical potential of the novel for altering the political consciousness of the reader, and the use of form and style to dramatize 'evils that are too frequently overlooked, and to drag into light those details of oppression, of which the grosser and more insensible part of mankind make little account'. The novelist is a political artist, a member of the revolutionary vanguard able to politicize 'the grosser and more insensible part of mankind', thereby effecting a non-violent, intellectual, moral and cultural revolution – a reading revolution. Somewhat misleadingly, Godwin claims Wollstonecraft's work for the English Jacobin novelists' version of the professional cultural revolution; Wollstonecraft herself aimed to transform that revolution by her Revolutionary feminism, in this case as applied to the English Jacobin novel.

Wollstonecraft completed what survives of *Maria* by May 1797, and spent the summer preparing to deliver her child, whom she thought would be a boy and was to be called William. In June Godwin toured the Midlands with Basil Montagu, visiting the Wedgwoods, Robert Bage and others, and viewing the natural and man-made sights in the heartland of the new Industrial Revolution. Absence again made Wollstonecraft's heart grow fonder, but Godwin's vagueness about the date of his return exasperated her. She apologized for poaching his friends to pass the time – their agreement was to socialize separately. She found it difficult to work, preferring distraction with a newspaper or novel, and consulted with Anthony Carlisle, surgeon at Westminster Hospital, on her pregnancy. Meanwhile, she was sitting for a portrait to John Opie. The picture, now in the National Portrait Gallery, London, contrasts to earlier ones, showing her relaxed, domestic and even matronly. But in July she was alarmed at the interest of a Miss Pinkerton in Godwin and had to forbid the young woman her house. Wollstonecraft reproved Godwin for not treating the matter seriously enough. She also felt hurt at his continuing disregard of her religious faith.

On 30 August Wollstonecraft delivered a daughter, named Mary. Godwin was not present and Wollstonecraft, who wished to employ women professionals wherever she could, was attended by a midwife from the Westminster Lying-In Hospital. But the midwife failed to ensure that the entire placenta was expelled and Wollstonecraft developed puerperal fever. After several days of struggle she died at twenty minutes to eight on the morning of 10 September 1797. Even her independent 'mind' could not withstand one of the all too common 'wrongs of woman' in her time.

Her friends were shocked; Godwin was distraught. Like a true professional intellectual he buried himself in work and collected her surviving papers into the four volumes of *Posthumous Works of the Author of A Vindication of the Rights of Woman*, published in January 1798 with his *Memoirs of the Author of A Vindication of the Rights of Woman*. The titles indicate how he wished to memorialize her as the Revolutionary feminist in domestic as well as public life. At the same time, as Mitzi Myers points out, he emblemizes 'himself and Wollstonecraft as representatives of the discursive and the intuitive', the masculine and feminine as complements within the same revolutionary culture, consistent with the politicizing of domesticity in the vanguard of the professional cultural revolution.[27] A few months after her death he also began a new novel, set in the sixteenth century and published in 1799 as *St Leon*, in which he presented an idealized portrait of Wollstonecraft as Marguerite de Damville, calm domestic refuge in an earlier and turbulent age of revolutions. But in the growing reaction against the French Revolution in the later 1790s, Godwin's candour in describing his late wife's personal battle against 'the wrongs of woman' made her seem a transgressor of the bourgeois domestic ideal to many social critics, and cast a long shadow over her reputation and her Revolutionary feminism in the century ahead.[28]

She and *A Vindication of the Rights of Woman* continued to interest feminists, social reformers, intellectuals and ordinary women through the early and mid-nineteenth century.[29] The novelist Elizabeth Benger was reported to have made a pilgrimage to Wollstonecraft's grave and thrown herself on it, pouring out 'a rapturous eulogy of the departed'. A writer in the 1840s claimed: 'No woman (with the exception of the greatest woman, Madame de Staël) has made any impression on the public mind during the last fifty years, to be compared with Mrs Godwin.' The same writer claimed: 'This was more especially true in the provinces, where her new and startling doctrines were seized with avidity, and acted upon in some particulars to a considerable extent, particularly by married women.' The French feminist Flora Tristan wrote enthusiastically in 1840, *'Le livre de Mary Wollstonecraft est une oeuvre impérissable!* . . . *parce que le bonheur du genre humain est attaché au triomphe de la cause que défend* the vindication of the rights of woman.'[30]

But even those sympathetic to Revolutionary feminism often regretted what they saw as the excesses of Wollstonecraft's life and the seeming indiscipline and excess of her writing. Writing in 1843, the American feminist Margaret Fuller compared Wollstonecraft to George Sand and thought her 'existence better proved the need of some new interpretation of woman's rights, than anything she wrote'; Harriet Martineau wrote that Wollstonecraft 'was, with all her powers, a poor victim of passion'. On the other hand, George Eliot found Wollstonecraft 'nothing if not rational' and the *Vindication* 'eminently serious, severely moral, and withal rather heavy'; Maria Jane Jewsbury thought it would have to be remodelled to become again 'attractive' and 'useful'.[31]

Interest and admiration flourished with the late nineteenth-century campaigns for women's suffrage and educational equality, and continued to grow through the feminist movements of the twentieth century.[32] Writing in 1893, the suffragist Millicent Garrett Fawcett thought that the women's rights movement of her time owed as much to Wollstonecraft as political economy owed to Adam Smith. Writing in 1929, Virginia Woolf thought that 'we hear her voice and trace her influence even now among the living', and that the two *Vindication*s 'are so true that they seem now to contain nothing new in them – their originality has become our commonplace'.[33] By the 1960s Wollstonecraft seemed to have an established position in the history of feminism. Françoise Basch calls *A Vindication of the Rights of Woman* the 'first truly "modern"' manifestation of feminism. Rosalind Miles describes Wollstonecraft's life as the 'stuff of penny-dreadful romance', but calls the *Vindication* 'one of the most powerful and assured of feminist critiques'. More recently Wollstonecraft has been repositioned as a founder of bourgeois feminism. Rosemarie Tong treats Wollstone-craft as the first major 'liberal feminist', who demanded that women be allowed and enabled to participate in 'personhood' as defined and constructed for males – that is, in the uniquely human capacity for rationality.[34]

More recently still, feminist critics, especially those engaging with psychoanalytical and Lacanian theory, are disturbed by what they see as Wollstonecraft's denial of female sexuality and desire, especially in the *Vindication*, and have offered varying accounts of the relation of that denial to the social reality of her time. Mary Jacobus sees the *Vindication* as the beginning of the 'demand for education' that 'provides the emancipatory thrust of much nineteenth- and twentieth-century feminism'; but she argues that Wollstonecraft's appropriation of 'the language of Enlightenment Reason for her own sex' brought with it 'alienation, repression, division – a silencing of the "feminine", a loss of women's inherit-ance'. Similarly, Mary Poovey argues that Wollstonecraft's books 'reveal her difficulty in launching a frontal assault on the values of her society', because Wollstonecraft 'became emotionally ensnared by the network of rationales, social functions, and cultural fears' of the dominant gender ideology of her time, that of the 'proper lady'. Cora Kaplan notes the 'polarization of social and psychic explanation' in modern feminists' treatment of writers such as Wollstonecraft, and tries to bring these together by arguing that Wollstonecraft initiated the 'long and fascinating history in "left" feminist writing' of interest in 'the psychic life of women as a crucial element in their subordination and liberation'; thus Wolls-tonecraft 'set the terms for a debate that is still in progress'.[35]

Different and differing feminisms continue to read Wollstone-craft and Revolutionary feminism in diverse ways; if feminism is not settled and singular neither will such readings be. What should be clearer from the preceding chapters is that, whatever she means to followers and successors, Wollstonecraft was also a feminist of her time, responding to both broad and particular conditions of class and gender conflict that she experienced, especially cultural revolution as state formation in Britain, and the more violent and cataclysmic parallel Revolution in France. The cultural revolution worked largely through those practices – subjectivity and domes-ticity – that women conventionally presided over and that 'woman' was constructed to represent, especially through writing, then becoming the cultural property of the professional bourgeoisie. But

Wollstonecraft rejected the gendering of subjectivity. She developed her own 'mind' and identity as critical consciousness in response to her experience and internalization of class, gender and cultural differences, and took up writing as a way of turning her 'mind' into a career. But 'mind', writing and career were all fields of struggle, instruments of class and gender conflict and themes in the bourgeois cultural revolution. Wollstonecraft grasped these instruments and intervened in these themes by means of her Revolutionary feminism – a feminism conditioned by its time in its very attempt to transcend or transform those conditions.

Of necessity, then, she was also a relentless experimenter in form and style, contesting the order of discourse in her time because she saw it as reproducing an oppressive social order. But as a consequence of this experimenting her writing was widely perceived in her time and since as simply 'bad' – incoherent, unlearned, inartistic and ineffective. Even those who appreciated her work (especially men such as Godwin) often saw it as merely personal, rather than political by virtue of being personal, and preferred the lovable 'softness' and 'tenderness' of the woman writer to the 'harshness and ruggedness' of the political philosopher. In fact, Wollstonecraft's writing should be viewed as a Revolutionary feminist challenge to the contemporary discursive order, including the judging of writing as 'good' or 'bad' in itself, apart from political considerations – a process that always seemed to downgrade, denigrate or dismiss women's writing. At the same time, the development of what Elaine Showalter defines as 'the female tradition' in literature of the nineteenth and twentieth centuries, pursuing professionalism in the *belles-lettres* alongside yet differently from men writers, left Wollstonecraft behind, as a 'pioneer' and merely polemical writer.[36]

The discursive order was revolutionized in the 1790s and early 1800s, but not by Wollstonecraft. Such developments as the professionalization of *belles-lettres*, the founding of literature as a national institution, the dissemination of professional method, the imposition of the utilitarian agenda, the *embourgeoisement* of the sublime – in short, the re-masculinization of writing against the subversive feminizations of the 1780s and early 1790s – left Wollstonecraft's writing, and women's writing of all kinds, outside or subject to the dominant (men's) discursive order of the professional middle-class cultural revolution. As this revolution moved to its triumph and consolidation in the nineteenth and twentieth centuries it remained a field of struggle, where feminisms contend for leadership among themselves, largely within the dominant professional culture. Meanwhile most women, like other subordinate social groups, rely on their skills at resistance, in the bricolage of everyday life, improvising in the interstices of the dominant order, practising feminisms not yet written. In a similar way Wollstonecraft improvised in the interstices of the dominant and gendered discursive order of her time, to effect a 'revolution in female manners' by means of a writing revolution.

Notes

Notes to Chapter 1: Gender, Class and Cultural Revolution

1. On cultural revolution and state formation, see Philip Corrigan and Derek Sayer, *The Great Arch: English State Formation as Cultural Revolution* (Oxford and New York: Basil Blackwell, 1985); on revolutionary élites and state formation, see Theda Skocpol, *States and Social Revolutions: A Comparative Analysis of France, Russia, and China* (Cambridge: Cambridge University Press, 1979); on culture, domination, and resistance, see Joan Cocks, *The Oppositional Imagination: Feminism, Critique and Political Theory* (London and New York: Routledge, 1989) chs 1–3.
2. Philippa Levine, *Victorian Feminism, 1850–1900* (London: Hutchinson, 1987) p. 14.
3. See, for example, Anne M. Haselkorn and Betty Travitsky (eds), *The Renaissance Englishwoman in Print: Counterbalancing the Canon* (Amherst, Mass.: University of Massachusetts Press, 1990); Elaine Hobby, *Virtue of Necessity: English Women's Writing, 1649–88* (London: Virago Press, 1988); Katharine M. Rogers, *Feminism in Eighteenth-Century England* (Brighton, Sussex: Harvester Press; Urbana, Ill.: University of Illinois Press, 1982); Alice Browne, *The Eighteenth-Century Feminist Mind* (Detroit, Mich.: Wayne State University Press, 1987).
4. Mary Poovey, *The Proper Lady and the Woman Writer: Ideology as Style in the Works of Mary Wollstonecraft, Mary Shelley, and Jane Austen* (Chicago, Ill. and London: University of Chicago Press, 1984) ch. 1.
5. For a review of the problems of definition and a survey of accounts of class in this period, see R. J. Morris, *Class and Class Consciousness in the Industrial Revolution, 1780–1850* (London: Macmillan, 1979); for a broader treatment, see R. S. Neale, *Class in English History, 1680–1850* (Oxford: Basil Blackwell, 1981).
6. Gordon E. Mingay, *The Gentry: The Rise and Fall of a Ruling Class* (London and New York: Longman, 1976); Lawrence Stone and Jeanne C. Fawtier Stone, *An Open Elite? England, 1540–1880*, abridged edn (Oxford and New York: Oxford University Press, 1986).
7. Geoffrey Holmes, *Augustan England: Professions, State and Society, 1680–1730* (London and Boston, Mass.: George Allen and Unwin, 1983); Harold Perkin, *The Origins of Modern English Society, 1780–1880* (London: Routledge and Kegan Paul; Toronto and Buffalo: University of Toronto Press, 1969) pp. 213–17, 428–9. On the triumph of the professional bourgeoisie in the present century, see Harold Perkin, *The Rise of Professional Society: England since 1880* (London and New York: Routledge, 1989), which argues that 'the professional society' superseded a society based on class.
8. Penelope J. Corfield, *The Impact of English Towns, 1700–1800* (Oxford: Oxford University Press, 1982).

9. Alan D. Gilbert, *Religion and Society in Industrial England: Church, Chapel and Social Change, 1740–1914* (London and New York: Longman, 1976).

10. For an account of the process in Scotland, see Charles Camic, *Experience and Enlightenment: Socialization for Cultural Change in Eighteenth-Century Scotland* (Chicago, Ill.: University of Chicago Press, 1983). See also Wilfred Prest (ed.), *The Professions in Early Modern England* (London: Croom Helm, 1987).

11. Edward P. Thompson, 'The Moral Economy of the English Crowd in the Eighteenth Century', *Past and Present*, vol. 50 (Feb. 1971) pp. 76–136; Robert W. Malcolmson, *Popular Recreations in English Society, 1700–1850* (Cambridge: Cambridge University Press, 1973); Bob Bushaway, *By Rite: Custom, Ceremony and Community in England, 1700–1880* (London: Junction Books, 1982).

12. On the 1790s, see Carl B. Cone, *The English Jacobins: Reformers in Late 18th Century England* (New York: Charles Scribner's Sons, 1968); Albert Goodwin, *The Friends of Liberty: The English Democratic Movement in the Age of the French Revolution* (London: Hutchinson, 1979).

13. For a brief survey of the social position of women, see Roy Porter, *English Society in the Eighteenth Century*, rev. edn (London: Penguin Books, 1990) pp. 21–34.

14. Neale, *Class in English History*, pp. 199–200. See also Joan Kelly, *Women, History, and Theory* (Chicago, Ill. and London: Chicago University Press, 1984) pp. 1–18; Christine Delphy, *Close to Home: A Materialist Analysis of Women's Oppression*, trans. Diana Leonard (London: Hutchinson, with The Explorations in Feminism Collective, 1984) pp. 71–6; Pamela Abbott and Roger Sapsford, *Women and Social Class* (London and New York: Tavistock Publications, 1987).

15. Ivy Pinchbeck, *Women Workers and the Industrial Revolution, 1750–1850* (1930; London: Virago, 1969).

16. See Nancy Armstrong, 'The Rise of Domestic Woman', in *The Ideology of Conduct: Essays in Literature and the History of Sexuality*, ed. Nancy Armstrong and Leonard Tennenhouse (New York and London: Methuen, 1987) pp. 96–141.

17. Neil McKendrick, John Brewer and J. H. Plumb, *The Birth of a Consumer Society: The Commercialization of Eighteenth-Century England* (London: Hutchinson, 1982); Maxine Berg, *The Age of Manufactures: Industry, Innovation and Work in Britain, 1700–1820* (London: Fontana, 1985); Colin Campbell, *The Romantic Ethic and the Spirit of Modern Consumerism* (Oxford and New York: Basil Blackwell, 1987).

18. John Feather, *A History of British Publishing* (London and New York: Routledge, 1988) Part 2.

19. Devendra P. Varma, *The Evergreen Tree of Diabolical Knowledge* (Washington, D.C.: Consortium Press, 1972).

20. Anthony Grafton and Lisa Jardine, *From Humanism to the Humanities: Education and the Liberal Arts in Fifteenth- and Sixteenth-Century Europe* (London: Duckworth, 1986).

21. Benedict Anderson, *Imagined Communities: Reflections on the Origin and Spread of Nationalism* (London: Verso, 1983).

22. See J. W. Saunders, *The Profession of English Letters* (London: Routledge and Kegan Paul; Toronto: University of Toronto Press, 1964) ch. 7.
23. See Walter J. Ong, *Orality and Literacy: The Technologizing of the Word* (London and New York: Methuen, 1982) pp. 178–9; François Furet and Jacques Ozouf, *Reading and Writing: Literacy in France from Calvin to Jules Ferry*, English trans. (Cambridge: Cambridge University Press; Paris: Éditions de la Maison des Sciences de l'Homme, 1982) p. 310; and Luther H. Martin, Huck Gutman, and Patrick H. Hutton (eds), *Technologies of the Self: A Seminar with Michel Foucault* (Amherst, Mass.: University of Massachusetts Press, 1988).
24. Stephen D. Cox, *'The Stranger Within Thee': Concepts of the Self in Late Eighteenth-Century Literature* (Pittsburgh, Pa: University of Pittsburgh Press, 1980).
25. On court culture, see Norbert Elias, *The Court Society*, trans. Edmund Jephcott (Oxford: Basil Blackwell, 1983).
26. See Raymond Williams, *Keywords: A Vocabulary of Culture and Society* (Glasgow: Fontana/Croom Helm, 1976).
27. Eli Zaretsky, *Capitalism, The Family, and Personal Life*, rev. edn (New York: Harper and Row, 1986); Lawrence Stone, *The Family, Sex and Marriage in England, 1500–1800*, abridged edn (Harmondsworth, Middx: Penguin Books, 1979); Randolph Trumbach, *The Rise of the Egalitarian Family: Aristocratic Kinship and Domestic Relations in Eighteenth-Century England* (New York: Academic Press, 1978); Leonore Davidoff and Catherine Hall, *Family Fortunes: Men and Women of the English Middle Class, 1780–1850* (London: Hutchinson, 1987); Philippe Ariès and Georges Duby (eds), *A History of Private Life*, vol. 3, *Passions of the Renaissance*, trans. Arthur Goldhammer (Cambridge, Mass., and London: Harvard University Press, 1989).
28. On the place of needlework in the construction of femininity, see Rozsika Parker, *The Subversive Stitch: Embroidery and the Making of the Feminine* (New York: Routledge, 1984) ch. 6.
29. Gerald Newman, *The Rise of English Nationalism: A Cultural History, 1740–1830* (New York: St Martin's Press, 1987).
30. Anderson, *Imagined Communities*, pp. 39–40.
31. 'Woman' is now thought to indicate an essentialist view of women, in contrast to a 'materialist' view that treats women and the gender category 'woman' as socially and historically specific. See Annette Kuhn and AnnMarie Wolpe (eds), *Feminism and Materialism: Women and Modes of Production* (London and New York: Routledge and Kegan Paul, 1978); Denise Riley, *'Am I That Name?': Feminism and the Category of 'Women' in History* (Minneapolis: University of Minnesota, 1988) ch. 1. I use 'woman' throughout, often with quotation marks, to refer to the cultural and rhetorical figure of the late eighteenth century, and 'a woman' or 'women', though usually without quotation marks, to refer to people who would have been considered women at that time.
32. See John Mullan, *Sentiment and Sociability: The Language of Feeling in the Eighteenth Century* (Oxford: Clarendon Press, 1988) ch. 2.
33. See Jane Rendall, *The Origins of Modern Feminism: Women in Britain,*

France and the United States, 1780–1860 (London: Macmillan, 1985) ch. 1; and Genevieve Lloyd, *The Man of Reason: 'Male' and 'Female' in Western Philosophy* (London: Methuen, 1984).

34. See Jean Bethke Elshtain, *Public Man, Private Woman: Women in Social and Political Thought* (Princeton, N.J.: Princeton University Press, 1981) ch. 3.

35. See Campbell, *The Romantic Ethic and the Spirit of Modern Consumerism*, ch. 7; Jean Bethke Elshtain, *Meditations on Modern Political Thought: Masculine/Feminine Themes from Luther to Arendt* (New York: Praeger, 1986) pp. 46–7.

36. Lawrence Stone, *The Family, Sex and Marriage in England, 1500–1800*, abridged edn (Harmondsworth, Middx: Penguin Books, 1979) p. 404.

37. Nancy Armstrong, 'The Rise of Domestic Woman', in *The Ideology of Conduct: Essays in Literature and the History of Sexuality*, ed. Nancy Armstrong and Leonard Tennenhouse (New York and London: Methuen, 1987) pp. 96–141; Joyce Hemlow, 'Fanny Burney and the Courtesy Books', *Publications of the Modern Language Association of America*, vol. 65 (1950) pp. 732–61.

38. See Peter Berger, *The Social Reality of Religion* (1967; Harmondsworth, Middx: Penguin Books, 1973).

39. Paul Hoffmann, *La Femme dans la pensée des lumières* (Paris: Ophrys, 1977); *French Women and the Age of the Enlightenment*, ed. Samia I. Spencer (Bloomington, Ind.: Indiana University Press, 1984) Part 5.

40. Nancy Armstrong, *Desire and Domestic Fiction: A Political History of the Novel* (New York and Oxford: Oxford University Press, 1987).

41. For 'an attempt at definition' of Sensibility, see R. F. Brissenden, *Virtue in Distress: Studies in the Novel of Sentiment from Richardson to Sade* (London: Macmillan, 1974) pp. 11–55, and the works cited there.

42. James Fordyce, *Sermons to Young Women* (1766), 8th edn, corrected and enlarged (Dublin, 1796) pp. 11, 18.

43. Margaret Walters, 'The Rights and Wrongs of Women: Mary Wollstonecraft, Harriet Martineau, Simone de Beauvoir', in *The Rights and Wrongs of Women*, ed. Juliet Mitchell and Ann Oakley (Harmondsworth, Middx: Penguin Books, 1976) p. 305.

44. On discourse and power, see Diane Macdonell, *Theories of Discourse: An Introduction* (Oxford and New York: Basil Blackwell, 1986). For a different way of envisaging language and culture as a field of struggle, relying on a Lacanian model of the construction of the subject, see Margaret Homans, *Bearing the Word: Language and Female Experience in Nineteenth-Century Women's Writing* (Chicago, Ill., and London: University of Chicago Press, 1986).

45. Virginia Woolf, *Women and Writing*, ed. Michèle Barrett (London: Women's Press, 1979) p. 98; Toril Moi, *Sexual/Textual Politics: Feminist Literary Theory* (London and New York: Methuen, 1985) p. 64.

Notes to Chapter 2: Self, Social Conflict and Writing

1. Modern biographies of Wollstonecraft to which I am indebted here include Ralph M. Wardle, *Mary Wollstonecraft: A Critical Biography* (1951; repr. Lincoln, Neb.: University of Nebraska Press, 1966); Eleanor Flexner, *Mary Wollstonecraft* (New York: Coward, McCann and Geoghegan, 1972); Claire Tomalin, *The Life and Death of Mary Wollstonecraft* (London: Weidenfeld and Nicolson, 1974); Emily Sunstein, *A Different Face: The Life of Mary Wollstonecraft* (New York: Harper and Row, 1975); Margaret Tims, *Mary Wollstonecraft: A Social Pioneer* (London: Millington, 1976); and William St Clair, *The Godwins and the Shelleys: The Biography of a Family* (London: Faber and Faber, 1989).
2. *The Collected Letters of Mary Wollstonecraft*, ed. Ralph M. Wardle (Ithaca, N.Y., and London: Cornell University Press, 1979) p. 60. All subsequent references to Wollstonecraft's letters are to this edition.
3. Throughout I capitalize 'Sensibility' and 'Sentimental' when referring to the particular late eighteenth-century cultural movement, its manifestations and products, and I use uncapitalized 'sensibility' and 'sentimental' when referring to the late eighteenth-century idea of physical and mental sensitivity or the quality of emotionalism in experience, literary works and so on.
4. William Godwin, *Memoirs of the Author of 'A Vindication of the Rights of Woman'* (1798), with Mary Wollstonecraft, *A Short Residence in Sweden, Norway and Denmark*, ed. Richard Holmes (Harmondsworth, Middx: Penguin Books, 1987) pp. 10–11. All subsequent references to these *Memoirs* are to this edition.
5. Roy Porter, *Mind-Forg'd Manacles: A History of Madness in England from the Restoration to the Regency* (1987; Harmondsworth, Middx: Penguin Books, 1990) pp. 105–7.
6. She went to hear Price in his chapel at Newington Green, was introduced to him and in 1786, before she went to Ireland, told her sister Eliza that Price had 'been uncommonly friendly to me' (*Letters*, p. 113).
7. See D. O. Thomas, *The Honest Mind: The Thought and Work of Richard Price* (Oxford: Clarendon Press, 1977).
8. Hester Chapone, *Letters on the Improvement of the Mind, Addressed to a Young Lady*, 2 vols (London, 1773) vol. 2, p. 5.
9. See Mitzi Myers, '"Servants as They are Now Educated": Women Writers and Georgian Pedagogy', *Essays in Literature*, vol. 16 (Spring 1989) pp. 51–69.
10. Mary Wollstonecraft, *Thoughts on the Education of Daughters* (London: J. Johnson, 1787) pp. 5, 13, 123. All subsequent references are to this edition.
11. Wollstonecraft, *Letters*, pp. 146–7. The letter is misdated 25 March; according to my examination of the original letter the postmarks read 28 April and 2 May 1787.
12. See Mitzi Myers, 'Pedagogy as Self-Expression in Mary Wollstonecraft: Exorcising the Past, Finding a Voice', in *The Private Self: Theory and Practice of Women's Autobiographical Writings*, ed. Shari Benstock

(Chapel Hill, N.C., and London: University of North Carolina Press, 1988).

13. See R. F. Brissenden, *Virtue in Distress: Studies in the Novel of Sentiment from Richardson to Sade* (London: Macmillan, 1974) pp. 56–64, 'Sentimentalism and Ideology: a Note on the French Revolution'.

14. Mary Wollstonecraft, *Posthumous Works of the Author of 'A Vindication of the Rights of Woman'*, 4 vols (London, 1798) vol. 4, pp. 97–155.

15. Mary Wollstonecraft, *Mary and The Wrongs of Woman*, edited by Gary Kelly (London: Oxford University Press, 1976) p. xxxi. All subsequent references to the novel are to this edition.

16. See Janet Sayers, *Biological Politics: Feminist and Anti-Feminist Perspectives* (London and New York: Tavistock Publications, 1982).

17. My reading of *Mary* and Wollstonecraft's later *Maria; or, The Wrongs of Woman* as political novels differs from that of Tilottama Rajan in her important essay 'Wollstonecraft and Godwin: Reading the Secrets of the Political Novel', *Studies in Romanticism*, vol. 17 (Summer 1988) pp. 225–8.

18. Patricia Meyer Spacks, *The Adolescent Idea: Myths of Youth and the Adult Imagination* (New York: Basic Books, 1981) p. 120.

19. Graeme Tytler, *Physiognomy in the European Novel: Faces and Fortunes* (Princeton, N. J.: Princeton University Press, 1982) chs 1 and 2.

20. See Nicholas Hudson, *Samuel Johnson and Eighteenth-Century Thought* (Oxford: Clarendon Press, 1988) ch. 4; Richard B. Schwartz, *Samuel Johnson and the Problem of Evil* (Madison, Wis., and London: University of Wisconsin Press, 1975).

Notes to Chapter 3: 'The First of a New Genus'

1. George Godfrey Cunningham, *Lives of Eminent and Illustrious Englishmen*, vol. 6 (Glasgow and Edinburgh: A. Fullarton, 1837) p. 247.

2. Mitzi Myers, 'Impeccable Governesses, Rational Dames, and Moral Mothers: Mary Wollstonecraft and the Female Tradition in Georgian Children's Books', *Children's Literature*, vol. 14 (1986) pp. 31–59.

3. See Jack Zipes, *Fairy Tales and the Art of Subversion: The Classical Genre for Children and the Process of Civilization* (New York: Wildman Press, 1981) ch. 2.

4. Mary Wollstonecraft, *Original Stories* (London: J. Johnson, 1788) p. 101. This text was revised for the second edition, but all subsequent references are to the 1788 edition.

5. Myers, 'Impeccable Governesses, Rational Dames, and Moral Mothers', p. 39.

6. Emily Sunstein, *A Different Face: The Life of Mary Wollstonecraft* (New York: Harper and Row, 1975) p. 161.

7. [Joseph Johnson,] 'A Few Facts', Shelley MSS, Bodleian Library.

8. Padraig O'Brien, *Warrington Academy, 1757–86: Its Predecessors and Successors* (Wigan: Owl Books, 1989).

9. Mary Wollstonecraft, *The Female Reader* (London: J. Johnson, 1789;

repr. Delmar, N. Y.: Scholars' Facsimiles and Reprints, 1980) p. v. All subsequent references are to this edition.

10. Dick Leith, *A Social History of English* (London: Routledge and Kegan Paul, 1983) ch. 2, 'Standardisation and Writing'.

11. W. Benzie, *The Dublin Orator: Thomas Sheridan's Influence on Eighteenth-Century Rhetoric and Belles Lettres* (Leeds: University of Leeds School of English, 1972) pp. 37–8; Moira Ferguson, 'Introduction', in Wollstonecraft, *The Female Reader*.

12. Ralph M. Wardle, *Mary Wollstonecraft: A Critical Biography* (1951; repr. Lincoln, Neb.: University of Nebraska Press, 1966) pp. 100–1.

13. [Johnson], 'A Few Facts'.

14. According to dates on the engravings illustrating the book, volume 1 was published in October 1790, volume 2 on 1 January 1791, and volume 3 on 14 March 1791; see Wardle, *Mary Wollstonecraft*, p. 123.

15. Ibid., pp. 124–5.

16. Mitzi Myers, 'Sensibility and the "Walk of Reason": Mary Wollstonecraft's Literary Reviews as Cultural Critique', in *Sensibility in Transformation: Creative Resistance to Sentiment from the Augustans to the Romantics: Essays in Honor of Jean H. Hagstrum*, ed. Syndy McMillen Conger (Rutherford, N.J.: Fairleigh Dickinson University Press; London: Associated University Presses, 1989) p. 120.

17. Information on the *Analytical* may be found in Walter Graham, *English Literary Periodicals* (1930; London: Frank Cass; New York: Octagon Books, 1966) pp. 220–2; Derek Roper, *Reviewing before the Edinburgh: 1788–1802* (Newark, N.J.: University of Delaware Press, 1978); Gerald P. Tyson, *Joseph Johnson: A Liberal Publisher* (Iowa City: University of Iowa Press, 1979) pp. 95–103; and Alvin Sullivan (ed.), *British Literary Magazines: The Augustan Age and the Age of Johnson, 1698–1788* (Westport, Conn., and London: Greenwood Press, 1983) pp. 11–14. On the politics of the *Analytical* during the 1790s, see Brian Rigby, 'Radical Spectators of the Revolution: the Case of the *Analytical Review*', in *The French Revolution and British Culture*, ed. Ceri Crossley and Ian Small (Oxford and New York: Oxford University Press, 1989).

18. Graham, *English Literary Periodicals*, p. 209.

19. These included Dr John Aikin, his sister Anna Laetitia Barbauld, Arthur Aikin, William Enfield, Joshua Toulmin, Alexander Geddes (a Catholic), George Anderson and George Dyer. Wollstonecraft's friend the Anglican clergyman John Hewlett contributed, as did Henry Fuseli, the poet Cowper, Henry Crabb Robinson, the mathematician John Bonnycastle, with whom Wollstonecraft's brother James studied for a time, Alexander Chalmers, William Turner, Alexander Crombie, Robert Burns's biographer James Currie and John Mason Good, orientalist and M.D. Other contributors in the early years may have included the inventor William Nicholson, Thomas Beddoes, Sarah Trimmer and Joseph Priestley

20. Quoted from C. H. Timperley, *Encyclopedia of Literary and Typographical Anecdote*, 2nd edn (1842), in Graham, *English Literary Periodicals*, p. 189n.

21. Quoted in Tyson, *Joseph Johnson*, p. 97.
22. Ibid., p. 100. Anna Seward, the poet and a leading figure in the provincial Enlightenment, told Christie: 'of all things I approve of its being a day-light business! To have the names of its authors and compilers known, will be the great guards of its integrity.' Quoted in Ibid., p. 98.
23. For a review of the various attempts to identify Wollstonecraft's contributions see Myers, 'Sensibility and the "Walk of Reason"', note 6. Myers and others accept reviews signed 'T.' as Wollstonecraft's, but I do not feel this attribution can be made as confidently as with 'M.' and 'W.'. Accordingly I do not consider such reviews here, though doing so would not significantly change my account.
24. The review is unsigned, but is followed by one signed 'M.'.

Notes to Chapter 4: From the Rights of Man to Revolutionary Feminism

1. On Fuseli, see John Knowles, *The Life and Writings of Henry Fuseli*, 3 vols (London: Henry Colburn and Richard Bentley, 1831); Eudo C. Mason, *The Mind of Henry Fuseli* (London: Routledge and Kegan Paul, 1951); Frederick Antal, *Fuseli Studies* (London: Routledge and Kegan Paul, 1956); Marcia Allentuck, 'Henry Fuseli: the Artist as Man of Letters and Critic', unpublished Ph.D. dissertation, Columbia University, 1964; Peter Tomory, *The Life and Art of Henry Fuseli* (London: Thames and Hudson, 1972); Nicolas Powell, *Fuseli: The Nightmare* (London: Allan Lane, 1973); Carol Louise Hall, *Blake and Fuseli: A Study in the Transmission of Ideas* (New York and London: Garland, 1985) Part 1; and John Barrell, *The Political Theory of Painting from Reynolds to Hazlitt* (New Haven, Conn., and London: Yale University Press, 1986).
2. Knowles, *Fuseli*, vol. 1, pp. 161–2.
3. See J. G. A. Pocock, 'The Political Economy of Burke's Analysis of the French Revolution', in *Virtue, Commerce, and History: Essays on Political Thought and History, Chiefly in the Eighteenth Century* (Cambridge: Cambridge University Press, 1985).
4. Donald Cross Bryant, 'The Contemporary Reception of Edmund Burke's Speaking', in *Historical Studies of Rhetoric and Rhetoricians*, ed. Raymond F. Howes (Ithaca, N.Y.: Cornell University Press, 1961).
5. Michael Meehan, *Liberty and Poetics in Eighteenth-Century England* (London: Croom Helm, 1986).
6. Cf. James T. Boulton's account of the *Vindication*, in *The Language of Politics in the Age of Wilkes and Burke* (London: Routledge and Kegan Paul; Toronto: University of Toronto Press, 1963) pp. 167–76.
7. Mitzi Myers, 'Politics from the Outside: Mary Wollstonecraft's First *Vindication*', *Studies in Eighteenth-Century Culture*, vol. 6 (1977) p. 119.
8. Mary Wollstonecraft, *A Vindication of the Rights of Men*, 1st ed (London: Joseph Johnson, 1790). The text was thoroughly rewritten for the second edition of December 1790; although this revision is richer and subtler than the first version, I quote from the earlier edition as

Wollstonecraft's first expression of her political voice. All subsequent references are to this edition.
9. See G. J. Barker-Benfield, 'Mary Wollstonecraft: Eighteenth-Century Commonwealthwoman', *Journal of the History of Ideas*, vol. 50 (1989) pp. 95–115.
10. Edmund Burke, *Reflections on the Revolution in France*, ed. Conor Cruise O'Brien (Harmondsworth, Middx: Penguin Books, 1968) p. 197.
11. Bodleian Library, Shelley MSS, Dep. c. 514. I am grateful to Lord Abinger for permission to use this material.
12. [Joseph Johnson,] 'A Few Facts', Bodleian Library, Shelley MSS.
13. *The Literary Diary of Ezra Stiles*, ed. Franklin Bowditch Dexter, 3 vols (New York: Charles Scribner's Sons, 1901) vol. 3, pp. 502–3.
14. *Analytical Review*, vol. 10 (May 1791) p. 102. The review is unsigned but it is followed by a review of another novel that is signed 'M.'.
15. Knowles, *Fuseli*, vol. 1, p. 163. Knowles was the only person besides Fuseli and the family of Wollstonecraft's grandson, Percy Florence Shelley, to see Wollstonecraft's letters.

Notes to Chapter 5: 'A Revolution in Female Manners'

1. See Joan B. Landes, *Women and the Public Sphere in the Age of the French Revolution* (Ithaca, N.Y., and London: Cornell University Press, 1988).
2. The review was signed 'T.', attributed by some to Wollstonecraft.
3. For a different account of Wollstonecraft's themes and rhetorical strategies, see Mary Poovey, *The Proper Lady and the Woman Writer: Ideology as Style in the Works of Mary Wollstonecraft, Mary Shelley, and Jane Austen* (Chicago, Ill., and London: University of Chicago Press, 1984) ch. 2.
4. Mary Wollstonecraft, *A Vindication of the Rights of Woman*, ed. Carol Poston, 2nd ed (New York: W. W. Norton, 1988) p. 78 note 3. This edition uses Wollstonecraft's second, also published in 1792, records significant variants from the first edition, and makes 'nonsubstantive changes in styling . . . to bring the eighteenth-century text into conformity with modern printing practices'. It records significant alterations from the first edition in footnotes. As Wollstonecraft's first edition is not widely available but the Poston edition is, I use the latter here. The edition by Miriam Brody (Kramnick) for Penguin Books (1975) is also widely available, but it alters the order of the first three sections, does not identify quotations and allusions and makes a large number of minor changes, such as eliminating many of the dashes, thus altering the impression Wollstonecraft wished to give of an improvised, spontaneous, expressive text. Ulrich Hardt's edition (Troy, N.Y.: Whitston Publishing, 1982) makes available Wollstonecraft's first with variants from the second; Marilyn Butler and Janet Todd's edition (London: Pickering and Chatto, 1989), with textual editing and annotation by Emma Rees-Mogg, makes available Wollstonecraft's second edition and records significant variants from the first, but in fact it differs very little from the Poston edition.

5. Christine Battersby, *Gender and Genius: Towards a Feminist Aesthetics* (London: Women's Press, 1989) p. 83.
6. See Gary Kelly, *English Fiction of the Romantic Period, 1789–1830* (London and New York: Longman, 1989) pp. 42–6.
7. See *The Dialogic Imagination: Four Essays by M. M. Bakhtin*, ed. Michael Holquist, trans. Caryl Emerson and Michael Holquist (Austin, Tx.: University of Texas Press, 1981). For a reading of Chapter 5 of *A Vindication* in relation to Bakhtin, see Patricia Yaeger, *Honey-Mad Women: Emancipatory Strategies in Women's Writing* (New York: Columbia University Press, 1988) pp. 149–76.
8. In the first edition the first three sentences read: 'In the government of the physical world it is observable that the female, in general, is inferior to the male. The male pursues, the female yields – this is the law of nature; and it does not appear to be suspended or abrogated in favour of woman. This physical superiority cannot be denied – and it is a noble prerogative!' This suggests that male superiority has more to do with sexual aggression.
9. On Wollstonecraft's reply to Rousseau see Diana H. Coole, *Women in Political Theory: From Ancient Misogyny to Contemporary Feminism* (Hemel Hempstead, Herts: Harvester Wheatsheaf, 1988) ch. 5.
10. R. M. Janes, 'On the Reception of Mary Wollstonecraft's "A Vindication of the Rights of Woman"', *Journal of the History of Ideas*, vol. 39 (1978) pp. 293–302; repr. in Mary Wollstonecraft, *A Vindication of the Rights of Woman*, ed. Carol H. Poston, 2nd edn (New York and London: W. W. Norton, 1988).
11. *Letters of Anna Seward*, 6 vols (Edinburgh and London, 1811) vol. 3, p. 117 (26 February 1792); Anne MacVicar Grant, *Letters from the Mountains*, 3 vols (London, 1807), vol. 2, p. 268; Bodleian Library, Shelley MSS, Dep. c. 526; Maria Josepha Holroyd, *The Girlhood of Maria Josepha Holroyd [Lady Stanley of Alderley]*, ed. J. H. Adeane (London, 1896) p. 347; *Extracts of the Journals and Correspondence of Miss Berry from the Year 1783 to 1852*, ed. Lady Theresa Lewis, 3 vols (London: Longmans, Green, 1865) vol. 1, p. 92. On the relation of Wollstonecraft and More, see Mitzi Myers, 'Reform or Ruin: "A Revolution in Female Manners"', *Studies in Eighteenth-Century Culture*, vol. 11 (1982).
12. *A Reply to Mr Burke's Invective against Mr Cooper, and Mr Watt, in the House of Commons, on the 30th of April, 1792* (London and Manchester, 1792) p. 81n.
13. Eleanor Flexner, *Mary Wollstonecraft* (New York: Coward, McCann and Geoghegan, 1972) p. 164; Claire Tomalin, *The Life and Death of Mary Wollstonecraft* (London: Weidenfeld and Nicolson, 1974) p. 105; Ellen Moers, *Literary Women* (Garden City, N.Y.: Anchor Books, 1977) p. 225.
14. For example, two important essays dealing with Wollstonecraft by Cora Kaplan, 'Wild Nights: Pleasure/Sexuality/Feminism' (1983) and 'Pandora's Box: Subjectivity, Class and Sexuality in Socialist Feminist Criticism' (1985), both republished in *Sea Changes: Culture and Feminism* (London: Verso, 1986).
15. Poovey, *The Proper Lady and the Woman Writer*, pp. 78–80.

Notes to Chapter 6: From Revolutionary Feminism to Revolutionary Paris

1. [Joseph Johnson,] 'A Few Facts', Shelley MSS, Bodleian Library.
2. John Knowles, *The Life and Writings of Henry Fuseli*, 3 vols (London: Henry Colburn and Richard Bentley, 1831) vol. 1, p. 167. Here again the passage in double quotations is Knowles's quotation from one of Wollstonecraft's letters to Fuseli, with appropriate alteration of the personal pronoun.
3. Ibid., p. 163.
4. See Michael Ackland, 'The Embattled Sexes: Blake's Debt to Wollstonecraft in The Four Zoas', *Blake*, vol. 16 (Winter, 1982-3) pp. 172-83; Nelson Hilton, 'An Original Story', in *Unnam'd Forms: Blake and Textuality*, ed. Nelson Hilton and Thomas A. Vogler (Berkeley, Cal.: University of California Press, 1986) pp. 69-104.
5. Hays's copy of *A Vindication* is in the Pforzheimer Library, New York Public Library, along with a significant collection of her letters.
6. *Letters*, p. 223. The letter is undated and Ralph Wardle thinks it refers to proofs of Hays's *Cursory Remarks*, reprinted in 1792. But Wollstonecraft remarks: 'I have just cast my eye over your sensible little pamphlet, and found fewer of the superlatives, exquisite, fascinating, &c, all of the feminine gender, than I expected.' This suggests the *Letters and Essays* rather than *Cursory Remarks*. *Letters and Essays* was published very late in 1792 or early in 1793, just after Wollstonecraft left for Paris, according to a letter to Hays from Hugh Worthington dated 9 December 1792.
7. George Chandler, *William Roscoe of Liverpool* (London: Batsford, 1953) p. 389.
8. See Eleanor Flexner, in *Shelley and His Circle*, ed. Kenneth Neill Cameron (New York and London: Oxford University Press, 1970) vol. 4, pp. 871-2.
9. Lionel D. Woodward, *Une anglaise amie de la Révolution Française: Hélène-Maria Williams et ses amies* (Paris: Honoré Champion, 1930) p. 79.
10. On Marie Roland, see Gita May, *Madame Roland and the Age of Revolution* (New York and London: Columbia University Press, 1970) esp. Part 3, 'Passion and Politics'.
11. Woodward, *Williams et ses amies*, p. 57, quoting Williams's *Souvenirs de la Révolution Française*, trans. C. Coquerel (Paris, 1827).
12. *Posthumous Works of the Author of 'A Vindication of the Rights of Woman'*, ed. William Godwin, 4 vols (London, 1798) vol. 4, p. 43. Subsequent references are to this text.
13. Richard Price, *Observations on the Importance of the American Revolution* (1784).
14. William Godwin, *Memoirs of the Author of 'A Vindication of the Rights of Woman'*, with Mary Wollstonecraft, *Letters Written During a Short Residence in Sweden, Norway, and Denmark*, ed. Richard Holmes (Harmondsworth, Middx: Penguin Books, 1987) pp. 239-40. Subsequent references are to this edition.

15. Reported by von Schlabrendorf and quoted in Claire Tomalin, *The Life and Death of Mary Wollstonecraft* (London: Weidenfeld and Nicolson, 1974) p. 132.
16. See also Meena Alexander, *Women in Romanticism: Mary Wollstonecraft, Dorothy Wordsworth and Mary Shelley* (London: Macmillan, 1989) ch. 3, 'Of Mothers and Mamas'.
17. On the suppression of women's participation in the Revolution during this period, see Joan B. Landes, *Women and the Public Sphere in the Age of the French Revolution* (Ithaca, N.Y., and London: Cornell University Press, 1988) ch. 4.
18. Ernst Breisach, *Historiography: Ancient, Medieval, and Modern* (Chicago, Ill., and London: University of Chicago Press, 1983) p. 248.
19. E. P. Thompson, 'The Moral Economy of the English Crowd in the Eighteenth Century', *Past and Present*, vol. 50 (1971) pp. 76–136; George Rudé, *The Crowd in History: A Study of Popular Disturbances in France and England, 1730–1848* (New York: John Wiley, 1964).
20. Landes, *Women and the Public Sphere in the Age of the French Revolution*, p. 149.
21. Elizabeth Fox-Genovese, *The Origins of Physiocracy: Economic Revolution and Social Order in Eighteenth-Century France* (Ithaca, N.Y., and London: Cornell University Press, 1976) p. 47; see also Georges Weulersse, *La physiocratie à l'aube de la Révolution* (Paris: Éditions de l'École des Hautes Études en Sciences Sociales, 1985).

Notes to Chapter 7: 'A Solitary Wanderer'

1. Per Nyström, 'Mary Wollstonecraft's Scandinavian Journey', *Acts of the Royal Society of Arts and Sciences of Gothenburg*, Humaniora, no. 17 (1980); Mary Wollstonecraft, *Letters Written during a Short Residence in Sweden, Norway, and Denmark*, as *A Short Residence in Sweden, Norway and Denmark*, with William Godwin, *Memoirs of the Author of 'The Rights of Woman'*, ed. Richard Holmes (Harmondsworth, Middx: Penguin Books, 1987) 'Introduction', pp. 21–6. All subsequent references are to this edition.
2. See Charles L. Batten Jr, *Pleasurable Instruction: Form and Convention in Eighteenth-Century Travel Literature* (Berkeley, Cal.: University of California Press, 1978).
3. Mitzi Myers, 'Mary Wollstonecraft's *Letters Written . . . in Sweden*: Toward Romantic Autobiography', *Studies in Eighteenth-Century Culture*, vol. 8 (1979) p. 166.
4. Mary Poovey, *The Proper Lady and the Woman Writer: Ideology as Style in the Works of Mary Wollstonecraft, Mary Shelley, and Jane Austen* (Chicago, Ill., and London: University of Chicago Press, 1984) p. 85.
5. Wollstonecraft, *Letters*, ed. Holmes, p. 166.
6. Ibid., 'Introduction', p. 33.
7. John R. Gillis, *For Better, For Worse: British Marriages, 1600 to the Present* (New York and London: Oxford University Press, 1985) pp. 110–11.

8. Roy Porter, *English Society in the Eighteenth Century* (Harmondsworth, Middx: Penguin Books, 1982) p. 311.
9. See Thomas Preston Peardon, *The Transition in English Historical Writing, 1760–1830* (New York: Columbia University Press, 1933) chs 4 and 5.
10. Gerald Newman, *The Rise of English Nationalism: A Cultural History, 1740–1830* (New York: St Martin's Press, 1987) p. 127.
11. Myers, 'Mary Wollstonecraft's *Letters Written . . . in Sweden*', p. 179.
12. Ibid., p. 170.
13. Robert Southey, 'To A. S. Cottle', in A. S. Cottle, *Icelandic Poetry; or, The Edda of Saemund Translated into English Verse* (Bristol and London, 1797) p. xxxvi.
14. Thomas Brown, *The Wanderer in Norway, with other Poems*, 2nd edn (London: J. Murray, 1816).

Notes to Chapter 8: Love, Marriage and the Wrongs of Woman

1. Bodleian Library, Shelley MSS, Dep. b. 214/3.
2. There are several accounts of Godwin's philosophy, but see Don Locke, *A Fantasy of Reason: The Life and Thought of William Godwin* (London: Routledge and Kegan Paul, 1980); and Mark Philp, *Godwin's Political Justice* (Ithaca, N.Y.: Cornell University Press, 1986).
3. Gina M. Luria, 'Mary Hays: A Critical Biography', unpublished Ph.D. dissertation, New York University, 1972, p. 233.
4. William Godwin, *Memoirs of the Author of 'A Vindication of the Rights of Woman'*, with Mary Wollstonecraft, *A Short Residence in Sweden, Norway, and Denmark*, ed. Richard Holmes (Harmondsworth, Middx: Penguin Books, 1987) p. 256. All subsequent references to *Memoirs* are to this edition.
5. *Godwin and Mary: Letters of William Godwin and Mary Wollstonecraft*, ed. Ralph M. Wardle (Lawrence, Kan.: University of Kansas Press, 1966) p. 16.
6. In the second edition of *Memoirs* Godwin revised the passage to be clearer about the advisability of conforming to 'the established rules and prejudices of mankind'.
7. William St Clair, *The Godwins and the Shelleys: The Biography of a Family* (London: Faber and Faber, 1989) Appendix 1.
8. Ibid. p. 502.
9. *Posthumous Works of the Author of a Vindication of the Rights of Woman*, 4 vols (London: J. Johnson and G. G. and J. Robinson, 1798) vol. 2, pp. 175–96.
10. Ibid., vol. 4, p. 57.
11. Republished with slight changes in ibid., vol. 4, pp. 159–75; quotations here are from this text.
12. Ibid., vol. 4, pp. 179–95.
13. On the increase of conduct or 'advice' books addressed to women, see St Clair, *The Godwins and the Shelleys*, Appendix 2, p. 511.

14. See Gary Kelly, *The English Jacobin Novel* (Oxford: Clarendon Press, 1976).
15. See Marilyn Butler, *Jane Austen and the War of Ideas* (Oxford: Clarendon Press, 1975) Part I; Gary Kelly, *English Fiction of the Romantic Period, 1789–1830* (London and New York: Longman, 1989) pp. 59–64.
16. Mary Wollstonecraft, *'Mary' and 'The Wrongs of Woman'*, ed. Gary Kelly (London: Oxford University Press, 1976) p. 73. All subsequent references are to this edition.
17. S. D. Harasym, 'Ideology and Self: a Theoretical Discussion of the "Self" in Mary Wollstonecraft's Fiction', *English Studies in Canada*, vol. 12 (June 1986) p. 164.
18. For a different reading of the novel as political, see Tilottama Rajan, 'Wollstonecraft and Godwin: Reading the Secrets of the Political Novel', *Studies in Romanticism*, vol. 27 (Summer 1988) pp. 228–39.
19. Christopher Hibbert, *George IV* (1972, 1973; London: Penguin Books, 1976) chs 13–14.
20. Godwin's MS journal, Bodleian Library Oxford.
21. Cited in Mitzi Myers, 'Unfinished Business: Wollstonecraft's *Maria*', *Wordsworth Circle*, vol. 11 (Spring 1980) p. 110.
22. Robert D. Bass, *The Green Dragoon: The Lives of Banastre Tarleton and Mary Robinson* (New York: Henry Holt, 1957) ch. 32.
23. Roy Porter, *Mind-Forg'd Manacles: A History of Madness in England from the Restoration to the Regency* (1987; Harmondsworth, Middx: Penguin Books, 1990) pp. 148–55.
24. The translation was published by Joseph Johnson in the same year, as *An Appeal to Impartial Posterity by Citizeness Roland*, 2 vols; later editions were published as the *Memoirs of Mme Roland*.
25. Jane Spencer, *The Rise of the Woman Novelist: From Aphra Behn to Jane Austen* (Oxford and New York: Basil Blackwell, 1986) p. 134.
26. Wollstonecraft's appropriation of the conventionally masculine domain of the sublime anticipates certain themes in modern feminist theory; see Patricia Yaeger, 'Toward a Female Sublime', in *Gender and Theory: Dialogues on Feminist Criticism*, ed. Linda Kauffman (Oxford and New York: Basil Blackwell, 1989).
27. Mitzi Myers, 'Godwin's *Memoirs* of Wollstonecraft: the Shaping of Self and Subject', *Studies in Romanticism*, vol. 20 (Fall 1981) p. 316.
28. See R. M. Janes, 'On the Reception of Mary Wollstonecraft's *A Vindication of the Rights of Woman*', *Journal of the History of Ideas*, vol. 39 (1978) pp. 293–302; Marcelle Thiébaux, 'Mary Wolstonecraft in Federalist America: 1791–1802', in *The Evidence of the Imagination: Studies of Interactions between Life and Art in English Romantic Literature*, ed. Donald H. Reiman *et al.* (New York: New York University Press, 1978).
29. Barbara Taylor, *Eve and the New Jerusalem: Socialism and Feminism in the Nineteenth Century* (London: Virago, 1983) p. 9.
30. William Bates, *The Maclise Portrait Gallery* (London: Chatto and Windus, 1883) p. 274; Anne Katherine Elwood, *Memoirs of the Literary Ladies of England, from the Commencement of the Last Century*, 2 vols (London: Henry Colburn, 1843) vol. 1, p. 152, quoting a private communication from 'a well-known living writer', who is not named;

Flora Tristan, *Promenades dans Londres*, 2nd edn (Paris: H. L. Delloye; London: W. Jeffs, 1840) p. 323.

31. Margaret Fuller, 'The Great Lawsuit', *The Dial*, vol. 4 (July 1843) p. 29; *Harriet Martineau's Autobiography* (1877; repr. London: Virago, 1983) vol. 1, p. 400; George Eliot, 'Margaret Fuller and Mary Wollstonecraft' (1855), in *Essays of George Eliot*, ed. Thomas Pinney (London: Routledge and Kegan Paul, 1963) p. 201; Maria Jane Jewsbury reported in Elwood, *Memoirs of the Literary Ladies of England*, vol. 1, p. 153.

32. See Janet Todd, *A Mary Wollstonecraft Bibliography* (New York: Garland, 1976).

33. M. G. Fawcett, Introduction to Mary Wollstonecraft, *A Vindication of the Rights of Woman* (London: T. Fisher Unwin, 1891) p. 30; Virginia Woolf, *Women and Writing*, ed. Michèle Barrett (London: Women's Press, 1979) pp. 103, 98.

34. Françoise Basch, *Relative Creatures: Victorian Women in Society and the Novel*, trans. Anthony Rudolf (New York: Schocken Books, 1974) p. 10; Rosalind Miles, *The Women's History of the World* (London: Paladin, 1988) p. 234; Rosemarie Tong, *Feminist Thought: A Comprehensive Introduction* (Boulder, Col. and San Francisco, Cal.: Westview Press, 1989) pp. 13–17.

35. Mary Jacobus, 'The Difference of View', in *Women Writing and Writing about Women*, ed. Mary Jacobus (London: Croom Helm with Oxford University Women's Studies Committee; New York: Barnes and Noble, 1979) p. 10; Mary Poovey, *The Proper Lady and the Woman Writer: Ideology as Style in the Works of Mary Wollstonecraft, Mary Shelley, and Jane Austen* (Chicago, Ill., and London: University of Chicago Press, 1984) p. 46; Cora Kaplan, 'Pandora's Box: Subjectivity, Class and Sexuality in Socialist Feminist Criticism', in *Making a Difference: Feminist Literary Criticism*, ed. Gayle Green and Coppélia Kahn (London and New York: Methuen, 1985) p. 154.

36. Elaine Showalter, *A Literature of Their Own: British Women Novelists from Brontë to Lessing* (Princeton, N.J.: Princeton University Press, 1977).

Index